EL MUNDO ZURDO 5

SELECTED WORKS FROM THE 2015 MEETING OF THE SOCIETY FOR THE STUDY OF GLORIA ANZALDÚA

EDITED BY
DOMINO RENEE PEREZ,
LARISSA M. MERCADO-LÓPEZ,
AND SONIA SALDÍVAR-HULL

aunt lute books
San Francisco

Aunt Lute Books
P.O. Box 410687
San Francisco, CA 94141
www.auntlute.com

Cover design: Amy Woloszyn, Amymade Graphic Design
Cover art: "Voces de la Tierra," Hector Garza © 2015
Text design: Amy Woloszyn, Amymade Graphic Design
Senior Editor: Joan Pinkvoss
Managing Editor: Shay Brawn
Production: Andrea Ikeda, Micaela Clark, Ali Giordani, Zhayra Palma, Kari Simonsen, Maya Sisneros, and Taylor Hodges

Library of Congress Cataloging-in-Publication Data

Names: Mundo Zurdo (Conference) (5th : 2015 : University of Texas at Austin) | Perez, Domino Renee, 1967- editor. | Mercado-Lâopez, Larissa M. editor. | Saldâivar-Hull, Sonia, 1951- editor. | Society for the Study of Gloria Anzaldâua.
Title: El Mundo Zurdo 5 : selected works from the 2015 meeting of the Society for the Study of Gloria Anzaldâua / edited by Domino Renee Perez, Larissa M. Mercado-Lâopez, and Sonia Saldâivar-Hull.
Other titles: Mundo Zurdo Cinco | Mundo Zurdo Five
Description: San Francisco : Aunt Lute Books, 2016. | Consists of SSGA conference proceedings held May 27-30, 2015, at The University of Texas at Austin.
Identifiers: LCCN 2016039943 | ISBN 9781879960961
Subjects: LCSH: Minorities--Education (Higher)--United States--Congresses. | Hispanic Americans--Education (Higher)--Congresses. | Anzaldâua, Gloria--Criticism and interpretation--Congresses. | Anzaldâua, Gloria--Philosophy--Congresses.
Classification: LCC LC3731 .M86 2016 | DDC 378.1/9820973--dc23
LC record available at https://lccn.loc.gov/2016039943

Printed in the U.S.A. on acid-free paper

10 9 8 7 6 5 4 3 2 1

CONTENTS

EL MUNDO ZURDO 5

SELECTED WORKS FROM THE 2015 MEETING OF THE SOCIETY FOR THE STUDY OF GLORIA ANZALDÚA

RE-MEMBERING GLORIA ANZALDÚA

ARCHIVE, LEGACY, AND THOUGHT

DOMINO RENEE PEREZ

Gloria Anzaldúa drew inspiration from many sources throughout her life. The Mexican diosas Coatlicue, Cihuacoatl, Tlazolteotl, and Coyolxauhqui, along with other powerful figures, held particular meaning for her and appeared prominently in her critical and creative works. She also found kinship with La Llorona, her "musa bruja," that wailing woman who wanders the night, plucking children from the darkness ("Putting Coyolxauhqui" 242). Anzaldúa stated that she saw herself as both "the daughter of La Llorona" and La Llorona, who was characterized not by motherhood but by the search for the self ("Llorona Coyolxauhqui" 295). La Llorona shares similar characteristics with the Cihuateteo, women who are honored among warriors in the afterlife. They alone achieve this esteemed position as a result of dying in the process of creating, of giving birth. Some have argued that the Cihuateteo provide one originary source for La Llorona's story. According to myth, they help the sun to set each night, bringing it down from the sky to rest below the horizon. The Cihuateteo are also said to haunt crossroads, awaiting victims or stealing children. Half of their lives are spent safeguarding the source of light and life, the other half as night predators wielding power over life and death. The Cihuateteo represent the power of simultaneity of being both/neither, all/nothing, light and/or dark, life and/or death, all at once. There, in the darkness, they make way for Coatlicue's daughter Coyolxauhqui, the moon, who was dismembered by her brother and thrown into the night sky so that their mother might gaze upon her daughter at night, easing the longing for her lost child. Coyolxauhqui's severed head also served as a reminder of the punishment for her defiance. Anzaldúa saw Coyolxauhqui as a "symbol for both the process of emotional psychical dismemberment, splitting body/mind/spirit/soul, and the creative work of putting all the pieces together in a new form [...] a labor of re-visioning and re-membering," a kind of work that is often done at night or in solitude ("now let us shift" 546). It is difficult to think of the Cihuateteo merely standing and staring passively at a severed fellow warrior, the subject and symbol of such profound violence, alone in the dark, waiting, watching. But "[t]here is darkness and there is darkness," one debilitative, the other liberatory (*Borderlands* 71). So imagine, instead, in the mantle of night, the hands of warriors working, weaving, re-membering, re-making the unmaking of the whole.

Academics, artists, activists, and healers convened on May 27–30, at the University of Texas at Austin for El Mundo Zurdo 2015: Memoria y Conocimiento: Interdisciplinary Anzaldúan Studies—Archive, Legacy, and Thought. The conference theme was inspired by both a memorial tribute for Gloria Anzaldúa that took place at UT eleven years earlier on October 22–23, 2004 and the location of Anzaldúa's archive, which measures an impressive 125 linear feet and is one of the most visited holdings at the Nettie Lee Benson Latin American Collection. The 2004 memorial event was held by the Center for Mexican American Studies, in conjunction with numerous other UT affiliates, including the Lozano Long Institute for Latin American Studies (LLILAS), the College of Liberal Arts, the Graduate School, the Office of the Dean of Students, the Centers for African and African American Studies, Asian American Studies, Gender and Sexuality, and Women's and Gender Studies, and the Américo Paredes Center for Cultural Studies, as well as ALLGO, a statewide queer people of color organization; Resistencia Bookstore; Red Salmon Arts; BookWoman; and the City of Austin Commission for Women. People traveled from across the country to participate in a celebration of Anzaldúa's spirit and legacies. They also shared their loss through performances, readings, and testimonios, speaking from the borderlands of sorrow and joy, as they re-membered a person whose life and work had such a profound impact on their own.

The following year, in 2005, the Benson became the repository for the Anzaldúa papers and made them available to the public in 2006. Since that time, scholars, activists, and artists have traveled from Germany, Poland, Russia, Israel, Japan, Australia, Scotland, and England, among other places, to work with the papers, which include "correspondence, written works, audio tape interviews, reviews, clippings, photographs, posters, artwork, and collected materials" ("Descriptive Summary"). At the 2015 conference, the featured roundtable with former LLILAS-Benson Fellows, who presented their research on such issues as education, visual and virtual texts, and the borderlands, highlighted the diversity of the archival collection.

"Records of the Memorial Tribute to Gloria Anzaldúa, 2004" have also become a part of the Benson's rich holdings available to Anzaldúa scholars from across the globe, consisting of one box and eight folders that include "invitations, publicity, publications, and *recuerdos* generated in memory of Anzaldúa, and video recordings of the events" ("Scope and Contents Note"). The availability of these materials is an important means of remembering and re-membering, even for those original participants, for, as Anzaldúa herself reminds us: "Memory is not infallible. Memory has gaps. Memory has silences. Memory has wrong imprints" *(Interviews/Entrevistas* 224). The archives can begin to fill the gaps, disrupt silences, and inspire new imprints.

El Mundo Zurdo 2015 was designed to engage the wealth and variety of the archive, as well as Anzaldúa's work more broadly, through a wide range of panels, performances, and cultural events. Dr. María Cotera, in the opening plenary, demonstrated the urgency of creating and making accessible a Chicana and Latina archive that documents and re-members a multi-generational, feminist, activist history. An archive, like Coyolxauhqui, represents pieces, sometimes fragmented, sometimes whole, that fit, not so much as interlocking parts but rather like something meant to be *puzzled out*, theorized, or applied. Each visitor to the popular library collection, whether knowingly or not, enacts the Coyolxauhqui imperative, which Anzaldúa describes as "an ongoing process of making and unmaking" ("let us be the healing of this wound" 312). Discovering, uncovering, arranging, or rearranging are all acts associated with the fragmented Coyolxauhqui, whose body is scattered, waiting to be found and remade. As Anzaldúa explains,

> One of the visuals I use is Coyolxauhqui, the Aztec moon goddess and first sacrificial victim. Her brother threw her down the temple stairs and when she landed at the bottom she was dismembered. The act of writing for me is this kind of dismembering of everything I'm feeling—taking it apart to examine and then reconstituting or recomposing it again but in a new way. (*Interviews/Entrevistas* 257)

Conference attendees and participants who took part in the archive workshop, curated by the staff of the LLILAS-Benson and facilitated by graduate students from different departments and disciplines across campus, engaged in the process of collectively examining materials selected from the Anzaldúa holdings to begin conversations about and around the items from different methodological and epistemological perspectives to discover and/or see them again in "a new way," as a part of archive, memory, thought, or something yet to be imagined.

The essays and creative writing that follow extend the work initiated at El Mundo Zurdo 2015. Dr. Marisa Belausteguigoitia's essay opens the collection with a consideration of how Anzaldúa's Coyolxauhqui imperative ("the vision of reaching out, of being all in this together") directly impacts learning environments, re-making them into transformational spaces (Alarcón 192). The Coyolxauhqui imperative, Belausteguigoitia argues, is explicitly a pedagogical imperative. It offers a conceptual and political frame for thinking about the body or bodies, such as "the forgotten body of the nation," "sexuality hidden by shame," or, in the case of the forty-three students from Guerrero, the disappeared. These bodies can make visible for students that which often "dis/appears" inside the classroom, such as political or cultural histories, and they can inspire a re-membering of that which is lost or concealed. The direct impact of educational practices, informed through the implementation of Anzaldúan theory or thought, sets the stage for the essays that follow in the first two sections.

Section One, "Anzaldúan Visions of Higher Education," theorizes through the extreme obstacles we can and do face in our efforts to bring Anzaldúa's work, along with other marginalized voices, into places of higher learning. Like Cihuateteo working to make whole what is fragmented or incomplete, these educators have navigated oppressive cultural, systemic, and corporatized environments to meet their own educational objectives, instead of those imposed by other regulating bodies. The results of these efforts help to empower students against what Margaret Cantu-Sanchez calls the "in/civilities" of the state. In "Forging Spaces of Teaching and Learning," Section Two, the authors offer teaching methods that account for linguistic diversity (not simply in theory but also in practice) or can lead to greater understanding of spatial bodies through, for example, *amasamiento* and the study of Chicana rhetoricians, respectively. These authors show us how Anzaldúa's work encourages us to think about how to transform educational practices at the K–12 level and within the academy, a place where, too often, scholars of color take up as border dwellers, stretched over time, space, and geographies.

Any collection of writing about Anzaldúa would seem incomplete without a section on spirituality. Section Three turns toward "Epistemologies of the Body/Mind/Spirit." Anzaldúa possessed a vast array of spiritual knowledge and practices, ranging from "New Age thought, transcendental and metaphysical philosophies, and spiritualism," according to David Hatfield Sparks. These and other philosophical and spiritual practices informed her ongoing effort to bridge the mind, body, and spirit on the path to *conocimiento*. The journey can be a fearful one through un-safe spaces, requiring us to call upon our *facultad*. Rather than being debilitative, these spaces can be sites of personal and social transformation. Spiritual activism, too, has a role to play in healing, through such forms as Spoken Word Arts Performance Activism (SWAPA) that reaches out to our mestiza consciousness, inviting us into a performance to be transformed by the experience. Crossroads, those places favored by the Cihuateteo, can also be places of healing. We must be watchful, ready to transform and transmute knowledge and knowledge production, to change the world and ourselves.

The final section of essays, "Archives and Trajectories of Anzaldúan Thought," challenges us to think about Anzaldúa and archives, her own as well as the ones she helped to create. Her archive-building efforts, according to Annette Portillo, in the form of anthologies filled with *testimonios*, have both filled and exposed gaps in critical conversations about such issues as race, gender, sexuality, and immigration. Anzaldúa's own archive, while home to an impressive array of materials, is also a place of gaps, ones occupied by the unexpected, as Trevor Boffone discovered, when he happened upon an unpublished drawing of La Llorona. Her archive is also a place of critical inspiration, prompting an enactment of Anzaldúan archival methods inclusive of collaboration, multivalent analyses, and operations both independent and in concert that challenge how we think about one item in the collection and the scholarly production about it. Finally, Anzaldúa's archive includes a legacy of thought that can lend understanding to other contested spaces, including the borderlands between Haiti and the Dominican Republic, and philosophical issues such as hospitality, a conversation that places Anzaldúa alongside Kant, Levinas, and Derrida.

As others before me have noted, *Borderlands/La Frontera* closes with poetry that extends the major themes and theories in the essays into complex lyrical expression. Poetry constitutes the final selections of the collection, not as the last word, but as a re-membering of Anzaldúan thought in ways that disrupt convention. The cultural capital of particular kinds of consumer goods, especially as they are associated with gender and class, form the frame of Veronica Sandoval's piece presented as an epistle to Santa Claus. Seemingly an expression of a child's longing for gift, the prose poem takes a sharp turn to engage with immigration, demonstrating that the borderlands are always present, though sometimes they remain hidden beneath the surface, revealed through the slightest effort. Similarly, Veronica Solis's poem is both an expression and enactment of the Coyolxauhqui imperative as the narrator searches for her queer familia, desiring to assemble or re-assemble it, while doing away with binaries in the process. The search is urgent, the longing made palpable, as she calls out for her familia and for social justice to end the violence, including self-harm.

El Mundo Zurdo and the essays in this collection attend to Anzaldúa's intellectual and activist legacy. Through critical and creative means, the authors and artists contribute greater understanding as a part of an ongoing project to transform the world, a longing Anzaldúa expressed a number of times but never more powerfully than post 9/11. In a time of deep national mourning, Anzaldúa sought out a healing, one that would bring people together instead of deepening divisions among us. She once again found inspiration in Coyolxauhqui: "I stare up at the moon, Coyolxauhqui, and its light in the darkness. I seek a healing image, one that re-connects me to others" ("Let us be the healing" 304). Each year, El Mundo Zurdo brings people together. Anzaldúa's words and creative spirit connect us as we continue the work she laid out before us. We are the hands in the darkness.

WORKS CITED

Alarcón, Norma. "Anzaldúan Textualities: A Hermeneutic of the Self and the Coyolxauhqui Imperative." *El Mundo Zurdo 3.* Eds. Larissa M. Mercado-López, Sonia Saldívar-Hull, and Antonia Castañeda. San Francisco: Aunt Lute Books, 2013. 189–208. Print.

Anzaldúa, Gloria E. *Borderlands/La Frontera: The New Mestiza.* 2nd ed. San Francisco: Aunt Lute Books, 1999. Print.

---. *Interviews/Entrevistas.* Ed. AnaLouise Keating. New York: Routledge, 2000. Print.

---. "Let us be the healing of the wound: The Coyolxauhqui imperative—la sombra y el sueño." *The Gloria Anzaldúa Reader.* Ed. AnaLouise Keating. Durham: Duke University Press, 2009. 303–314. EBL. Web. 1 May 2016.

---. "Llorona Coyolxauhqui." *The Gloria Anzaldúa Reader.* Ed. AnaLouise Keating. Durham: Duke University Press, 2009. 295–297. EBL. Web. 1 May 2016.

---. "now let us shift...the path of conocimiento...inner work, public acts." *this bridge we call home: radical visions for transformation.* Eds. Gloria E. Anzaldúa and AnaLouise Keating. New York: Routledge, 2002. 540–578. Print.

---. "Putting Coyolxauhqui Together: A Creative Process." *How We Work.* Eds. Marla Morris, Mary Aswell Doll, and William F. Pinar. New York: Peter Lang, 1999. 241–259. Print.

"Descriptive Summary." Gloria Evangelina Anzaldúa Papers, 1942-2004. The Nettie Lee Benson Latin American Collection, The University of Texas at Austin, Austin, TX. Texas Archival Resources Online. Web. 1 May 2016.

"Scope and Contents Note." Records of the Memorial and Tribute to Gloria Anzaldúa, 2004. The Nettie Lee Benson Latin American Collection, The University of Texas at Austin, Austin, TX. Texas Archival Resources Online. Web. 1 May 2016.

DIS/APPEARANCE AS PEDAGOGICAL IMPERATIVE IN ANZALDÚA'S THEORY AND WRITING

MARISA BELAUSTEGUIGOITIA RIUS

Guilt lay folded in the tortilla.

–Gloria Anzaldúa, "La Prieta" 224

ON DISAPPEARANCE

In these closing plenary panel remarks, I will focus on the way in which Latina/o and Chicana/o Studies knowledge and cultural practices produced in the US have traveled "back" and are being appropriated and taught in the Mexican academic scenario. I will focus on a pedagogical scene, the uses of Anzaldúa inside the classroom at UNAM (National Autonomous University of México) in México City, precisely in an undergraduate class on culture and education that I taught in Fall 2014.

One of the accents of Chicano/a and Latino/a knowledge—at least during the last decade—has been on a *pedagogical imperative.* I draw this sort of imperious tension from what Anzaldúa called the *Coyolxauhqui imperative,* "the vision of reaching out, of being all in this together" (Alarcón 192). And when in contact with an urgent pedagogical intervention, it is understood as a particular approach to epistemologies, politics, and aesthetics that may transform the classroom into a critical space where students may find not only knowledge, but knowledge that favors the understanding of political, racial, and sexual codes and practices of desire, sexuality, and identity that make up their bodies. In this presentation, I will concentrate on a particular experience that interrogates the paradoxical role of two opposite materialities: the "body of the other" (the forgotten body of the nation, the racialized one) and the "other body" (the re-membered body of desire, the sexual one). These two forms of materiality of the body and the (racial and sexual) "other" collide, but also forge coalitions. The first one (the "body of the other") underlines identity and its forms of "disappearance" inside the cultural and political codes of the nation; the second one (the "other body") addresses "appearance" by the presence of desire and what may become visible through it. According to Alarcón, Western philosophy can be said to begin and end with the question of the Other (193); Anzaldúa's psychic, spiritual, political, and intellectual journey, however, starts with inquiries into her own otherness within, which compels her to pierce the "mystery of the self" (*This Bridge Called my Back* 169). This shift from "the body of the other" outside the self to "the other body" as a structural one is found in Anzaldúa's work. She speaks about the pervasiveness of these bodily divisions and of the necessity of dissolving the body/mind/spirit split and, with that, of the possibility of wholeness. She states: "Though your body is still la otra and though pensamientos dualisticos still keep you from embracing and uniting corporally con esa otra, you dream of the possibility of wholeness" ("now let us shift" 562). A variety of questions emerge around these tensions: What may dis/appear inside the classroom? What kind of tensions, paradoxes, and national formations can be visible through the conceptual maneuvers of Chicana theory and writing? What kind of responses are produced when the classroom—as scene of enactment of identity and desire—is appropriated by Chicana/Latino discourse and writing? Anzaldúa did work on what may be called a pedagogical imperative, a mandate interwoven in our teaching practices. According to Norma Alarcón in "Anzaldúan Textualities," this imperative means the relentless pursuing of personal, political, and collective meaning, derived from the *Coyolxauhqui imperative*. Alarcón deploys this imperative into three actions:

– Develop the freedom to carve and chisel my own face,
– Staunch the bleeding with ashes,
– Fashion my own gods out of my entrails

These three actions concentrated on bodily materialities—face, blood, and entrails—tend to construct the mask of identity very close to your own face, stop the bleeding and consumption, and diminish what threatens self-integration. They do allude to the materiality and substances of the body at the border of desire and identity. Anzaldúa addresses these *imperatives* inside the teaching act, by equating the production of theory with the presence of the flesh: "theory from the flesh" through the exploration of personal, collective, and political structures of experience, memory, and history. What I propose in these closing remarks is the reading—inside the classroom—of the pedagogical imperatives (the pursuing of personal, political, and collective meaning) through these three actions (freedom of a face-carving, stopping of the bleeding, and fashioning from the inside).

ON APPEARANCE: THE CLASS

Last spring, I taught an undergraduate course whose goal was to reflect on the forms of violence reproducing in México, particularly the one that has to do with disappearing bodies. I called the course "Antigone's claim: Pedagogies of disobedience (voice, gaze and body in the classroom)." It concentrated on the type of violence that is proliferating in México: state violence, criminal violence, military and paramilitary violence. The course reflected on dispossession and forced disappearance, events that are reorganizing public opinion due to the strong protests on the street and in public and private institutions. The syllabus I taught worked around both acts, disappearance and dispossession, and was strongly inspired by the recent disappearance of forty-three students in Ayotzinapa, Guerrero on September 26th, 2014. This course was taught at UNAM in the department of Education and Latin American Studies, inside a public university with the mandate not only to produce academic knowledge but also to intervene in social urgencies, as defined by Boaventura de Sousa Santos in *La Universidad en el Siglo XXI.* The disappearance of the forty-three students, an extreme act of violence, happened in Guerrero, a region in South East México that has been subjected to radical violence for the last fifty years. During the seventies and the so called "Guerra Sucia" (Dirty War), the rural population—mainly those related to the uprising of rural teachers, who organized and fought back against the shortage of the state—were persecuted and violently disappeared. The original rebellion erupted because of the precarious conditions of schools and the deficiencies of teaching. During the sixties and seventies, that precise region fought for better classrooms and better education for peasants and indigenous people. An extreme repression began in Guerrero during the presidential period of Luis Echeverría Álvarez (1970–1976). One of the repercussions of this kind of violence was the slow consolidation of guerrilla movements organized due to the perverse state violence and, specifically, as an effect of the assassination of Genaro Vázquez and Lucio Cabañas, two important peasants' leaders and teachers who were forced to hide and use guerrilla tactics to survive and be heard. Ayotzinapa, site of the students' school "Isidro Burgos," is historically marked by the fight for education, which makes the empty classroom of the disappeared Indian young men a major offense and an ongoing act of violence.

Several questions emerge: How did our course problematize the issues on disappearance? In which ways does Anzaldúa depict an "empty classroom" and the faces, entrails, and bodies of those disappeared? How does Gloria Anzaldúa's theory and writing offer conceptual and practical frames to think on the body, disappearance, and the possibility of "talking back" on disappearance from the space of the classroom?

For sixteen weeks, we reflected on these and the following questions: When and how does the body dis/appear in the classroom? How does appearance get enacted inside the classroom? How can we make the bodies of the "other" appear? What kind of texts, practices, discourses make them reappear? And the most important ones: What does Anzaldúa have to do with the appearance of the bodies of the others and of "other" bodies? In which ways may we use her theory and pedagogy to reflect on the most fundamental losses and appearances in academia? Is this theory useful to develop a critique around the two most significant wounds—dispossession and disappearance—in México today? The course presented an invitation to make body, face, and voice appear through the production of dissident and dissonant questions, as a pedagogical *imperative* inside the classroom.

THE PROTEST

The dramatic and forced disappearance of forty-three students and the empty classroom they left deepened a big national wound. For months, and still today, hundreds of thousands of protesters took over streets and squares in México City and other cities of the nation and abroad following the students' disappearance in September 2014. Students and professors at UNAM in México City—undergraduate and graduate alike—marched into the streets and squares and overflowed to barrios, corners, and dirt roads. The protest also hit classrooms and walls at UNAM, most heavily at the Facultad de Filosofía y Letras (Humanities and Education programs), which were loaded with posters, scratches, graffiti.

Figure 1. Demonstration in México City three weeks after the students' disappearance

One image on the walls at UNAM was poignant: the faces—portraits—of the forty-three Indian students aligned; they had similar gestures, the same brown color, the same military haircut, the same blank face. These mug shots forced them to be seen as anonymous strangers. They could hardly be one's son, one's lover; instead of familiarity, fear and a sort of danger might be encountered (Kumar 39). This kind of portrayal enhances the walls and separation of "us" vs. "them." How could this "framing" travel and serve to be a framing of any body's self?

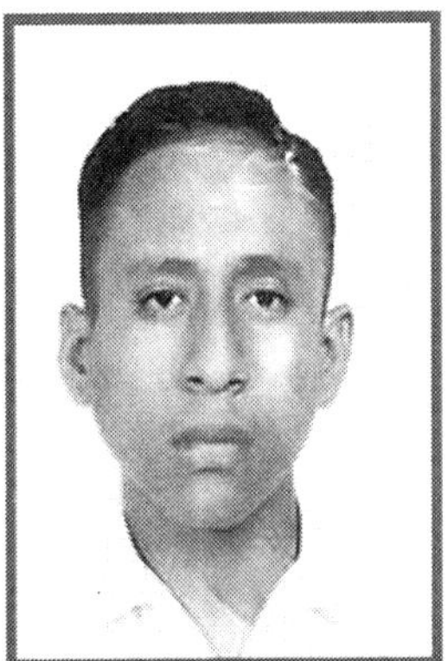

Figure 2. Portrait of Dorian González Parral

In *Making Face, Making Soul/Haciendo Caras,* Anzaldúa makes an intervention for theorizing from the flesh. Theory's main goal, according to her critical theory, is related to the transformation of the chaos of experience into order, an order that is constantly in peril of becoming chaos again. This experience-based definition derives from a Mexican colloquial expression to represent dissent: *No estés haciendo caras / Stop making faces.* This saying means that you do not agree to a command, you are close to disobeying. Anzaldúa translates dissonant experiences, these gestures of disobedience, into acts of political and theoretical intervention related to pedagogy as an imperative to dissent and disagree by "making faces."

One of the most radical acts of violence done to the students of "Isidro Burgos" school appears to be the pulling off of the face of one of the students, Julio César Mondragón. De-facing students represents an extreme act of silencing. In *Borderlands/La Frontera,* Gloria specifies the work that has to be done to make oneself appear—*facing* what has been deprived, stopping what is bleeding, doing it from within: "I want the freedom to carve and chisel my own face, to staunch the bleeding with ashes, to fashion my own gods out of my entrails" (44), which defines her pedagogical *imperative*. How can we manage to confront and resist when faceless? What is it about a face? What is to be seen in the face of an Indian student? How many of our students as "others" are faceless?

A couple of weeks after the students' disappearance, along with the overflow of images and taking-over of walls, streets, and patios, I found inside Facultad de Filosofía y Letras at UNAM a disconcerting scene. At every door of the building's classrooms, somebody placed an image of each one of the forty-three students.

Figure 3. Classroom in the Humanities at UNAM, México City

In a couple of days, the student faces transited into the classroom. The students' faces could be seen at the classroom door and every image appeared, occupying one seat each in the classroom. Facebook and other media showed an international multiplication of images of empty classrooms with forty-three seats waiting for the missing students. A collective act of indignation proliferated internationally and many classrooms of different universities, public and private, hosted forty-three empty seats taken by portraits of the missed young men: a performance of absence marked by their missing presence that shocked the nation.

Figure 4. UNAM, Universidad Autónoma Metropolitana, México City

The classroom was transformed into a transnational agent of both dissent and assertion of the missing presence of the students, which allowed for a representation of appearance of the forty-three inside one of the most excluded spaces: a public university, the classroom, the space for the connection of social urgencies and conceptual emergencies.

In this way, the function of university intervention inside the public space has been reversed, this time going from public space to the classroom, as an urgent space to be intervened: as the place for the demand for knowledge about exclusion and disappearance. My students, many of whom come from working class neighborhoods, live at the margins of a highly stratified society in México City. The majority, women and men of color, began to interrogate their own bodies, the carving with which they may craft their own faces and their most inner images. In one word, they crafted their responses and their resilience to vulnerability from their entrails, their faces, and their own bodies.

Through this pedagogical *imperative* to dissent, this "making (of) faces" when faceless, they constructed a political action, an unexpected transit: they went from the demand to find the bodies of the "other," the Indian students, to the search for their "other body," their own bodies, the bodies which would grant them "face" only when protesting.

THE SYLLABUS

Our syllabus was organized around the economy and epistemology of the "protest" through the revision of the tragedy of Antigone. We concentrated on the appearance of voice and body of the thousands of disappeared bodies in México since 2006, the excluded and those rendered invisible. We read texts organized around the main function of the public university, connection and contagion with social urgencies, but the course concentrated on *Borderlands*, "La Prieta," and "A Letter to Third World Women," combined with *Antígona* by Sófocles, *Antígona* by the Peruvian José Watanabe, and *Antígona González* by Sara Uribe. Double A: Antigone and Anzaldúa, disobedience and dissent. The bodily contours of the forty-three began to be clearer inside the academic institution, when, just beside the Main Library at UNAM, the families of the students took the tribune and, with it and their words and their desperation, gave materiality and individual and collective history to the anonymity of sons.

After this appearance, my students began to interrogate their own visibility, stigmatization, and exclusion around racism, normative sexuality, and, most of all, around the politics and the aesthetics of shame. Guilt about being a "dirty" woman, an indecent one; issues around heterosexuality and living in a traditional family; tension over masturbation and queer love appeared and were discussed inside the classroom. So much death and so much life. This interrogation of shame and passivity presented by Anzaldúa, particularly in "Entering the Lives of Others: Theory in the Flesh," allowed for a return of the "other" body, the invisible one, the one hidden behind the pervasiveness of shame, "*bridging*" from the disappeared body to the hidden sexual one: the "other" body. *Theory in the flesh* is what Anzaldúa and Moraga called this transition as early as 1983: "theory in the flesh means one where the physical realities of our lives—our skin color, the land or concrete we grew up on, our sexual longings—all fuse to create a politic born out of necessity" (*This Bridge Called My Back* 19). Anzaldúa and Moraga state that "we do this bridging by naming our selves and by telling our stories in our own words" (19). In her text "La Prieta," Gloria writes endlessly about vergüenza/shame; the scenes that produce shame proliferate: her mother in every corner, her color, her tongue, the food she prepares, Spanish and Spanglish, her lack of education. Everything that makes her different was a reason for being ashamed: "…eating at school out of sacks, hiding our 'lonches' *papas con chorizo* behind cupped hands and bowed heads, gobbling them up before the other kids could see. Guilt lay folded in the tortilla" [italics in original] (224).

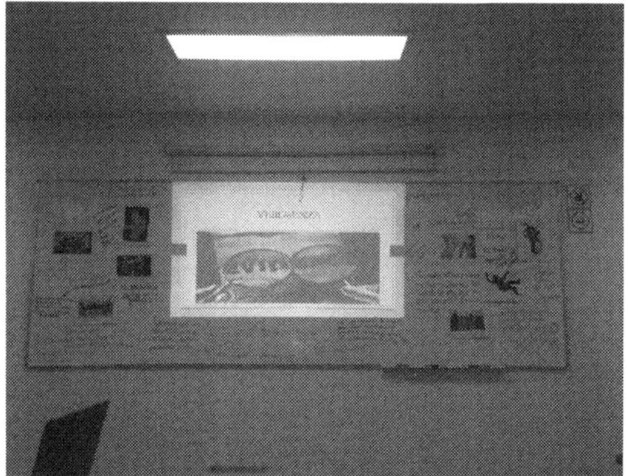

Figure 5. Images in my class on Anzaldúa's readings (Spring 2015)

In "La Prieta," she writes about two practices that helped her raise her head: one related to the body, the other attached to the tongue. The first one manufactured her way out of femininity: transgressing/transdressing—boots, jeans, attire to look like a man. The second practice relied on the use of her tongue: the search and claim for both precise words that could help her materialize her anger and her rage, and words, "palabras," which would not tie their meaning to previous signification, particularly the ones that escape premeditation on sexuality, gender, and the unexpected routes of her desire.

Figure 6. One of my students in this class

ON SHAME

An extraordinary work on translation takes place in Gloria's work related to shame. Both semiotic strategies on body and tongue brought her to build an uneven equation between the repulsion that the odor of her mother's food (papas con chorizo) would produce inside the classroom, with the smell of pesticide thrown from airplanes when her family was working in the fields. The word justice emerged between odors: "...the planes swooping down on us, the fifty or a hundred of us falling onto the ground, the cloud of insecticide lacerating our eyes, clogging our nostrils" ("La Prieta" 225). *Hunger of words*. Through both strategies, precision and relocation of signification and odor, Anzaldúa unlearns the belief that white is better than brown or black, that heterosexuality and maternity are the future. The process of fighting shame provokes the further process of unlearning sexual, racial, and gender normativity and social hierarchies, something that, Anzaldúa remarks, many people of color will never unlearn. She states:

> Being lesbian and raised Catholic, indoctrinated as straight, I *made the choice to be queer* [...]. It's an interesting path, one that continually slips in and out of the white, the Catholic, the Mexican, the indigenous, the instincts. In and out of my head. It makes for *loquería*, the crazies. It is a path of knowledge—one of knowing (and of learning) the history of oppression of our *raza*. It is a way of balancing, of mitigating duality. [italics in original] (*Borderlands* 41)

The students, most of them of color, produced a significant act. They draw their own faces with chalk on white sheets of paper. Mugshots facing disappearance, exclusion, and discrimination. They generated a vocabulary from la desvergüenza, from a shameless body, the body of sexuality, desire, and dissent. They made their bodies appear inside a queer/cuir classroom, where *deslen-*

*guados y descarados (*tongue-less and faceless) face their future. In such way, they responded to the pedagogical imperatives of both calls, Anzaldúa's and Antigone's. They fought shame and gained words that faced the shortness of the state and its mechanisms of invisibility.

Figure 7. Figure identifying crossroads in the body in Anzaldúa's text "La Prieta"

The "other body" (the body of desire, of sexuality hidden by shame) could only appear surrounded by critical knowledge, border thinking, counter-visuality, and decolonial discourses. Gloria was a major provider of these tools and concepts with her pedagogical imperative based on the dismembering of *Coyolxauhqui,* the restoration of that which has been ripped apart, the completion of broken stories, inner completeness. The "other body" hidden by shame was visible only when crossed by tensions regarding the visibility of hierarchies around language race, sexuality, gender, and class.

Figure 8. A moment of my class on Anzaldúa's "La Prieta"

This axis and its frame of visibility appeared when we questioned the relations of power by transgressing and transdressing the body and by intervening with words that could grant integrity to the self. They will preserve and multiply the same strategies, the same hunger of words, *hambre de palabras,* until the bodies of the other forty-three students appear.

Figure 8. My students presenting Gloria Anzaldúa

WORKS CITED

Alarcón, Norma. "Anzaldúan Textualities: A Hermeneutic of the Self and the Coyolxauhqui Imperative." *El Mundo Zurdo 3,* Eds. Mercado-López, L., Saldívar-Hull, S., Castañeda, A. San Francisco: Aunt Lute Books, 2014. 189–208.

Anzaldúa, Gloria E. *Borderlands/La Frontera: The New Mestiza.* San Francisco: Aunt Lute Books, 1987.

---. *The Gloria Anzaldúa Reader.* Ed. AnaLouise Keating. Durham: Duke University Press, 2009.

---. "Speaking in Tongues. A Letter to Third World Women Writers." *This Bridge Called My Back: Writings by Radical Women of Color.* 4th Edition. New York: SUNY Press, 2015. 163–72.

---. "La Prieta." *This Bridge Called My Back: Writings by Radical Women of Color.* 4th Edition. New York: SUNY Press, 2015. 198–209.

---. "now let us shift...the path of conocimiento...inner work, public acts." *this bridge we call home.* Eds. Gloria E. Anzaldúa and AnaLouise Keating. London: Routledge, 2002. 540–578.

---, ed. *Making Face, Making Soul/Haciendo Caras.* San Francisco: Aunt Lute Books, 1990

Anzaldúa, Gloria and Cherríe Moraga, eds. *This Bridge Called My Back: Writings by Radical Women of Color.* 4th Edition. New York: SUNY Press, 2015

De Sousa Santos, Boaventura. *La Universidad en el Siglo XXI. Para una reforma democrática y emancipatoria de la universidad.* La Paz, Bolivia: CIDES-UMSA, 2007.

Kumar, Amitava. *Passport Photos.* Berkeley: University of California Press, 2000.

Saldívar-Hull, Sonia, Norma Alarcón, and Rita Urquijo-Ruiz, eds. *El Mundo Zurdo 2: Selected Works from the 2010 Meeting of the Society for the Study of Gloria Anzaldúa.* San Francisco: Aunt Lute Books, 2012.

Sófocles. *Antígona.* México: Pehuén, 2001.

Uribe, Sara. *Antígona González.* México: Surplus ed, 2012.

Watanabe, José. *Antígona. Versión libre de la tragedia de Sófocles.* Perú: COMIDESH, 2000.

ANZALDÚAN VISIONS OF HIGHER EDUCATION

HOW TO TAME A WILD ACADEMIC

TEACHING ANZALDÚAN THOUGHT IN THE POLISH CONTEXT

GRAŻYNA ZYGADŁO

In Poland, feminism is a "bad word"; gender, nowadays, is even worse. An interdisciplinary approach looks good in various grant proposals, but is undervalued in the reality of the academic environment, which is still fond of the old, clear division of disciplines. Hence, crossing borders is not welcome. To teach about a queer philosopher and writer who believed in spirits in a rather conservative Catholic country is a challenge. Yet, challenge is something that Nepantleras confront every day of their existence. Therefore, being a devoted believer in Gloria Anzaldúa's philosophy, I had to try to teach a course on her at my university. And I did it. As a result, together with my students we managed to create a real El Mundo Zurdo in our classroom, and this paper describes the process, with its complications, barriers, and gains. However, I would like to begin by shedding light on some "taming" aspects of the Polish context.

TAMING TOOLS

To address the problems and differences one has to face to include Anzaldúa's work in a teaching program in Polish academia, I have to start with the general attitude towards, and situation of, feminism and gender studies in Poland. First of all, gender studies is not classified as an official academic discipline by our

Ministry of Science and Higher Education, which is a central governmental institution responsible for evaluating academics' work and distributing funds. Therefore, those who want to do research or teach about gender have to do it by incorporating women's issues in various programs ranging from American literature and sociology to cultural studies. The analogous situation can be seen in queer studies. In the social context, feminism, or "genderism," as it is referred to nowadays, is one of the most hated terms in Poland. In the media, almost every day we have ongoing discussions about the harm done to children because of gender education, or how gender discourse in general is used as a backdoor for introducing gay marriage and destroying the traditional Polish family, etc.

These discussions are also a reflection of a widespread attitude toward minority and ethnic groups and studies. In Poland, which is an overwhelmingly homogeneous country, at least in the official political debate, society is very suspicious of such ideas as multiculturalism, and *mestizaje* and difference are perceived as a threat rather than an advantage to our cultural identity. Actually, with the growing migration from African and Middle East countries, this suspicion is recently a dominating tendency in the whole European Union; still, the hostility towards migrants is worse in the former Soviet bloc countries, for example, Hungary. This harsh stand is expressed by numerous objections articulated by different European countries, Poland being one of them, to the European Commission's proposal for accepting a proportional number of immigrants by all European Union members. Other evidence of this appalling attitude is the very poor conditions in the refugee camps, as recorded in *testimonios* of bad treatment experienced by various exiles.

Secondly, interdisciplinary approaches are not easily and willingly accepted in Polish academia, including crossing genres, or questioning the established norms and systems, which, in my opinion, is related to the fact that the vast majority of our academics are, quoting Anzaldúa, "dependant scholars." Thus, using "alternative ways of knowing" becomes a completely unacceptable idea and may even disqualify you as a researcher. Moreover, feminist criticism is still being questioned and trivialized, especially such viewpoints as "writing with your body" or "putting yourself in the words you write" (Keating).

Finally, the lack of any deep knowledge of Mexican-American Diaspora in the US, or Latinos/as in general, can also be an obstacle to including Anzaldúa and her writings in the curriculum. Similarly, the absolute lack of any translation of her work into Polish means that only people who are fluent in English (and Spanish) can read her. This limits the body of students with whom we can incorporate Anzaldúan studies to mostly American Studies and Literature departments. However, if an effort to translate her writings into Polish is made, we have to bear in mind that her extraordinary code switching, which is a recognizable and intentional feature of her creation, will probably be lost in translation. Nonetheless, I believe that such a translation, at least of *Borderlands/ La Frontera*, is needed and looked for by many scholars. In addition, a dictionary of the most important terms and vocabulary concerning Anzaldúan terminology could also be created.

What makes understanding Anzaldúa's work and philosophy vital for Polish students is the fact that we are defined as a Catholic patriarchal society, which has powerful implications for our political and everyday life, but can also bring us closer to the comprehension of the Latino/a Diaspora and its problems in the US As a nation, we also share a long history with a troubled past—partitions, wars, communism—which gave us the experience of being an oppressed ethnicity, a cheap labor force emigrating to Western Europe, and the emergence of a specific culture of endurance and resistance. Furthermore, we have our own cult of the Black Madonna of Częstochowa (Matka Boska Częstochowska), which can be perceived as our version of La Virgen de Guadalupe. Our Black Madonna is a role model for traditional Polish female identity that reinforces the ideal of a dutiful and subservient wife and mother. Even her face is surprisingly dark, in spite of the fact that Poles are generally of light complexion. Unfortunately, we are still waiting for our Coatlicue.

TEACHING GLORIA ANZALDÚA IN POLAND

Bearing all these cultural similarities and difficulties in mind, I would now like to concentrate on particular classes that I have taught for years to show how Anzaldua's theory works in practice. Since 2004, I have been teaching classes about Latino/a Diaspora in the US, borderlands, and Gloria Anzaldúa. At first, these were mostly classes for Polish MA program students in American and International Gender Studies. Then I started to teach a class entitled "*La Frontera* and the *New Mestiza* Consciousness: Race, Ethnicity and Gender at the US–Mexican Border," which is my original course offered within the Erasmus Mundus Master's Degree in Women's and Gender Studies Program (GEMMA). This is a unique "program of excellence" supported by the European Commission and offered, since 2006, by a consortium of six European universities for international students from all over the world. In fact, this class is the primary focus of this essay; but I would also like to discuss my students' diversity over the years, their numbers, ethnic origin, gender and sexual identification, as well as their previous experience with gender studies, Mexican-American Diaspora, and Anzaldúa herself.

Within the MA program for Polish students in American Studies and International Gender Studies, I have taught classes on Latino/a Diaspora in the US, and a large part of these courses covered the history of the borderlands,

Chicano/a culture, and elements of Anzaldúan theory. Throughout the course of this class, I have taught over a hundred students, mostly women and only nineteen men, with men making up 15–20% of a class. The reasons for this disproportion may be the following facts: in Poland, more women study than men in general. Also, some of the classes were optional, and men usually do not choose courses that are devoted to gender issues. All classes were conducted in English, yet the majority of students have never heard of Gloria Anzaldúa.

Since 2008 I have also used Anzaldúa's writings in the class entitled "Women's Movements Worldwide," which is a part of the first year of the Erasmus Mundus Program, GEMMA, and where we predominantly discuss problems faced by the Third World and women of color. Over the years, twenty-seven people coming from twenty-one countries participated in this class. Again, the majority of them were women. As for their ethnic and religious background, fourteen were people of color and at least five of them identified as Muslim. Table 1 presents the countries of origin of students in this class.

GEMMA class first year			
Women's Movements Worldwide			
Number of students	Men	Ethnicity	Countries of Origin
27	2	14	21 Bangladesh Belgium Cameroon China Colombia Croatia Ethiopia Finland France Germany India Indonesia Italy Netherlands Pakistan Romania Spain Syria Taiwan Uzbekistan Vietnam

Nonetheless, since the title of this paper introduces me as the wild academic, at this point I would like to acquaint the readers with the chronicle of me going wild.

GOING WILD

The most interesting and inspiring group, as far as the reception of Anzaldúa's texts is concerned, has always been the second year of the MA GEMMA program.[1] Here, I have been teaching a class, "*La Frontera* and the *New Mestiza* Consciousness: Race, Ethnicity and Gender at the US–Mexican Border," annually since 2008. Students in this class, so far nineteen, come from twelve to thirteen different countries (one person was from Cuba, but with American citizenship and lived permanently in the US). There were only two men, eight people were other than white and some of them identified as bi- or homosexual. Some of them, because their countries of origin were in Latin America, had heard about Anzaldúa, but had never read her texts. Still, because of their programs of study, they had quite a thorough knowledge of gender studies, feminism, and feminist criticism. Four people admitted to choosing my university as their mobility direction because of the existence of this particular class. Some were feminist activists in their countries or workers in non-governmental organizations.

GEMMA Class: Second Year			
La Frontera and the New Mestiza Consciousness: Race, Ethnicity and Gender at the US–Mexican Border			
Number of students	Men	Etnicity	Countries of Origin
19	2	8	12/13 Argentina Bangladesh Colombia Cuba / USA Italy Mexico Peru Philippines Puerto Rico Serbia Slovenia Spain

The syllabus for the course and the list of readings are mostly based on Anzaldúan texts, with *Borderlands/La Frontera* as our key source. We also discuss some other texts and short excerpts from the writings of other contemporary Chicana authors, such as Sandra Cisneros, Ana Castillo, Norma Cantú, or Cherríe Moraga, chosen by me and varying from year to year depending on class participants, their background and interests, etc. Since one of the main goals in the curriculum is also to acquaint the students with basic concepts and themes in Chicano/a and Border Studies and to explain the historical, socio-political and cultural situation of Chicanas in the present-day US, during the classes we discuss the life of Mexican-American women in the borderlands from different perspectives. The following subjects are covered: Border Theory, issues of multiple identities, displacement and homeplace, the redefinition of Mexican-American gender mythology, means of oppression and racism, violence against women at the Border, and the role of cultural activities for the formation of Chicanas' identity. In all those aspects, Anzaldúa's life and theory are exemplary models.

The major requirements for completion of this course include participation in class discussions and the final essay and presentation. The course is divided into three parts. In Part I, which is a kind of introduction, there is a thorough discussion of Anzaldúa's biography and work; here students also get acquainted with the basic terminology concerning Mexican–American Diaspora in the US. They learn about the socio-political context, Mexican–American relations over the centuries, history of the US–Mexican border, Chicano/a movement and feminism, and Chicano/a mythology (Aztlán, La Virgen de Guadalupe, La Malinche, La Llorona, *curanderismo*).

In Part II we pay attention to the literary and aesthetic value of Anzaldúa's works, placing her in the context of Chicano/a literature in general and specifically comparing her works with the ones of other female ethnic authors, such as Sandra Cisneros, Ana Castillo, Cherríe Moraga, Norma Cantú, Toni Morrison, bell hooks, and Alice Walker. This part is devoted to close readings of Anzaldúa's essays, children's literature, and primarily *Borderlands*. We also discuss how her work and activism have influenced different groups in the US, but also all over the world and look for various strategies to put her theory into practice. Finally, the last part is the most noteworthy for the purpose of this paper since it includes students' own work with Anzaldúa's texts. Firstly, they have to write an essay relating Anzaldúa's theory to their own lives and secondly, the have to deliver a presentation connecting a chosen poem from *Borderlands* with some current issue concerning women or minority groups from their countries or communities. Here they revise their own experiences, put this lived knowledge in their presentations, and thus re-read and translate Anzaldúa's concepts for their own goals and environments. For this assignment, they can use visual media, performance, or any other form of expression they come up with. This empirical work with the strategic use of one's own experience becomes the process of knowledge construction and, for me, students' attempts to illustrate the poems are professionally very rewarding and inspiring. Some of the most remarkable presentations included dance performances, a song, and drawings. As for the topic of the written works, they can be divided into two major categories: traditional essays based only on the material presented and discussed during class and very personal, often interdisciplinary projects comparing a student's own culture with Anzaldúa's concepts. I will briefly discuss some of them.

One of the students, Cristina, analyzed Anzaldúa's texts through queer theory in the context of biopolitics and showed how concepts such as Nepantla allow for transgressing many systems. Julie juxtaposed Anzaldúa's New Mestiza Consciousness with the nomadic subject presented by Rosi Braidotti. Ana compared the situation of women from different ethnic minority groups in the US and Europe—Latinas and African Americans in the US and Arabs and Muslims in Europe, respectively. In her essay, she points out that domination and power mechanisms that were created under colonialism are still present in Western culture, though they operate in a much subtler way so they can often be unnoticeable for those unfamiliar with the problem or who have no knowledge of power structures or colonialism. Yet, scholars classify this as "neoracism" and see it working in theories such as Huntington's clash of civilizations, which results in minority cultural practices being presented in terms of binary oppositions, always as something inferior to the dominant model. This racism based on cultural difference has become especially popular in the contemporary European Union, which is observable in the tightening policy and very strict regulations concerning immigrants. This in turn results in "blaming minority cultures" for the difficulties related to assimilation or even the impossibility of acclimatization in a particular country. Media representation and stereotypes play a vital role in this process. They are a constant repetition of preconstructed knowledge—Arabs are always terrorists, and rich sheiks and Arab women are either over sexualized and demonized or presented as subjugated slaves hidden behind hijab. According to Ana, the process of Latina stereotyping is very similar. What also significantly joins the two groups together is the presentation of religion as an absolutely oppressive institution for women without really hearing their opinions on that matter.

Another student, Barbara, wrote an essay in a similar vein. She presented Italy as an example of European borderlands due to the current huge influx of immigration from African countries. Since immigrants are represented in the media as a threat to the European identity and are highly stereotyped, this rhetoric is parallel to the one used to discuss the US–Mexican border. Barbara sees a resemblance not only to the discourse related to the immigrants alone, but also in the humiliating way they are treated by the border guards. Kept for months in refugee centers without any legal justification and in poor conditions, those immigrants suffer in a world that is supposed to protect human rights. Moreover, immigrant women are also frequently raped and abused. In addition, she describes the care system,[2] fields in the South of Italy, and the construction business as "Italian *maquiladoras*" since these are the sectors of the Italian economy that hire the biggest number of illegal immigrants, using their helplessness and lack of possibilities to exploit them. Furthermore, even though there is a high demand for female labor in domestic services and the care system, it is easier for immigrant women to legalize their status. Nonetheless, according to Barbara, this whole procedure is based on racial and gender prejudice. She also claims that despite its geographical location and history, which have made Italy a laboratory for Mestiza culture, activists today have to fight with a system that penalizes people who want to take full advantage of the ideals promised by democracy and globalization such as freedom, equality, and free movement of people, information, and goods.

These are just some examples of how Anzaldúa's theory is used in a multinational classroom, but I propose that they clearly prove how well it can integrate students who come from various backgrounds and bring with them different cultural experiences. What I also strongly believe is that my students and I have managed to bring Anzaldúa's concept of El Mundo Zurdo into life.

CLASSROOM AS EL MUNDO ZURDO

For Anzaldúa, El Mundo Zurdo was an imagined space where left-handed people from various places and with different needs could co-exist side by side working together on a change. My classroom is actually a real place where multicultural students relate Anzaldúa's ideas to the multiplicity and diversity of their own experiences, thus putting her theory of inclusivity "in the flesh." Anzaldúa writes:

> Bridges span liminal (threshold) spaces between worlds, spaces I call Nepantla, a Náhuatl word meaning *tierra entre medio*. Transformations occur in this in-between space, an unstable, unpredictable, precarious always-in-transition space lacking clear boundaries. Nepantla *es tierra desconocida*, and living in this liminal zone means being in a constant state of displacement—an uncomfortable, even alarming feeling. ("Preface" 1)

In a broad sense, Nepantla, in Poland, can be the discipline of gender studies that is constantly being attacked and represented as a field where suspicious knowledge, or rather ideology, as its opponents call it, is born. For many, our politicians and scholars as well, it is *tierra desconocida,* which rejects and crosses the limits of established disciplines and is unpredictable and dangerous. Reflecting restrictions and limitations of our culture and society, the feminist classroom becomes open space for creativity and new possibilities, where anger is a part of the process of teaching. Educating about gender and using feminist discourse in this hostile environment become our subversive gestures, yet, in the words of Anzaldúa, "by sending our voices, visuals and visions outward into the world, we alter the walls and make them a framework for new windows and doors [...] Only then can we make a home out of the cracks" ("Haciendo Caras" xxiv–xxv).

Moreover, according to Anzaldúa, Nepantla is also a concept that describes a state of mind in which we get rid of old ideas and come up with new ones; we reject stereotypes and myths to gain new perspectives and viewpoints and we re-configure our identities transgressing all the borders and barriers—thus, the feminist classroom in Poland becomes a perfect symbol of Nepantla. In this space we learn about alternative ways of knowledge, question the existing systems of power, and open up to the Other. In my opinion, every person in Poland who teaches about gender, oppression, and violation of women's rights is a Nepantlera. As instructors, we oppose the prevailing beliefs in rationality and objectivity of knowledge construction, broaden or even dispose of the existing canons in various disciplines, and we always loudly demand our space in the Academy. Anzaldúa describes Nepantleras the following way:

> Where others saw borders, these Nepantleras saw links; where others saw abysses, they saw bridges spanning those abysses. For Nepantleras, to bridge is an act of will, an act of love, an attempt toward compassion and reconciliation, and a promise to be present with the pain of others without losing themselves to it. ("Preface" 4)

In that context, the feminist classroom becomes a bridge, since most feminist teachers are reaching out to everybody who wants to cross and are open to the ideas that have been silenced and rejected. The liminality and multiplicity of Nepantla can also enrich our quest for *conocimiento*.

Therefore, I see my international "*La Frontera* and the *New Mestiza* Consciousness" classroom as an example of El Mundo Zurdo, of *almas afines* in which together with my students, we are all willing to engage in open conversations about what is common and what separates us, exploring and using our differences not against each other but treating them as something positive, enriching, and as potential for transformation. We have cherished our bodies and experiences, built new coalitions and alliances, and avoided categorization, thus putting in practice Anzaldúa's theory of *nos/otras* and working towards the New Tribalism in which we could become a part of a "collective mind-set and collective dream" ("now let us" 547).

In the Introduction to *The Gloria Anzaldúa Reader*, AnaLouise Keating writes that what strikes her most about Gloria's texts are "the profound ways that her words resonate with so many different types of people [...] They are shocked by the intimacy of Anzaldúa's insights; they feel like she's speaking directly to them, like she's describing their own deeply buried secrets and beliefs [...] When they read Anzaldúa they feel a sense of familiarity more intense than they experienced with most other authors." Further Keating attributes Anzaldúa's "ability to generate such complex intimacies [...] to her willingness to risk the personal" ("Introduction" 1).

I must admit that these are precisely my experiences with my students. First of all, thanks to the diversity of the participants in my classroom and their enthusiastic reception of the texts we discussed, I could really see and appreciate the versatility, receptivity, and applicability of Anzaldúa's theory in multiple and diverse environments. Secondly, what students usually like most about Gloria's texts is her involvement, directness, or even "nakedness," as well as her openness to a dialogue with the reader. Finally, teaching this class for so many years and to so many diverse people allowed me, as a teacher, not only to open up more to the Other and to an intercultural dialogue, but it has always been an invaluable source of knowledge for me. This transnational flow of knowledge is not oriented to one-side. It was not only me teaching people who have never heard about Anzaldúa before, about Mexican-American Diaspora, Chicana politics and culture, and so on. My students have also been teaching me and I have learned from them. They have changed my views and approaches to many issues and allowed me to get to know other socio-cultural contexts in which I could locate Anzaldúa's writings. This internationalized environment has opened completely new directions and themes in my research and teaching, which, for me, is the fulfillment of Anzaldúa's life's motto "I usually learn the most when I teach" (Keating 42).

NOTES

1 Within the GEMMA program, one semester is called mobility because during this period all the students have to move to another chosen country and study there for at least one semester —therefore, at the end, they are granted two diplomas from two different institutions and countries.

2 "Care system" in Poland means nurseries and kindergartens for little kids and special homes for elderly people who cannot live by themselves. Similar institutions exist in many countries in Europe within different state organizations, yet, because European societies are "aging societies" and because women nowadays work professionally instead of staying at home with children as it was in the past, there are not enough state operated places for children and not enough care for the elderly so to fill the gap immigrant women are hired in all these professions that are related with taking care of somebody, thus the "care system."

WORKS CITED

Anzaldúa, Gloria. *Borderlands/La Frontera: The New Mestiza.* 2nd Ed. San Francisco: Aunt Lute Books, 1999. Print.

---. "Haciendo caras, un entrada." *Making Face, Making Soul. Haciendo Caras. Creative and Critical Perspectives by Feminists of Color.* San Francisco: Aunt Lute Books, 1990. Print.

---. "now let us shift ... the path of conocimiento ... inner work, public acts." *This Bridge We Call Home. Radical Visions for Transformation* Gloria Anzaldúa and AnaLouise Keating, eds. New York: Routledge, 2002. 540- 548. Print.

---. "Preface." *This Bridge We Call Home. Radical Visions for Transformation.* New York: Routledge, 2002. Print.

Keating, AnaLouise. ed. *Interviews. Entrevistas.* New York: Routledge, 2000. Print.

---. "Introduction." *The Gloria Anzaldúa Reader*. Durham: Duke University Press, 2009. Print.

IN/CIVILITIES OF THE AMERICAN CLASSROOM

A CLASH BETWEEN A CHICANA TEACHER AND AN ANGLOCENTRIC SCHOOL SYSTEM

MARGARET CANTÚ-SÁNCHEZ

Gloria Anzaldúa began her teaching career in a high school in the Rio Grande Valley of Texas where, as a Chicana teacher teaching a primarily Anglocentric discipline, English, Anzaldúa experienced numerous dilemmas. The most problematic issue Anzaldúa describes in "How to Tame a Wild Tongue" is the experience of attempting to incorporate literature written by Latinas/os into an Anglocentric curriculum (40). To accomplish this task, Anzaldúa had to swear her students to secrecy and proceed with caution. Though Anzaldúa spoke of this experience nearly thirty years ago, similar problems persist in the education system today. The question of how to incorporate culturally relevant literature into the curriculum continues to haunt Chicana/o teachers in the US education system.

An exploration of the teaching experiences of secondary teachers and core curriculum instructors at colleges and universities divulges how the US education system is utilized by the government to seek control of its citizens, specifically its Latina/o students, by first exerting power over those supposedly in charge: teachers. Especially problematic are arguably racist attempts to "civilize" students, which ensure that they continue to uphold Anglocentric ideologies, through a whitewashed curriculum. This exertion of power, this attempt to "civilize," emerges in policies designed to establish what Michel Foucault calls "docile bodies" [1]of students and teachers, to which I also add "docile minds," through the use of standardized testing, restrictions on what texts may or may not be taught, and, more importantly, the questioning of identity that occurs in Latino/a students, causing an in/civility of self. Foucault's "docile bodies" refers to the figure of the ideal soldier as

> something that can be made; out of a formless clay, an inapt body, the machine required can be constructed; posture is gradually corrected; a calculated constraint runs slowly through each part of the body, mastering it, making it pliable, ready at all times, turning silently into the automatism of habit. (135)

Originally, these disciplinary methods emerged in the military and were gradually adopted and adapted by schools and hospitals. Among schools and other institutions,

> [t]he meticulousness of the regulations, the fussiness of the inspections, the supervision of the smallest fragment of life and of the body will soon provide, in the context of the school, the barracks, the hospital or the workshop, a laicized content, an economic or technical rationality for this mystical calculus of the infinitesimal and the infinite. (Foucault 140)

The slightest rules of discipline and punishment as used by the military slowly begin to be implemented in varied contexts such as prisons and schools. I argue that Foucault's concept of the docile body is further exaggerated by the US education system to include docile minds. The purpose of the school system, like Foucault's prison, is to mold Latina/o and other minority students' minds in an effort to maintain control over them. The docile minds of Latina/o students are ultimately necessary so that the Anglo hegemony remains in power.

Because there is the desire to control and eventually mold students into the ideal American citizen, Latina/o and other minority students are forced to forgo their cultural affiliations or risk rejection from mainstream society. Teachers and professors are the tools used to exert this control and mold students into patriotic students, with allegiance to Anglocentric ideologies. Through the implementation of standardized testing, strict adherence to state-mandated curriculums, and Anglocentric pedagogies, the bodies and minds of teachers and professors can also become "docile" and malleable. In light of these striking issues, it is necessary to understand that a need for Anzaldúan pedagogies, transformative pedagogies, like a mestizaje of epistemologies, the blending of cultural knowledge of the home with that of school, must find a way into K–12 curriculum via the implementation of multi-ethnic studies into literary core curriculum university courses.

Anzaldúa sums up the experience of minority teachers and professors working against an Anglocentric system. She explains, "I am an outsider/insider in academic circles. This allows me to look at American Studies from three points of view: the distance of the outsider, the closeness of the insider, and the in-between zone, the space between worlds I call 'nepantla'" (Anzaldúa, *Reader* 239). It is this revelation that allows many of us, Chicana teachers, professors, and instructors of secondary and university classes, to acknowledge that we too come to the Anglocentric school system and academia as outsiders, insiders, and those who must negotiate from in between worlds. As a Chicana teacher/professor I am caught in the precarious position of adhering to strict academic guidelines and criteria that often clash with my desire to include more multicultural/multiethnic texts, develop unorthodox teaching approaches, and get to know my students on a more personal level than the current K–12 and university systems allows.

As a former high school English teacher, I, like Anzaldúa, found myself inundated with specific curriculum criteria that I had to adhere to. The criteria necessary for sophomore English courses includes the teaching of classification essays, a traditional and outdated approach to composition, and a small list of texts, with very few authors of color, from which to choose. All of these requirements are mandatory, in addition to focusing on the successful completion of STAAR testing.[2] With such restrictive requirements, it becomes problematic for a teacher of color, a Chicana, to truly "teach" while maintaining Texas's mandated criteria. To utilize the words of Foucault, it seems that teachers must succumb to the concept of "docile minds and bodies," allowing school boards and administrators to dictate what is best for students. So what exactly can be done about such restrictions? How can teachers work against school systems which exert power over those who really do have the "power to change not only our students' lives but our own?" (Anzaldúa, *Reader* 240). The answers to such questions lie in the core curriculums of universities and colleges, where a diverse body of students from multiple disciplinary backgrounds can come together, learn, engage in classrooms as places of social transformation and take that with them into the world beyond graduation.

Gloria Anzaldúa explains that

> [t]ransformation does not happen unless we explore what threatens us as teachers and students [. . .] what we silence; what we're angry about; what causes us anxiety; what brings us into conflict and disagreement; and what cultural prescriptions and cultural teachings we're rebelling against. (*Reader* 241)

From this statement, she calls for transformative approaches to teaching that re-conceptualize homogenous pedagogies in the literature classroom. Although the plight of minority students fights to help people of color obtain access to institutions of higher education, one of the main reasons we continue to need such changes in pedagogy is not only to retain access but also to address the education/educación split so many of us find ourselves experiencing at home and at school. One way to combat such a conflict is through the critical examination of transformative pedagogies that invites awareness, civic engagement, transformations of identity, and empowerment in the classroom. It is the study of these disciplines within Literature Core courses which may help teachers/professors accept and formulate what I refer to as a mestizaje of epistemologies. Often core curriculum classes are subjected to certain criteria, however, every once in a while a professor is given the opportunity to design such a course in whatever way they please. One such opportunity presented itself to me, and I decided to design this core course as a multi-ethnic literature class with the knowledge that I would have students from multiple classifications and disciplines joining me.

One of the first questions I pose upon entering my Literature Core class is whether students are familiar with some of the texts we intend to examine including: *George Washington Gómez, Canícula: Snapshots of a Girlhood en la Frontera, Ceremony,* and *Paradise.* More often than not, most students stare blankly at me and admit that they've never heard of such texts let alone the authors of those works. Even more interesting is the fact that when I introduce such texts, I provide historical/cultural contextual background which most students also admit they have never heard of or encountered in previous history or literature courses. Some of the historical context surrounding *George Washington Gómez* includes discussions regarding the Treaty of Guadalupe-Hidalgo, the treatment of Mexican American students at the time, and the lynching of many Mexican Americans by the Texas Rangers. Students react with shock and horror and, most interestingly, with the fact that they were taught to be ignorant about such historical events.

As a professor, it is important to note that much of the information provided in multi-ethnic courses has never been accessed by many students, often resulting in an education/educación split in which their cultural and academic identities and epistemologies split and contradict one another. Such a split can emerge especially in literature courses where Chicana/o and/or Latina/o students cannot relate and respond to the literature they are reading. Gloria Anzaldúa speaks about this conflict from the perspective of a student and teacher in "How to Tame a Wild Tongue." She explains, "In the 1960s, I read my first Chicano novel. It was *City of Night* by John Rechy, a gay Texan, son of a Scottish farmer and a Mexican mother. For days I walked around in stunned amazement that a Chicano could write and get published" (*Borderlands* 40). Though Anzaldúa is writing about the 1960s, some of the same issues she encountered still exist today. Exposure to texts like Anzaldúa's *Borderlands*, Américo Paredes's *George Washington Gómez*, and Norma Elia Cantú's *Canícula* in core curriculum literature courses reveal the education/educación conflict not only of the protagonists and authors, but also of the student-readers themselves. Such works allow students to begin to confront their own complex identity, how that identity has been shaped, formed, and manipulated by a society engaged in various "isms," especially via an Anglocentric school system.

This recognition emerges especially through the composition of essays and Blackboard journals in which students are asked to simply respond to the readings or literature of the day with their own thoughts, expressions, opinions, stories, experiences, testimonios, etc. Such an invitation to write about what students know sends them into frenzy because they must confront their own split in identity and so much more. Many students initially find themselves continuously asking me for prompts or clarifying that it's ok to speak about their own lives. Like Anzaldúa, many student-writers realize, "writing is dangerous because we are afraid of what the writing reveals: the fears, the angers, the strengths of a woman under a triple or quadruple oppression. Yet in that very act lies our survival because [those] who write ha[ve] power" (Anzaldúa, *Reader* 33). It is this confrontation that signals the beginning of a mestizaje of epistemologies, a blending of cultural and academic epistemologies in home and school spaces, as a method of transformative pedagogy.

Exposure to literature written by minority authors brings an awareness of this education/educación split to the student. This becomes especially evident as I ask students to write about and contemplate the dilemmas encountered by protagonists of our texts, while drawing on their own life experiences, an experience they initially find awkward. Education scholars like Laura Rendón explain that once in the school system,

> [n]o one asked me to write about what I knew best—*mi familia, mi barrio,* my life experiences and what I had learned from them. Instead, I attended classrooms with teachers who seemed so far removed from what I represented, teachers who had been socialized to not get too close to their students, to teach the basics, day in and day out.(3)

Rather than continue such methodologies that separate my student's cultural epistemologies from those of school, I invite them to do just the opposite. I often invite students to relay similar stories of alienation and a conflict of identity which emerges once exposed to Anglocentric pedagogies.[3] Along with this revelation comes the awareness that as a Chicana/o and/or Latino/a student, one exists between multiple education epistemologies and that one's subjectivity is constructed by an Anglocentric, hegemonic society. Anzaldúa refers to such awareness as she contemplates her graduate school experience:

> Bereft of your former frame of reference, leaving home has cast you adrift in the liminal space between home and school. In class you feel you're on a rack, body prone across the equator between the diverse notions and nations that comprise you. Remolinos (whirlwinds) sweep you off your feet, pulling you here and there. While home, family, and ethnic culture tug you back to the tribe, to the Chicana indígena you were before, the Anglo world sucks you toward an assimilated, homogenized, whitewashed identity. Each exhorts you to turn your back on other interpretations, other tribes. You face divisions within your cultures—of class, gender, sexuality, nationality, ethnicity. You face both entrenched institutions and the oppositional movements of working-class women, people of color, and queers. Pulled [...] between Chicano nationalists and conservative Hispanics. Suspended between traditional values and feminist ideas, you don't know whether to assimilate, separate, or isolate. ("now let us shift" 548)

From awareness, students are then guided into questioning and critiquing society's construction of their identity and dominant ideologies of the US school system.

The act of questioning one's self emerges because of exposure to multi-ethnic literature at the early stages of a liberal arts education that may allow students to achieve awareness of this education/educación conflict and, more importantly, challenge it by blending the ideologies of their home/culture with those of school. How does this tie in to the original dilemma of incorporating more multi-ethnic texts into Anglocentric secondary and elementary classrooms? By targeting the very people, from all disciplines who will go out into the work place and become administrators, teachers, politicians, school board trustees, parents, etc. If we can expose college students, who will shortly go out into the world as leaders, to the Anglocentrism of institutions, especially institutions of learning, then we may slowly begin to incorporate more Mexican American Studies programs at the high school levels, alter school district's reading lists to be more inclusive of multi-ethnic authors, and try alternative forms of education that teach a whole student, beyond simply teaching them how to take tests. Through such changes, understanding and compassion may emerge especially regarding the oppressions people of color continue to face in education and society. It is this awareness that propels students to take action and resist and transform academia for themselves and for future generations. Such transformations may eventually expand to the world beyond both literature and the classroom, inviting all to "heal the split" that has been imposed on us (Anzaldúa, *Borderlands* 102).

NOTES

1 Michael Foucault's concept of "docile bodies" refers to the description of the image of figure of an ideal soldier whose body and mind can be manipulated to achieve the objective of discipline and control.

2 State of Texas Assessments of Academic Readiness refers to the state student testing program for core subject areas including reading and writing. Students must pass each of these core exams in order to graduate from high school.

3 In using the term Anglo-centric pedagogy, I am referring to the teaching of literature composed by Anglos and Europeans.

WORKS CITED

Anzaldúa, Gloria. *Borderlands/La Frontera.* 2nd ed. San Francisco: Aunt Lute Books, 1999. Print.

---. *The Gloria Anzaldúa Reader.* Ed. AnaLouise Keating. Durham: Duke University Press, 2009. Print.

---. "now let us shift...the path of conocimiento...inner work, public acts." *this bridge we call home: radical visions for transformation.* Eds. Gloria E. Anzaldúa and AnaLouise Keating. New York: Routledge, 2002. Print.

Foucault, Michel. *Discipline and Punish: The Birth of the Prison.* New York: Random House, Inc., 1995. Print.

Rendón, Laura. *Sentipensante (Sensing/Thinking) Pedagogy: Educating for Wholeness, Social Justice, and Liberation.* New York: Stylus Publishing, 2008. Print.

TEACHING LIBERATORY CHICANA/O STUDIES IN THE CORPORATE UNIVERSITY

LINDA HEIDENREICH

The current struggles, issues and problems in Ethnic Studies are similar to the struggles, issues and problems for Ethnic Studies. The challenges from within and without are similar to those issues and problems faced thirty years ago: empowerment of people . . . pride . . . and social transformation of society on all levels.

–*Gloria Anzaldúa, "Nos/otros 'Us' vs. 'Them,' (Des)Conocimientos y Compromisos"*

In college I picked up this book, Yo Soy Joaquin, by Corky Gonzalez, a Chicano. It was a narrative poem about the history of Chicano people, and he took it down to the roots. Then I started reading everything I could get my hands on.

–*Gloria Anzaldúa, Interview with Linda Smuckler*

In an age of social corporatization, how do we teach empowerment, conocimiento y concientisación? As noted by J. Estrella Torrez, the neoliberal politics of today's dominant culture shapes today's university, "Students are viewed as consumers and learning is a commodity easily packaged on the Fordist conveyer belt of neoliberal education [...] a market-driven model [that] structures instruction around workforce preparation" (109). In far too many classrooms, the intersection of a Fordist approach with the rise of the "color-blind society" imposes formidable obstacles to creating spaces of conocimiento and concientisación.

For Anzaldúa, conocimiento was critical to the educational project. During the last two decades of her life she spoke about it in interviews; critical to this essay, she spoke of it in speeches given at college campuses throughout the 1990s. It was a central theme in a talk she gave at Simmon's College in 1997, in a 1999 speech at the University of Illinois, and in the speech she delivered at my own institution, Washington State University, in October of 1997. Conocimiento: knowledge about the self and about the self in relation to the world around us. It is rooted very much in Anzaldúa's earlier and now famous proclamation, "I change myself, I change the world" (*Borderlands* 92). Conocimiento emerges within us when we let down our blinders, face our fears, and reject the distractions the dominant culture sends our way to prevent self-knowledge. Once we know ourselves we can gaze, grounded, at the world around us—we can see it and we can change it (Anzaldúa, "Cracks and Remolinos"; Anzaldúa, "Quincentennial").

As educators grounded in Chicana feminisms, how do we pass on critical tools to the next generation when, as noted by C. Alejandra Elenes, those making curricular decisions at our institutions insist on a curriculum that meets the needs of a fictive *everystudent* (370)?[1] For me, in part, the answer is: we bring our histories and poetry into all our classrooms, whether a course is titled "Chicana/o Studies" or not. That is to say, if we do not consciously create and develop community-specific liberatory pedagogical frames, for those of us who teach in corporatized universities, we risk gradually drifting toward teaching to an environment of fictive *everystudents*. *Everystudents*, with their unmarked racial and ethnic status, of course, are white. Scholars of white privilege unmasked this phenomenon decades ago, yet with the emergence of Fordism in today's university, the problem is once again very pronounced (Elenes 360).

The struggles we face today where many Chicana/o Studies programs are under attack due to national trends toward corporate streamlining, to Fordism, and to the normalizing of assimilationist and Euro-centric presumptions about education, remind us of Gloria Anzaldúa's call to action well over a decade ago, "The current struggles...are similar to those issues and problems faced thirty years ago: Empowerment... social transformation of society on all levels ("Nos/otros"). In this article, I briefly outline the struggles for Chicana/o Studies at our land grant university in the Inland Northwest. The founding and dismantling of Chicana/o Studies at WSU is not unique; it is symptomatic of the neoliberal shift recently mapped by scholars such as Torrez and Slaughter and Rhoades.[2] Like the campuses described by Slaughter and Rhoades, WSU has embraced a corporate vision of the university; as with other campuses where Chicana/o Studies programs were founded in the 1970s, our programs have been dramatically streamlined. If there is a significant difference between WSU and the recent threats we have seen to Ethnic Studies, it is chronology: at WSU our battles with downsizing began long ago.[3] Our history, then, may aid others in their struggles to create and maintain liberatory pedagogies in this time of backlash. And so here I recount some of that struggle in a larger context of national backlash and of the continued need for conocimiento in all our classrooms.

Equally important to mapping the problems we face in any given time, is mapping remedies. Thus, I also map a pedagogy that I increasingly engage when working to create spaces of conocimiento and concientisación in today's corporate university: liberatory Chicana pedagogy through poetry and history. In addressing specific classrooms and specific lesson plans, I hope also to address the instances and contingencies for which Elenes calls when engaging in Chicana and borderlands pedagogy (371).

ORIGINS

From the mid-1960s through the early 1970s, students on high school, college, and university campuses in and beyond the Southwest began to demand programs in Chicana/o studies. Their struggles were successful, in part because they were a result of student, community, and faculty coalition and activism (San Miguel and Valencia 133-156; Delgado Bernal, "Chicana/o Education" 82-86; Pizzaro 5-6). The Chicana/o Studies program at Washington State University shared similar roots in community, activism, and coalition. Central to its formation was the participation of High School Equivalency Program (HEP) students in that activism (Rivera 95-96; Alamillo). In 1969, when WSU students formed their first Mexican American Student Association, HEP students were active in the organization. Later that year, when, due to increased politicization, the group became a MEChA chapter, HEP students were again involved in the decision. In the early years of Chicana/o activism at WSU, college and HEP students worked together and supported each other. As MEChistas, they soon formed strong coalitions with the Black Student Union, the Native American student group, and progressive white students. With their allies, they successfully organized campus and Safeway boycotts of non-union grapes and non-union lettuce; eventually they would stage a strike and sit-in demanding Chicana/o Studies on campus (Rivera 97-99; Rodríguez).[4] Further activism was required to secure funding for the program; finally, on May 28, 1970, WSU announced the establishment of a program in Chicano Studies.[5]

Beginning fall 1970, students were able to major in Chicano Studies. The course offerings were diverse; their common goal was to empower Chicana/o students with knowledge of their own communities and histories, and to equip students with tools to challenge structural inequality within and beyond the university. The founders of the program were committed to forming a program that could do more than teach white students about Mexican Americans (Rivera 99-100; Alamillo). In this insistence, the founders shared aspirations with those fighting for Chicana/o Studies throughout the country: the ability to create a curriculum of liberation—what those of us who study Anzaldúa's work call conocimiento: knowledge of the self and knowledge of one's social location in the world—knowledge that pushes us to action (Anzaldúa, "Quincentennial").

Throughout the 1970s, the program was headed by directors with strong commitments to engaged scholarship—scholarship rooted in community. Students and faculty alike were active in community groups such as Northwest Rural Opportunities, the State Advisory Migrant Education Committee, and the United Farm Workers Organizing Committee. The program formed a partnership with WSU's College of Education to work with bilingual teacher's assistants from the Yakima Valley's public schools so that they could complete their bachelor's degrees. The school of education came to embrace the importance of culturally relevant education and, in relation, to understand that bilingual education must also be bi-cultural. Its curriculum shifted to reflect that knowledge (Alamillo; Rodríguez). In the 1970s, the Chicano Studies program also saw its first tenured faculty member, and course listings grew from ten to more than thirty. Faculty strategically put forward classes for General Education Requirements, which in turn built enrollment and, as a consequence, increased the program's FTEs (Rodríguez).

BACKLASH OF THE 1980S

As the program moved into the 1980s, however, it also moved into the era of conservative backlash that was sweeping the nation. Conservatism affected the implementation of many of the social programs established in the 1960s and 70s. Even the courts backed away from enforcing civil and human rights legislation. According to Anderson and Shapiro, during the 1980s, there was a widespread "de-emphasis on combating discrimination" (273).[6] The rollback, in part was made possible by Reagan's promulgation of the myth of a "color-blind" society. Public discussions about inequality were out and fiscal conservatism was in.[7]

At WSU the administration moved to save overhead by streamlining all ethnic studies programs into a single unit. The dean of the college claimed that in order to save the programs, they would need to be consolidated; he threatened to cut Chicano Studies if they did not agree to the merger (Rodríguez). The program director conceded and in May of 1982, Chicano Studies, Asian

American Studies, and Black Studies were consolidated into the Department of Comparative American Cultures (Alamillo; Rodríguez).[8]

THE DEMISE

Further dismantling of the program occurred precisely at a time in the history of our state when our populations were/are expanding. As we entered the twenty-first century, Washington State shared the growing diversity of the nation-state, with 10.2% of the state population of Latina/o descent (Office of Financial Management). Even in 2000, for counties neighboring Whitman County (the home of WSU), the percentage population was much higher with Yakima, Grant, and Franklin counties all having Latina/o populations of between 20.1% and 47.2%. Between 2006 and 2010, Latinas/os grew from 14% to 18% of the total student population for Washington State (Office of the Superintendent of Public Instruction). As the population of the state shifted, however, Washington State University continued to cut its academic offerings in Chicana/o and Latina/o Studies. It also failed to replace Chicana/o faculty as they were recruited away to other universities.

From 2000 to 2009 various administrators at WSU sought to merge the American Studies Program, the Comparative Ethnic Studies Department and the Department of Women's Studies into one unit. For nine years the units successfully maintained their independence while working collaboratively to bring an interdisciplinary and counter-hegemonic curriculum to the students. Then, in 2009, the university hired a man who valued streamlining and efficiency as dean of the College of Liberal Arts. Today many of us who worked in the former units believe he was brought in to accomplish precisely what he did: he streamlined the college in part by cutting resources from the units most prone to challenging the status quo—completely eliminating the Department of Theatre, and merging American Studies, Comparative Ethnic Studies, and Women's Studies into a single unit. He eliminated departmental representation on the faculty senate and moved the bulk of administrative support out of departments and into service units supporting multiple departments (Geranios; Williams; Washington State University).

Today at WSU there are only two faculty members with any training in Chicana/o Studies who self-identify as Chicana or Chicano (neither of us teaching full-time in the field).[9] Further complicating our struggles, from 2010-2012 when the university streamlined general education requirements, the curriculum committee in charge of the new requirements agreed that only courses with comparative content would now satisfy university Diversity requirements. Their new approach to "diversity" ignored (either deliberately or due to historical amnesia) founding pedagogies rooted in community empowerment, where community knowledge was acknowledged as central, and Chicana/o and other minority knowledges were taught as of value in themselves (Bernal, "Critical Race Theory" 113; Moreno 210).[10] Thus, when I submitted Introduction to Chicana/o Studies for a Diversity designation, it was denied.

At our corporatized, predominately white institution in the Inland Northwest, what do we do when faced with the challenge of mentoring a new generation of students, of creating spaces of conocimiento and concientisación? In putting curriculum forward, we learn from those who built the foundation on which we continue to build: both the feministas who with their scholarship and actions taught us conocimiento, and the professors and activists who built the programs in our home institutions.

As at most universities throughout the nation, when the Chicano Studies program was first founded at WSU, there was no Diversity designation. I learned this when I had the opportunity to speak with one of the faculty members who helped build the program—the first faculty member to be tenured in the program: Prof. Pedro Rodríguez. From him I learned that an early successful strategy for building the curriculum was to locate courses throughout the curriculum with a variety of designations. Instructors crafted new courses and re-crafted old courses to fit general education requirements so that students could take Chicano Studies courses to meet humanities, social science, science, art requirements and more. Many students took one course and then were hooked. Or perhaps they just took one course and were so engaged from seeing themselves as knowledge producers that it gave them the confidence they needed to succeed in various majors. Today, in the twenty-first century, we continue to see studies that map how critical it is for students to be able to do just that (Cambrium, 44-49; Donald).[11]

I listened, learned, and then resubmitted our introductory course as a Humanities course, and it was accepted as such. Similarly, the Queer Identities course which I teach, comparing Queer Chican@ and Black Queer cultural production, I submitted as an Arts course. Such strategies, I believe position us to maintain the few courses we still have, while preparing us to argue and to fight for more resources. Yet, getting the courses on the books as Gen Ed classes is just one step: the second step is overcoming Fordism inside and outside of the classroom. To do this work, as one of two Chicana/o professors who sometimes teaches Chicana/o Studies, I absolutely rely on the work of graduate students. This next generation of scholar-activists is critical to our work not only because they are shaping the university and will continue to do so long after we are gone, but because they are eager to pitch-in with the mentoring of undergraduate students, to create a pedagogy of conocimiento in the classroom, and more. From our rural campus we network with faculty at neighboring campuses (in a rural area like Eastern Washington this means within a three hour drive). We also look to the tools created by our foremothers.

And we learn from our foremothers—especially foremothers who gave us the language of conocimiento, and of writing as soul-making—that "writing is a way of soul making or spirit making" (Anzaldúa, "On the Process of"). Writing is about arguing from facts and knowing how to cite sources, but it is so much more. It can also be, and must be, a means of reflection where students connect the knowledges they bring to the classroom with the knowledge we have to offer them. If we are to not only survive as critical educators in the twenty-first century, but to flourish and equip another generation with the tools to change the world—then writing as soul-making as well as writing as technical skill remains essential to our work.

We do this in a climate not only of academic Fordism, but one where the majority of our students grew up with politicians and social media insisting that "celebrating difference" while "not seeing color" is somehow a recipe for liberation. While color-blindness was promulgated by a long-past administration (three decades ago), popular culture, including reality shows such as *Survivor*, continue to reconstruct the myth. Even talk show hosts such as Ellen make statements such as "well you know I don't see color" (Hentges; Upworthy). Teaching a culturally relevant curriculum, where the *everystudent* is not the norm from which and for which we teach, then, results in pushback.

Yet, over two decades ago, in a commencement speech to students graduating from Kresge College, Anzaldúa reminded them that, "Going to the university is not just intellectual work, but also political" (Anzaldúa, "Another Rite of Passage"). The task at hand is very political; the stakes are high. Each day we walk into the classroom, we engage in either a pedagogy and politics of conocimiento, or a pedagogy and politics of Fordism—a pedagogy and politics of color-blindness and the *everystudent*, or a pedagogy and politics of community and empowerment. In the classroom this means integrating Chicana/o Studies into all courses I teach.

If, as prompted by our university curriculum committee, I teach to a fictive *everystudent*, I erase the realities of Chicana/o students in our classrooms. But if I construct the *everystudent* as Chicana, beautiful things can happen. For students from Chicana/o communities, the classroom becomes a place where they envision themselves as knowledge producers and connect with the long legacy of scholar activists who make our work today possible. For students from dominant cultures, they learn to connect with knowledges where they are not the center of attention—this is uncomfortable for them and so at times they do their best to make the experience uncomfortable for me—but it is an important lesson.[12] When they persevere, learning Chicana/o histories, culture, and epistemologies allows them to lift the veil of colorblindness and individualism to see how their own education, to date, has been biased and kept them from meaningful dialogue and coalition in meeting their own goals. For students from other marginalized communities, what I have seen in my classroom is that most of them make exciting and important connections about our communities and their own home communities.[13] In short, by utilizing Chicana feminist pedagogies, where the *everystudent* to whom I teach is assumed to be Chicana/o, students from a variety of backgrounds become "agents of knowledge who participate in intellectual discourse that links experience, research, community, and social change" (Delgado Bernal, "Critical Race Theory" 113).

And so here I return to my opening epigraph—where in reflecting on how she came to Chicana/o Studies – Gloria Anzaldúa remembered picking up a copy of *Yo Soy Joaquin*. It was one poem, as it intersected with her life experiences, which hooked her on our own creative community cultural production. In her own words, "In college I picked up this book, *Yo Soy Joaquin*, by Corky Gonzalez, a Chicano. It was a narrative poem about the history of Chicano people, and he took it down to the roots. Then I started reading everything I could get my hands on." Poetry is one of those tools that can speak to students in their own specific social locations. It can connect Chicana/o students to their internal and home knowledges; it can push other students to think critically of their relationship to other communities. In its soul and imagery, if read critically, it can dispel the myth of the *everystudent*, and, ironically, push every student to dig deeper.

And so I close this article with a lesson plan—a lesson plan based on a basic poem, one that Pat Mora wrote specifically for young people. The lesson plan is part of a larger project that integrates poetry into our classrooms with the goal of connecting students to our rich histories and to their lived experiences—of acknowledging our students as "holders and creators of knowledge" who can "transform the world into a more just place" (Delgado Bernal, "Critical Race Theory" 106, 108). It can be taught in one long session or broken into two—I often use bits and pieces at different times in the semester.

NEPANTLA POETRY 101

GOALS:

- Students will learn basic historical watersheds in Chicana/o history.
- Students will "meet" major Chicana poets and role models.
- Students will read, interpret, and respond to poems.
- Students will produce their own poetry.
- Conocimiento.

MATERIALS NEEDED:

- Student materials: Composition books, *My Own True Name* (Pat Mora).
- Faculty Materials: Background sheets (with poet biographies and quotations, for distribution), copies of accessible, historically grounded poems such as Gloria Anzaldúa's "Borderlands" and Carmen Tafolla's "Medina Magiadora" (*Five Poets of Aztlán*).

LESSON ONE: HOW TO READ A POEM

Students are introduced to "how to read a poem." Using Mora's "Strong Women," they identify images, use of simile, and are also encouraged to reflect on strong women in their own lives.

OVERVIEW:

1. Introduce the students to "How to Read a Poem" using overhead
2. Introduce students to the poet: Pat Mora
3. Walk students through reading a poem using "Strong Women"

1. INTRODUCTION OF "HOW TO" WITH VISUAL ON OVERHEAD:

How to Read a Poem

- Read it once to introduce yourself to the poem.
- Read it a second time, out loud, and underline phrases that are unclear to you; puzzle them (make notes).
- Read the poem a third time for the story it tells/message it conveys.
- Read the poem out loud once again; enjoy it.

[Narrative: Most poems are meant to move you either to action or to see beauty. This is especially true of Chicana/o poetry. So after you read a poem, ask yourself "what does this poet want me to do?" At a minimum, you will want to read any poem three times.]

2. BACKGROUND SHEET "PAT MORA": DISCUSS QUOTATION, TITLES OF BOOKS, BIOGRAPHY, AND DEFINITION OF NEPANTLA.

3. READ, DISCUSS, RESPOND TO "STRONG WOMEN":

- Have students read the poem silently to "introduce themselves" to the poem.
- Have students read the poem a second time writing down questions about the poem.
- Address the students' questions and then…
- Ask the students questions about the poem:
    - Discuss use of simile, then ask: how is it that the young woman in this poem might be "like cactus"?
    - Why don't the strong women catch her when she falls?
    - She repeats "some women hold me when I need to dream" four times in this one short poem. Why is it so important to dream?
    - Likewise she repeats the line "Strong women, teach me courage to esteem" four times. What or who does she esteem? Why does this take courage?
- Read the poem out loud to the class then encourage students:
    - Reflect for a few minutes on women who have let you dream and/or have taught you *courage to esteem*. These might be women you know, like an auntie, or they might be women you know through history or activism like Dolores Huerta, or Emma Tenayuca.
    - Write one or two paragraphs about that woman or those women and how they teach "courage to esteem."

NOTES

1 As Elenes points out, this is not only a problem in conservative educational spaces, but also in the work of some scholars engaged in Critical Pedagogy, such as Henry Giroux.

2 Slaughter and Rhoades argue that the shift to a corporate university also includes a shift to seeing students as a source of profit where "increased fees for services … increased charges in auxiliary units (e.g., residence life), and an increased tendency to make students foot the bill for new buildings and upgraded services (e.g., student union renovations and recreation centers)…" have made higher education inaccessible to many (74).

3 For example, it was in 2015, according to David Conde, that the University of Northern Colorado proposed to suspend the Mexican American Studies major due to a low number of majors.

4 In an interview, Pedro Rodríguez noted that the lettuce boycott was a significant political and educational struggle on campus, with President Terrell being called on the carpet to disclose whether or not his household used iceberg lettuce. Ultimately the student activists prevailed and the cafeteria offered a romaine alternative. Henceforth all students consuming lettuce in the cafeteria were compelled to make their politics known when they ordered any dish containing lettuce. Those who supported the farmworkers chose romaine, those supporting the growers, iceberg (Pedro Rodríguez, Oral History).

5 Ruben Durán, Zenaida Camacho, Pedro Rodríguez, Phil and Norma Durán, Rudy Cruz, Silvia Lemos Sharma (advisor to MEChA and an instructor for the HEP program), and MEChistA Margarita Mendoza de Sugiyama were all active in the founding and/or early building of the program (Rivera; Alamillo).

6 Anderson and Shapiro map how the 1989 Supreme Court decisions of Wards Cove Packing v. Antonio, Patterson v. McLeon, and Martin v. Wilks, sent a clear message to employers that anti-discrimination legislation would not be strictly enforced. This backlash trickled down to college campuses.

7 As pointed out by John E. Jacob, of the National Urban League, the language was used not only by Reagan, but also by his administration in general. The myth was used by the Justice Department, throughout the Reagan administration, to dismantle affirmative action ("NUL Assesses").

8 The unit was later renamed Comparative Ethnic Studies.

9 My own teaching is split between Women's Studies and Chicana/o Studies courses, and Dr. Brian McNeill teaches one upper division course when he is able.

10 Delgado Bernal maps how such knowledges have the power to unveil the bias of Euro-centric epistemologies. In Moreno's "Plática," it is Sammy Ybarra, a field representative for Senator Barbara Boxer, who notes the importance of community knowledges, insisting (to

Moreno): "If you are going to write the book, make it clear so these students can learn about themselves. Because you know, they are hitting us from all sides…"

11 Ironically, the Cambium Study of the Tucson Mexican American Studies Department, ordered by the Tucson Unified School District in an effort to discredit the program, contains one of the few quantitative studies mapping the positive impact of Mexican American Studies on student over-all academic performance.

12 One young man, for example, went so far as to wear a T-shirt that read "Anglo-Saxon" to class.

13 A key example of this is the work of Ms. J. Harris, an undergraduate who was intrigued by the role of colorism that continues to weave through both our communities (Chicana/o and African American). Energized with trying to understand this important and negative dynamic she went well beyond course requirements in her research project and eventually won the 2012 NACCS PNW Foco award in undergraduate research.

WORKS CITED

Alamillo, José. "A Brief History of Chicanos/as and Latinas/os at Washington State University, 1950-1990." Web. 1 Feb, 2015

Anderson, Debora and David Shapiro. "Racial Difference in Access to High-Paying Jobs and the Wage Gap between Black and White Women." *Industrial and Labor Relations Review* 49.2 (1996): 273 -286. *JSTOR.* Web. 6 Jul. 2016.

Anzaldúa, Gloria E. "Another Rite of Passage, Kresge College Commencement Address." TS. 1991. Gloria Evangelina Anzaldúa Papers, Benson Latin American Collection, University of Texas at Austin.

---. *Borderlands/La Frontera: The New Mestiza.* 4th Ed. San Francisco: Aunt Lute Books, 2012. Print.

---. "Cracks and Remolinos and Queer Conocimientos, keynote address at Washington State University." October 7, 1996. Video File. Gloria Evangelina Anzaldúa Papers, Benson Latin American Collection, University of Texas at Austin.

---. "Nos/otros 'Us' vs. 'Them,' (Des)Conocimientos y Compromisos." October 1999. TS. Gloria Evangelina Anzaldúa Papers, Benson Latin American Collection, University of Texas at Austin.

---. "On the Process of Feminist Image Making (workshop)." 1982. TS. Gloria Evangelina Anzaldúa Papers, Benson Latin American Collection, University of Texas at Austin.

---. "Quincentennial: From Victimhood to Active Resistance, Interview with Inés Hernández-Ávila." *Gloria E. Anzaldúa, Interviews: Entrevistas.* Ed. AnaLouise Keating. New York: Routledge, 2000. Print.

---. "Turning Points: An Interview with Linda Smuckler (1987)." *Gloria E. Anzaldúa, Interviews: Entrevistas.* Ed. AnaLouise Keating. New York: Routledge, 2000. Print.

Cambrium Learning, Inc. *Curriculum Audit of the Mexican American Studies Department, Tucson Unified School District, Tucson, Arizona.* Cambium Learning, Inc. 2011. Web. 19 June 2013.

Conde, David. "UNC Mexican-American Studies at a Crossroad." *La Voz Bilingue.* 15 April 2015. Web. 6 Jul. 2016.

Delgado Bernal, Dolores. "Chicana/o Education from the Civil Rights Era to the Present." In *The Elusive Quest for Equality: 150 Years of Chicana/Chicano Education.* Ed. José F. Moreno. Cambridge: Harvard Educational Review, 1999. Print.

---. "Critical Race Theory, Latino Critical Theory, and Critical Raced-Gendered Epistemologies: Recognizing Students of Color as Holders and Creators of Knowledge." *Qualitative Inquiry* 7.1 (2002): 105-126. Web. 18 September 2015.

Donald, Brooke. "Stanford Study Suggests Academic Benefits to Ethnic Studies Courses." *Stanford News*. Stanford University. 16 Jan. 2016. Web. 26 Jan. 2016.

Elenes, C. Alejandra. "Reclaiming the Borderlands: Chicana/o Identity, Difference, and Critical Pedagogy." *Educational Theory* 46.3 (1997): 359-375. *Education Full Text.* Web. 6 Jul. 2016.

Geranios, Nicholas K. "WSU Announces Final Cuts: 359 Jobs, Three Programs." *Spokesman Review.* 18 June 2009. Web. 8 July 2016.

Hentges, Sarah. "(In)Visible Fissures and the 'Multicultural' American: Interrupting Race, Ethnicity, and Imperialism through TV's Survivor." *Ethnic Studies Review* 31.2 (2008): 100-119. *JSTOR.* Web. 6 Jul. 2016.

Moreno, José F. "150 Years of Chicano/Chicana Education: Intergenerational Plática." In *The Elusive Quest for Equality: 150 Years of Chicano/a Education.* Ed. José F. Moreno. Cambridge: Harvard Educational Review, 1999. Print.

"NUL Again Assesses the Status of Blacks." *Washington Information.* 23.14 (1987). *Ethnic News Watch.* Web. 6 Jul. 2016.

Office of Financial Management, Executive Summary: Population by Age, Sex, Race and Hispanic Origin: 2000 and 2010. Web. 6 Jul. 2016.

Office of the Superintendent of Public Instruction, Washington State Report Card. Web. 6 Jul. 2016.

Pizarro, Marcos. *Chicanas and Chicanos in School: Racial Profiling, Identity Battles, and Empowerment.* Austin: University of Texas, 2005. Print.

Rivera, Ericka with Linda Heidenreich. "The Chicano/a Studies Program at Washington State University: Its Origins and Current Challenges." *McNair Journal* 3 (2005): 90-103. Print.

Rodríguez, Pedro. "Oral History Interview by Linda Heidenreich." 17 September 2013. Manuscripts, Archives, and Special Collections, Washington State University Libraries, Pullman, WA.

San Miguel Jr., Guadalupe and Richard R. Valencia. "From the Treaty of Guadalupe Hidalgo to Hopwood: The Educational Plight and Struggle of Mexican Americans in the Southwest." In *Legacies of Brown: Multiracial Equity in American Education.* Eds. Dorinda J. Carter, Stella Flores, and Richard J. Reddick. Reprint Series No. 40. Cambridge: Harvard Educational Review, 2004. Print.

Slaughter, Sheila and Gary Rhoades. "The Neo-liberal University." *New Labor Forum* 6 (2000): 73-79. Print.

Torrez, J. Estrella. "Translating Chicana Testimonios into Pedagogy for a White Midwestern Classroom. *Chicana/Latina Studies* 14.2 (2015): 101-130. Print.

Upworthy. "Here's Why You Don't Ask a Feminist to Hawk Your Sexist Product." 14 November 2013. Web. 27 January 2016.

Washington State University Faculty Senate Bylaws. Web. 28 Jan 2016.

Williams, June Audrey. "Careers, Interrupted." *Chronicle of Higher Education*. 28 September 2012. *Academic Search Complete*. Web. 6 Jul. 2016.

FORGING SPACES OF TEACHING AND LEARNING

ENACTING A CRITICAL PEDAGOGY OF *AMASAMIENTO* IN THE FIRST-YEAR WRITING CLASS

ELIZABETH BLOMSTEDT KEATING

Students' Right to Their Own Language was first presented at the 1974 meeting of the Conference on College Composition and Communication as a response to the influx of "nontraditional" college students who used dialects or languages other than Standard English. The resolution reads in part: "We affirm the students' right to their own patterns and varieties of language—the dialects of their nurture or whatever dialects in which they find their own identity and style" (*Students'*). Today, forty years after that resolution was originally presented, first-year-writing teachers continue to struggle with how exactly to enact this affirmation of student dialect and language within the first-year-writing classroom. As Geneva Smitherman describes the continued attempts to embrace language diversity in "The Historical Struggle for Language Rights in CCCC," the 1974 resolution was not an attempt by the CCCC at "being trendy, nor politically correct," but rather a response "to a developing crisis in college composition classrooms, a crisis caused by the cultural and linguistic mismatch between higher education and the nontraditional (by virtue of Color and class) students who were making their imprint upon the academic landscape for the first time in history" (19). In the decades since the resolution was passed, college campuses have continued to grow more diverse, creating a writing classroom that benefits from a wide range of perspectives and backgrounds. Nowhere is this more clear than at my own institution, the University of Houston, which boasts the second most diverse campus in the nation. And yet, this "cultural and linguistic mismatch" between the university and its changing student body continues as first-year-writing instructors struggle with how to address language diversity in our classrooms. As Jaime Mejía points out, those of us who teach in the Southwest are particularly at fault for failing to consider how to shape a pedagogy for our Mexican American students who often write and speak in complex, multilingual rhetorical situations. Mejía criticizes first-year-writing instructors for neglecting to create "pedagogical approaches [that] understand the robust dynamics of this hybrid rhetorical combination in countless discourses currently used throughout the Southwest and anywhere else Latinos/as find themselves" (52).

In search for a proper pedagogical approach to language diversity in the first-year-writing classroom, I turn to Gloria Anzaldúa's incomparable work, *Borderlands/La Frontera: The New Mestiza*. Much of Anzaldúa's work reads as a love letter to linguistic diversity, and I've found success teaching selections from "How to Tame a Wild Tongue" as a testament to the importance of language and dialect acceptance. But we can also see a potential pedagogical approach developing out of the text of *Borderlands* in Anzaldúa's chapter titled "*La conciencia de la mestiza* / Towards a New Consciousness," in which she lays out the potential for a new *mestiza* consciousness that embraces contradictions and ambiguities instead of policing them by erecting borders. She demonstrates how this new *mestiza* might be enacted through *amasamiento*:

> I am cultureless because, as a feminist, I challenge the collective cultural/religious male-derived beliefs of Indo-Hispanics and Anglos; yet I am cultured because I am participating in the creation of yet another culture, a new story to explain the world and our participation in it, a new value system with images and symbols that connect us to each other and to the planet. *Soy un amasamiento*, I am an act of kneading, of uniting and joining that not only has produced both a creature of darkness and a creature of light, but also a creature that questions the definitions of light and dark and gives them new meanings. (102–3)

This concept of *amasamiento* reflects Anzaldúa's own views of language, specifically the many different languages and dialects she describes as making up her own personal language practice. But we can also embrace *amasamiento* as a strategy for teaching writing. In "Discovering a 'Proper Pedagogy': The Geography of Writing at the University of Texas-Pan American," Dora Ramírez-Dhoore and Rebecca Jones describe the difficult position first-year-writing instructors often find themselves in, being caught "between the idea that students should be allowed to express their own language and culture and the need to teach them 'academic discourse' or 'the dominant language'" (77). The solution is to embrace both—to enact the new *mestiza* consciousness by making spaces for many forms of language in the first-year-writing classroom. By enacting a pedagogy of *amasamiento*, Ramírez-Dhoore and Jones argue we can "[create] another space where students can make sense of the theories and pedagogies that they face in the classroom in relation to their familiar space" (77). The question now is how to enact it. In this chapter, I present three broad approaches to enacting a pedagogy of *amasamiento*, each with its own potential classroom practices: to teach the dominant discourse in a way that acknowledges the systems of power that make it dominant, to teach the value of transcultural repositioning, and to embrace hybridity.

TEACHING LANGUAGE WITHIN THE CULTURE OF POWER

The first step to enacting this pedagogy is to teach the dominant discourse within the context of the systems of power that make it dominant. The difficult decision that first-year-writing instructors face when deciding how to respond to language diversity in their classes is often oversimplified as a choice between embracing languages and dialects students bring with them into the classroom *or* teaching them to write within the dominant discourse so that they can succeed in the university and beyond. We see strong arguments for embracing home languages and dialects in Anzaldúa's words from *Borderlands*:

> Until I can take pride in my language, I cannot take pride in myself. Until I can accept as legitimate Chicano Texas Spanish, Tex-Mex and all the other languages I speak, I cannot accept the legitimacy of myself. Until I am free to write bilingually and to switch codes without having always to translate, while I still have to speak English or Spanish when I would rather speak Spanglish, and as long as I have to accommodate the English speakers rather than having them accommodate me, my tongue will be illegitimate. (81)

This idea is affirmed in "Students' Rights to Their Own Language." We cannot downplay the ways that we harm our students when we dismiss their dialects or languages as "wrong." But, we also see the importance of the first-year-writing class preparing students for participation in academic discourse. David Bartholomae argues in "Inventing the University" that this expectation makes the first-year-writing class a class on language acquisition:

> [The students] have to invent the university by assembling and mimicking its language, finding some compromise between idiosyncrasy, a personal history, and the requirements of convention, the history of a discipline. They must learn to speak our language. Or they must dare to speak it,

> or to carry off the bluff, since speaking and writing will most certainly be required before the skill is "learned." And this, understandably, causes problems. (5)

Anzaldúa even acknowledged this in her interview with composition scholar Andrea Lunsford, stating that "to make it in this society you have to know the discipline, if it's teaching, if it's composition, if it's carpentry" (13). But as Bartholomae's description attests, this is not a small undertaking, and preparing students to participate in the dominant discourse could in itself take an entire semester.

But we can teach the dominant discourse in a way that points to the problematic nature of dismissing a student's personal language practice and empowers them to participate in that dominant discourse in order to change it, enabling language and dialect acceptance. We can follow the example critical pedagogue Lisa Delpit provides in *Other People's Children*: "I prefer to be honest with my students. I tell them that their language and cultural style is unique and wonderful but that there is a political power game that is also being played, and if they want to be in on that game there are certain games that they too must play" (40). In other words, we can teach Standard English in a way that recognizes the "culture of power" that privileges some forms of language over others, and we can empower students to change that culture. This method requires transparency—teachers must be willing to have uncomfortable discussions with students about how and why certain dialects and languages are more highly regarded than others. In my own writing class, I like to spur this discussion on the very first day of class by showing them a video: Jamila Lyiscott's "3 Ways to Speak English," in which she describes her own experiences speaking three different varieties of language in different situations in her life. Lyiscott presents her ideas in a slam-poetry style, explaining how she reacted when she was called "articulate" for speaking Standard English as an African American woman:

> Home, school and friends
> I'm a tri-lingual orator
> Sometimes I'm consistent with my language now
> Then switch it up so I don't bore later
> Sometimes I fight back two tongues
> While I use the other one in the classroom
> And when I mistakenly mix them up
> I feel crazy like ... I'm cooking in the bathroom
> I know that I had to borrow your language because mines was stolen
> But you can't expect me to speak your history wholly while mines is broken.

I have students write responses to the video and the ideas Lyiscott presents in it before leading a class discussion about the ways different languages and dialects are treated. For a composition class, Lyiscott's ideas also lead well into a discussion on rhetorical situation while still acknowledging the ways powerful entities in our culture police and privilege certain forms of language. It also gives me, as an instructor, an appropriate place to voice my own acceptance of other languages and dialects and explain why some of the major papers will be written in Standard English—because that is the language expected by other university professors and by future employers and a language students need to be comfortable with in order to change those rigid conventions.

TEACHING THE VALUE OF TRANSCULTURAL REPOSITIONING

Another strategy for enacting a pedagogy of *amasamiento* is to teach students the value of transcultural repositioning, a practice theorized by Juan Guerra. In "Emerging Representations, Situated Literacies, and the Practice of Transcultural Repositioning," Guerra warns writing instructors to be careful to teach dominant discourses "without having our students succumb to the socialization and acculturation inherent in the learning of dominant literacies to the point where they begin to deny the legitimacy of their experiences with other situated literacies" (15). Delpit's prescribed technique certainly helps prevent that, but so does what Guerra calls transcultural repositioning, the rhetorical skill of moving between different languages and dialects in different circumstances. Embracing transcultural repositioning creates a greater potential for overcoming the discrimination and inequality enacted through language, as Guerra explains:

> If enacted critically, transcultural repositioning can open the door to different ways of seeing and thinking about the increasingly fluid and hybridized world that is emerging around us. [...] By invoking the power and authority inherent in our literacy practices, and especially in the strategic rhetorical ability that more and more members of our community are developing as we learn to navigate our way through the perilous social and political waters of a nation in upheaval, we may yet chart our own destiny and ensure that everyone among us is granted the right to personal agency and self-determination. (8)

Beyond teaching the dominant discourse within a certain framework, transcultural repositioning teaches all discourses as valuable within certain circumstances, encouraging students to hone their language practices and use them to their advantage. Again, in a classroom dedicated to the teaching of rhetoric and writing, we can see how discussions of rhetorical situation could easily lead into discussions about utilizing different language practices in different circumstances. Guerra gives us three concrete ways to enact this transcultural repositioning in the classroom:

> 1. Making all students aware of "the ways in which the process of transculturation plays itself out in all of our lives" (18)
>
> 2. Having "students read selections from a number of autobiographies in which the authors grapple with the consequences of their hard-won identities" in order to "highlight the political implications of such restrictive and racist language policies" (19)
>
> 3. Sharing personal experiences and asking "students to delve into their own personal experiences in ways that will encourage them to reflect on how the practice of transcultural repositioning has played or can play itself out in their own lives" (19)

These three ideas can be carried out in a variety of ways, through both broad classroom strategies and specific assignments, but one assignment that I have found lends itself well to a careful study of transcultural repositioning is the literacy autobiography. However, when I've assigned the standard literacy autobiography assignment that appears in most textbooks, I've found that students often shy away from writing about their acquisition of other dialects or languages and instead recount how they learned Standard English, often in the classroom setting. Instructors must craft a specific assignment that pushes students to think about how they learned to use different languages and different "Englishes" in different circumstances.

There are several ways to go about creating this specific type of literacy autobiography. First, I prime students for thinking about language use other than Standard English through class discussions about code-switching, rhetorical context, and transcultural repositioning. These fit well at the beginning of the semester and can be instigated through discussion of the Lyiscott video or through brief excerpts from Guerra's work. I have also found success implementing sample literacy narratives that involve multiple languages or dialects, a nod toward Guerra's second suggestion. Students have responded particularly well to an excerpt from Jay Z's *Decoded* in which he describes his experiences becoming "literate" in the language conventions of hip-hop. These readings and the work we do with them encourage students to think about language acquisition beyond the grammatical and syntactical conventions they learned in an English classroom, and they also create space for continued discussion of the power at work in restrictive language policies. Finally, I craft the assignment sheet for the literacy autobiography so that it asks students to reflect specifically on the ways that they learned different languages or dialects, and which were privileged in what circumstances and why. In order to heed

Guerra's suggestion to encourage all students, even those who are well-versed in the dominant discourse, to consider how they engage in transcultural repositioning, I take a suggestion from Gail Okawa and encourage students who are unsure of what to write about to "do research on their own family language histories—the language(s) of their heritages, including stories passed down or remembered" (116). I'll also heed Guerra's advice and share with students what my own family language research revealed to me. Crafting the literacy autobiography in this way encourages students to think of their language as Anzaldúa does, as an *amasamiento* of different languages and dialects, and it helps instructors validate other forms of language and dialect by recognizing the value of being able to engage in the rhetorical work of transcultural repositioning.

TEACHING STUDENTS TO EMBRACE HYBRIDITY

Finally, we can begin enacting a pedagogy of *amasamiento* by embracing hybridity in writing—by making a space for students to make use of different languages or dialects other than Standard English. In "Inviting the Mother Tongue: Beyond 'Mistakes,' 'Bad English,' and 'Wrong Language,'" Peter Elbow provides one way that we might do this: by allowing students to write drafts in the dialect that they are most comfortable with and revise those drafts into a final paper written in Standard English. Certainly, this is one way to embrace hybridity, creating a space for students to work through ideas in another dialect before "translating" their work to Standard English, and I've embraced this in my classroom by being flexible about the type of drafts students turn in. This semester, I had two students who peer-reviewed each other's papers, which were both written in Standard English, by verbally discussing potential revisions in Spanish, a language one of the students was more comfortable speaking in. These approaches embrace *amasamiento* by accepting different languages and dialects at different steps of the writing process.

But like Kim Brian Lovejoy, I do not think that our embracing other languages and dialects in the writing classroom should end in the drafting process. As Lovejoy points out, "Not all pieces of writing can or should be transformed into SWE," citing the personal essay as a piece of writing that would almost always benefit from being written in a dialect other than Standard Written English (105). The literacy autobiography I described also fits this category; when asking students to write about experiences with different languages and dialects, it would be unreasonable to ask that students write only in Standard English. And as Jaime Mejía explains, this acceptance of other dialects and languages may include embracing a hybrid of languages and dialects, particularly for those of us who teach bilingual students in the Southwest:

> [F]or Mexican Americans in the Southwest and throughout the United States, as well as for other Latino/a groups, rhetorical situations and strategies often include a tactical mixture of both English and Spanish. These rhetorical situations and strategies include both colloquial and more formal usages of these two languages. Yet pedagogical approaches seldom understand the robust dynamics of this hybrid rhetorical combination in countless discourses currently used throughout the Southwest and anywhere else Latinos/as find themselves. (52)

Mejía calls for those in rhetoric and composition to embrace this hybridity, and one way we can do it is by being open to hybrid use of language in student writing. Just as we teach undergraduates about the rhetorical and strategic choices made by Anzaldúa and other writers who choose to write in multiple languages in the same text, we should encourage students to make those same choices when incorporating multiple languages and dialects in their writing. We should posit these decisions as not only rhetorical ones but acts of protest, a response to the power systems that have condemned other forms of language that are not Standard English. Though I want my students to learn Standard English in order to be taken seriously by the dominant discourse, I want them to embrace that *amasamiento* that Anzaldúa embraces in her own work in order to question the language policing that happens in the dominant culture.

In my classroom, I encourage the use of hybrid or alternative language practices in writing assignments other than the literacy autobiography. I often do so through use of a course blog, which I have used in both face-to-face and online classes. For their first blog posts, I ask students to consider the conventions of the "blog genre" by studying different blogs and to determine what kinds of language practices and rhetorical conventions bloggers employ. The conclusion we draw as a class is that this genre is far more flexible than the genre of "academic research paper," and thus, I encourage students to write in a manner that they would call "less formal," a manner that accommodates other dialects or hybridity. I do stress to students that even if their posts are in nonstandard English, they should still spend time crafting and editing their blog entries (since, after all, their blog genre study showed that bloggers do pay careful attention to detail and self-presentation). This ensures that students don't use this allowance to write less formally as an excuse for them to be careless or to post quick, shallow responses. Dedicating this space in the course to less formal writing enacts *amasamiento* by making my class hybrid in a different way; while many of the major papers, like the researched argument, are written in Standard English, students still have a space where they are free to employ their own personal dialect or language practices, including hybrid language. I've also found that opening the blog space up this way has led to more genuine and thoughtful responses from students, including hybridity in both language choices and in creating multimodal blog posts, and has made students more willing to engage meaningfully in the course.

"*Soy un amasamiento*, I am an act of kneading, of uniting and joining." As I embark on each new semester teaching students from a variety of language backgrounds, Anzaldúa's words serve as a reminder for how to craft a course that both embraces those personal language practices **and** teaches students to participate in the dominant discourse. Though the specific classroom strategies I've presented here are fairly adaptable, I encourage all first-year-writing instructors to find ways of embracing language diversity and enacting a pedagogy of *amasamiento* that works for their students and within their institutional constraints. The most important thing is to embrace rather than condemn. Instead of forcing students to adhere to Standard English in all of their writing, dividing students based on language practices, we can embrace *amasamiento* and make our classes a place where students are exposed to other dialects and languages and where students feel free to embrace their own complex identities.

WORKS CITED

Anzaldúa, Gloria. *Borderlands/La Frontera: The New Mestiza.* 4th ed. San Francisco: Aunt Lute Books, 2012. Print.

Bartholomae, David. "Inventing the University." *Writing on the Margins.* Palgrave Macmillan US, 2005. 60-85.

Delpit, Lisa. *Other People's Children: Cultural Conflict in the Classroom.* New York: The New Press, 2006. Print.

Elbow, Peter. "Inviting the Mother Tongue: Beyond 'Mistakes,' 'Bad English,' and 'Wrong Language.'" JAC 19.3 (1999): 358–99.

Guerra, Juan C. "Emerging Representations, Situated Literacies, and the Practice of Transcultural Repositioning." Kells, Balester, and Villanueva 1–23.

Kells, Michelle H., Valerie M. Balester, and Victor Villanueva, eds. *Latino/a Discourses: On Language, Identity & Literacy Education.* Portsmouth, NH: Boynton/Cook, 2004. Print.

Lovejoy, Kim Brian. "Practical Pedagogy for Composition." *Language Diversity in the Classroom: From Intention to Practice.* Eds. Geneva Smitherman and Victor Villanueva. Carbondale: Southern Illinois University Press, 2003. 89–108. Print.

Lunsford, Andrea. "Toward a Mestiza Rhetoric: Gloria Anzaldúa on Composition and Postcoloniality." JAC 18.1 (1998): 1–27. PDF.

Lyiscott, Jamila. "3 Ways to Speak English." Online video clip. TED. TED Conferences. Feb. 2014. Web. 8 Oct. 2015.

Mejía, Jaime. "Bridging Rhetoric and Composition Studies with Chicano and Chicana Studies: A Turn to Critical Pedagogy." Kells, Balester, and Villanueva 40–56.

Okawa, Gail Y. "'Resurfacing Roots': Developing a Pedagogy of Language Awareness from Two Views." *Language Diversity in the Classroom: From Intention to Practice.* Eds. Geneva Smitherman and Victor Villanueva. Carbondale: Southern Illinois University Press, 2003. 109–34. Print.

Ramírez-Dhoore, Dora and Rebecca Jones. "Discovering a 'Proper Pedagogy': The Geography of Writing at the University of Texas-Pan American." *Teaching Writing with Latino/a Students: Lessons Learned at Hispanic-Serving Institutions.* Eds. Christina Kirklighter, Diana Cardenas, and Susan Wolff Murphy. Albany: SUNY Press, 2007. 63–86.

Smitherman, Geneva. "The Historic Struggle for Language Rights in the CCCC." *Language Diversity in the Classroom: From Intention to Practice.* Eds. Geneva Smitherman and Victor Villanueva. Carbondale: Southern Illinois University Press, 2003. 7–39. Print.

Students' Right to Their Own Language. Committee on CCCC Language Statements. *College Composition and Communication* 25.3 (Fall 1974). Special Issue. Ed. Edward P.J. Corbett.

TERM PAPERS Y *TAQUERÍAS*

CHICANX *NEPANTLERAS* IN GRADUATE STUDY

ROBERTO C. OROZCO

ESTEE HERNÁNDEZ

Our institution is comprised of 15 percent Latinx undergraduate and graduate students. With this relatively high percentage of Latinx students, *hay comunidad*, and one that centers on the pan-ethnic Latinx experience. As Chicanxs in North Florida, our stories are not often represented in Latinx discourse. Additionally, this marginality is complicated by the severe underrepresentation of Latinxs in our respective graduate programs—so much so that we are often made to speak on behalf of a "singular" Latinx community, when that is not only impossible, but we do not even feel that we fully belong in said community.

In a way, our *chicanismo* is nested in a larger *latinidad*, which is then nested in an overarching Eurocentric academic culture. It engenders a compounded sense of marginalization—of being a minority within a minority. Straddling such simultaneous borderlands incites compounded dissonance. This dissonance elicits pain. However, we believe that *nepantla*—the margin—is also a site of liberation and resistance. From the dissonance, we develop *facultad* to "see through" marginality and to find consonance in our own lives as emerging scholars. *Nepantla* bears the potential for beautiful transformation and growth.

Our border perspectives—sitting on the border of *latinidad*, which sits on the border of academia—undergird our *autohistoria-teoría*. Our time as graduate students has focused on creating bridges between seemingly disparate parts of ourselves. As *nepantleras*, we are committed to mending the broken pieces of our spirits and finding the center—a place where mind.body.spirit coalesce. We do so in resistance to normative practices in academia and a pressure to flatten a diverse *latinidad*. This paper is a *testimonio* of our experiences. While our journey is necessarily specific to us, we believe that it can easily connect or be applied to other marginalized identities within graduate study and academia as a whole.

WHY WE WRITE

As first-generation students, we have experienced marginality throughout our entire postsecondary career at predominantly White institutions (PWIs). This marginality, however, has been exacerbated in graduate study—where a numerical presence of People of Color is even smaller, and where fewer interventions toward inclusion have taken hold. In fact, we are the only Chicanxs in our master's and doctoral programs, and we can count the Latinx students between both of our programs on two hands. Although Latinxs now comprise the largest Population of Color in U.S. higher education, our presence has not transferred to graduate study.

For those of us who have made it to graduate study, we are met with structures that have changed little to accommodate our diverse needs and ways of learning. This is frustrating, because we know that institutions benefit from our output and labor, yet we are expected to assimilate to the larger Eurocentric culture of academia. We are encouraged to pursue the kind of research that reduces experiences to numbers and variables. Our research is invalidated, our perspectives are dismissed as extreme, and we are accused of "navel-gazing" when we write about *nuestra gente*. Constantly challenging dominant discourse in class is exhausting and, sometimes, we let microaggressions slide. All of these things weigh on our spirit and prevent us from being fully ourselves.

Still, we recognize that it is a privilege to occupy space in academia. Our families made tremendous sacrifices for us to be here, and our younger siblings look to us as role models to follow. As student affairs administrators, we serve as visual representations of success to other im/migrant first-generation Chicanxs who participate in our programs and frequent our offices. While academia is fraught with problems, we believe that it bears the potential for transformation. As educators and as *nepantleras*, we are committed to being the bridges that engender growth and possibility. It is this sense of critical hope that sustains us despite the pervasive marginality. It is our journey towards equanimity that necessitates our resistance.

OUR CHICANX THEORETICAL EPISTEMOLOGY

As student affairs educators, we study and reference theoretical frameworks that have been constructed based on the experiences of White students. Existing theories often exclude the voices of people with marginalized identities. These theories influence how we see ourselves and how we understand our lived experiences. Scholars critique these theories, because they have not been applied to Students of Color. Infusing our voices within these theories comes at the expense of acculturating the voices of People of Color to fit within White models. To fit these models means to disassociate ourselves from our lived experiences—to take our authentic and unapologetic mind.body.spirit out of the narrative.

To have theory is to hold knowledge; therefore, theory is a set of knowledge ("Haciendo Caras" xxv). However, we have been excluded from theorizing spaces in academia. Dominant discourse marginalizes our ways of knowing. We must not allow ourselves to be invalidated and silenced. It is imperative that we insert ourselves in discourse, that we (re)center our "flesh and blood experiences" in theory, that we bring theory down from the ivory towers and into communities; "The physical realities of our lives [...] fuse to create a politic born out of necessity" (Moraga 23). Our daily lived experiences as Chicanx graduate students necessitate theory. Our politic, our ontology, lives in the margin. Our body is text (Anzaldúa, *Light in the Dark* 5).

Theory in the flesh pushes us into reconstructing our experiences as *nepantleras*. Anzaldúa used the word "nepantla," a Nahuatl word meaning "in-between space" to refer to individuals that move within multiple, conflicting spaces (Keating 6). Keating insists, "*Nepantleras* must be willing to open themselves to personal risks and potential woundings such as self-division, isolation, misunderstanding, and rejection" (6). *Nepantla* situates us in a place of dissonance, facilitating multiple lived realities as Chicanx graduate students. It fosters the *facultad* that makes us more agile, makes us *naguales*, facilitates our persistence, and fuels our activism. Occupying exclusionary spaces requires us to consciously build bridges between worlds. Such bridges allow us to move between and within *latinidad*—in the highly pan-ethnic geographic region in which we live.

SITUATING OUR AUTOHISTORIA-TEORÍA

This constancy of straddling borderlands situates us in a space with confounding truths that manifest themselves contextually. As Chicanxs in North Florida, a space like the taco truck fosters a sense of belonging that cultivates our *facultad*—a place of sensing and feeling without consciousness—as we dyadically process our discomfort in academia (*Borderlands* 60). When we are in a space like the taco truck, we are allowed to just Be, without questioning—stepping in and being welcomed as if this were our home. Within academia and our profession, we constantly negotiate how we "show up," as well as the potential consequences of just "being ourselves."

Our *autohistoria* is an amalgam of actual and fictive events and conversations retold as one narrative, with theoretical underpinnings ("now let us shift" 578). We employ *autohistoria-teoría* to honor ourselves as *nepantleras.* Crossing the bridge and constructing a new self in *conocimiento* is a spiritual (re)birth. *Autohistoria* affords the opportunity to anchor our voices as they intersect with theory, thoughts, and memories—to complicate what is real, true, and lived. We choose to use the word "I" to distinguish ourselves between narrations and our lived experiences.

Roberto C. Orozco identifies as a Chicano. Born near the Chicago area, Roberto spent a majority of his childhood in Irapuato, Guanajuato, Mexico. His family then decided to relocate to Sioux City, Iowa, where he later went on to become the first person in his family to pursue higher education. As a first-generation Chicano student, he has had to navigate complexities to persist through the educational pipeline. All of his degrees are from PWIs: two from the Midwest and one from the southeast region. Roberto's family members have always occupied intense labor positions, such as meat-packing plant workers, construction workers, and farm workers. Roberto is the oldest of four siblings.

Estee Hernández identifies as a Chicana/Tejana. She spent the earliest part of her childhood in Matamoros, Tamaulipas, Mexico and at about the age of five, her family relocated to Brownsville, Texas. Her parents affirmed her educational aspirations, but made it clear that they would not be able to finance a college degree. As a result, she navigated the college choice process independently and blindly. She has since leaned on her community of scholars and educators for her graduate program selection processes. All of her degrees are from PWIs. Both her mother and father are Mexican (her mother is a naturalized US citizen), and both stopped formal education in *secundaria.* Her father works in construction, and her mother is an assembly line worker. Estee has two younger siblings.

NUESTRA AUTOHISTORIA: VISITANDO LA TAQUERÍA

Estee sits in her corner cubicle, leaning into her double monitors, blinking twice as she cross-references student applications. Cubicles line the walls of the first floor of the department, and Estee's is unmistakable. Adorned with pictures, memories, sweet notes written by students on Post-its, and a money tree that has far outgrown its pot, it is a bright and colorful space. She stops typing, counts applications, tallies recommendations, squints. She can hear Roberto's projecting voice from across the office.

"Te tengo que decir algo!" Roberto exclaims, rushing towards Estee's cubicle.

Roberto walks into the cubicle and slumps in his usual spot: the chair directly in front of Estee's desk. He cannot contain his excitement.

"I finally found it."

"¿Qué encontraste ahora?"

"La taco truck!" Roberto says with accomplishment. "It felt like I was back home: the language, the food, *el estar con mi gente. Y la señora es de Guanajuato también!* It's a place where we can just be ourselves! We have to go. I have to take you."

Roberto spoke with urgency, because this discovery meant more than authentic Mexican food. It was an opportunity to assert Self without conscientiously thinking about the space in which they found themselves. *Mestizxs* in academe, they are *naguales*, shifting with context, thoughtfully considering, "How am I showing up today?" But at the taco truck, they could just Be. It represented the possibility of home, mind.body.spirit in sync.

On the drive to the taco truck, Estee prompts, "So you're done with your first year of graduate school. How do you feel?" Roberto feels his mind racing with thoughts and contrasting feelings, not knowing what he is about to say or how he is going to say it. He asks himself, "*¿Qué le digo?*" He recognizes the privilege it is to pursue a graduate degree, but he also does not want to continue to suppress how he feels. Still in thought, the topic shifts to how far the taco truck is from campus, how it is nearly in another world altogether.

EL CHICANO DEL MIDWEST: BUSCANDO LIBERACIÓN EN NEPANTLA

Thoughts of being in another world altogether resonate with me. I reminisce about a conversation I had with my mentor about how moving to North Florida would provide me with a challenging experience, because I would be around other Latinxs who were like me. I remember her mentioning how being in a space of people who are like you pushed one to think differently and contribute to similar passions in various ways. Reflecting on my first year in my graduate program at Florida State University, I began to think how far off that conversation was from my current lived experience.

Just as the taco truck seems as if it is nearly in its own world, I feel the same way when I show up in academic spaces with my peers. Validation and affirmation—these were the expectations I had when I accepted to pursue my graduate studies in North Florida. My heart is racing, as I think of responding with, "Everything's good," but deep down I know that I have to come to terms with my reality.

"Estee, it's almost as if I am constantly in a state of emotional survival." I look at her with disappointment. Cultural patriarchy has taught me that my emotions are to be suppressed, so I quickly think about how to handle this conversation, as my emotions began to manifest themselves outwardly in front of my Chicana peer.

Showing up authentically is a constant challenge for me, which has pushed me into a state of disengagement with my peers and my graduate program. I remember feeling a sense of belonging among my Mexican peers and family. That feeling quickly faded away after three months into my graduate program.

"I was not expecting it to be this difficult—trying to find community, to be seen, to be heard. I assumed since I was coming to Florida that I would be around my people all the time, and I, I guess I just haven't found that."

As a Chicano in a very Eurocentric academic space, I often found my voice being silenced by not only *otros, pero también mi gente.* The unconscious microaggressions within the program, by both non-Latinxs and Latinxs, constructed a singular Latinx experience. This singular experience was perpetuated through conversations within our classes, both consciously and unconsciously. The complexity in the Latinx identity made it harder for some to comprehend how six Latinxs in the same cohort did not have the same experience. *It's one thing to be Latinx in Florida, but being Chicanx—it throws the whole idea of a singular Latinx experience off.* A heightened sense of what it means to be Chicano overcomes my thoughts, as I struggle to find my space, the Third World, the place where I am, and can just Be.

"Chicana—nevermind Tejana! People *really* don't know what to do with that identity," Estee adds. "*Pero* I know what you mean, Robi. I don't know what I expected when I first got here. To some extent, I sort of expected something like, the Miami Sound Machine to immediately play on the radio when I traversed the state border, right? So not even necessarily Selena *ni nada*, but at least *some latinidad.* Did not expect for us to land in what essentially is South Georgia."

I laugh. It's funny, but it's not. "*Pos no sé.* Like, I don't know how I feel about my absence of community. There's feelings of dissonance, accomplishment, resistance, pain, invisibility. But then, like—I'm still here. So I guess I'm persisting, for now."

We finally pull the car into the *caliche* driveway and walk towards the truck. Familiar menu items are posted on plastic signs and edited with permanent marker. Signs soliciting roommates, *peluqueras*, *anunciando bailes*, are adhered on the windows with packing tape. *Pedimos nuestras órdenes de tacos al pastor*, and we sit on a nearby picnic table. Men wearing clothes splattered in paint, dusty with dirt, hardened by the sun walk past, order, walk away with their tacos to-go—in a constant loop. I am reminded of my brother who woke up early every Sunday morning to leave town for a new construction job.

I am suddenly overcome by emotion. Sitting here, watching the construction men, reminds me of the privilege I have to be in a space of higher education. Pictures of family members appear in my mind, imagining them working in the meat-packing plants, out in the fields, or in the hot sun on a high building as they construct a new roof. In the back of my mind I hear my mother and father say, *"Mi'jo, tú tienes que estudiar, para que puedas trabajar con la mente, y no tengas que matarte trabajando con tu cuerpo."* I begin to unpack the experiences my family goes through everyday and how I, in this educational position, do not have to undergo such experiences.

"El apoyo de nuestra familia means more than anything on this journey," *le digo a Estee, "Nos enseñaron a luchar para seguir adelante—no para nosotros mismos, pero para nosotros colectivamente." Es como decir, "Yo soy, porque tú eres."* I see this not only in the support I receive from my family but also in my Chicana sister. I am, because you are.

"¿Pero sabes qué?" I reflect on my entire first year of graduate school, "Engaging in the work of Anzaldúa has given me a sense of liberation. "How to Tame a Wild Tongue," yep, that was the chapter that pushed me to say, "*¡Ya basta! A mí me van a escuchar,* even if my voice shakes!" I remember handing in my final assignment for my first year. The title read: *Silencio, Conocimiento, y Movimiento.* The first paper in my educational trajectory in which I had infused Spanish—*mi lengua.* This later led me into building a strong mentoring relationship with my faculty advisor, who supported me as we began the long journey of writing a conceptual paper on gay Latino males using the process of *conocimiento.*

"El poder de Ser, to just Be, gave me a sense of liberation," I say to Estee as I bring my hands to my chest, "*Y tú, como mi hermana Chicana,* have helped me on this journey of liberation. Somos *nepantleras* for life. We will always be bridges."

LA CHICANA DE TEJAS: BUSCANDO VOZ EN NEPANTLA

I have grown to love Roberto very much over our time together in our respective graduate programs. I arrived to campus a year prior to Roberto, and it had been a very lonely year. I had developed friendships with my colleagues, but I missed connecting with Chicanxs. I do not believe in accidents. Roberto was meant to come into my life when he did, and we were meant to work in the same office. Our mentoring-friendship blossomed from the onset. We were pulled towards one another due to our common *chicanismo.* And although Roberto claims to look up to me, I honestly do not have my act together any better than he does.

Now in my second year in the doctoral program, I feel like I am just learning how to stand solidly on the ground. I am not only the sole Chicana in the doctoral program, but also the sole Latinx, made into the authoritative voice on the entire community, as if it were a singular community, a singular experience that could be parsed into dependent and independent variables. It is dismaying, because there is stratification even within *latinidad*. To feign unity is to cast a wide brush over something that is inherently complex.

Our tacos arrive, and we talk between bites. "Getting back to the conversation about being Chicanx here in Florida. Being Mexican American here carries baggage. People make assumptions about me before they even really know me. This goes beyond the typical, 'You're Latina, so you probably speak Spanish,' that I've come to expect from people who aren't Latinx. I feel the perception of being lesser-than within our own. Amongst our *gente*, I feel like I have to check people on assumptions based on skin color, education level, social class, immigrant status—which I think is frustrating, not only because it is endemic, but also because it's internalized within our own Latinx selves. We must do better!"

Roberto jumps in, "*Como*, how can we expect White people to be more inclusive of Latinxs, *cuando nos/otros,* within our own community, continue to marginalize and perpetuate hierarchies of nationalities within *latinidad*? *Mexicanos* are practically at the bottom of the proverbial totem pole! Estee, this shit happens all the time in my class. I try to speak up about my experience in broad Latinx terms, but my voice is not heard. But if my *Cubano* colleague asserts the same feelings, he is heard. My White peers think I am confusing, and my Latinx peers think I'm too fucking radical."

"*Es como dice la Anzaldúa,* Roberto: there is this notion of *nos/otras,* which theorizes an insider/outsider perspective, where the *nos* is the colonizer and the *otras* the colonized (Keating 10). But in honoring the dash between both, that duality begins to fade, and we live both *nos* and *otras* simultaneously. It is our responsibility to be the bridge—just like you were saying. We cannot give up and acquiesce."

I take a bite of my *taco al pastor* and wash it down with a big swig of my *soda de manzana*. Typically, being a bridge is easier to theorize than it is to practice. I initially approached the doctoral program pragmatically. I came in with an area of study in mind, had outlined a course sequence towards a quantitative methodological stance, and had mapped out opportunities to publish and present my work at conferences. I anticipated feeling challenged, as is typical for the next step in one's career. Because I had attended highly competitive PWIs for my other degrees and was accustomed to both academic rigor and being in the minority, I felt prepared for any challenge. But I could not foresee what I have actually experienced.

"Truthfully, I have never felt more marginal than I have here as a doctoral student, Robi. I attribute it to being a minority within a minority in an already oppressive environment. I feel very targeted whenever we read about how Mexican Americans have the lowest degree attainment rates among Latinxs. Research discourse always focuses on the deficit. What about the rest of us who have persisted despite adversity?" And the adversity has been greater at the doctoral level, where academic culture is pervasively competitive, individualistic, and unyielding. Academia does not affirm a *bienestar* that centers the mind. body.spirit in a way that is whole.

"So throughout my doctoral experience, I have committed to a praxis that aims towards consonance. This is my means of resistance. *En esta nepantla que es la academia, no me rindo ni me caigo.* It has been painful, it has not been easy, but I have grown so much. I have gotten closer to crystallizing my voice as a scholar. Centering narrative in my research praxis has been a way to lift our voices as marginalized peoples. Creating (counter)communities interrupts an individualistic academic culture that promotes and reproduces Whiteness. Where I might have intended my path to be more linear, it has actually looked more like a *remolino*—pulling me closer to the middle."

And I have let myself be okay with sitting in ambiguity and dissonance. The ambiguity has opened up endless dimensions and intersections of Being. It disrupts normative perceptions of Truth and Reality. It makes me a better researcher, scholar, and educator. It makes me a better human. I look at my watch and notice how much time has passed. "Time to go back to work, Robi! *Acabo, tú tienes que ir a* class." We couldn't possibly eat any more, but we still are sad to leave. It's as if we are leaving home, and it is so hard to leave home.

The more we frequent the *taquería*, however, the more we find ways to cross-pollinate. We invite friends—including White allies—to come eat lunch with us there, and we contract *Doña Vero* to cater some of our campus programs. We have found that these pieces of our lives do not necessarily have to be separate or isolated. We can honor both and be both at the same time.

CROSSING BRIDGES, *CONSTRUYENDOLOS AL ANDAR*

While our story is unique to us, we are not the only ones to navigate *nepantla* in graduate education. Likewise, we are not the only scholars to experience compounded marginality. We urge our *colegas* to also take on *nepantlera* identities and to find comfort in the margin. We implore our allies to also lift voice and center narrative, challenging pressures to conform and remain silent. We beseech you all to honor nuance and difference—to see all sides. Purporting hierarchies will not save us. *Nepantla* will.

Academia has broken us. Life has broken us. But in nepantla, *we can pick up the pieces and put them back together.*

Because we have claimed identities as *nepantleras*, we have committed to serving as bridges between our academic experiences and our cultural experiences, using mind.body.spirit to guide our healing and growing processes. We understand that as *nepantleras*, we must necessarily inhabit a space of dissonance. This space, while painful in many aspects, offers transformation and liberation. Here, we need not adhere to any singular Truth. We can entertain paradox.

The future belongs to us: the storytellers, the dreamweavers, the *naguales* that change with their surroundings (*Light in the Dark* 81). Our peer mentorship has enabled us to co-construct our experiences and to find comfort in the dissonance. Leaning on one another for support has empowered us to assert our cultural identity as Chicanxs and simultaneously persist as Scholars of Color—without losing soul. *Plática y reflexión* have helped us heal together. As we heal, we assist each other in forging paths and constructing our bridges.

Where there are borders, we will be bridges. As educators, we recognize the power inherent in being and building bridges between our students and colleagues. Actualizing *nepantla* as a site of resistance challenges Whiteness, challenges panethnicity, challenges singular dimensions, challenges a singular Truth. In adopting such a stance, we free others to do the same. And, together, our narratives manifest into acts of social change.

NOTES

1 According to NCES data cited in Krogstad & Fry, 2014

2 According to US Census data, located here: http://www.census.gov/hhes/socdemo/education/data/cps/2010/tables.html

WORKS CITED

Anzaldúa, Gloria. *Borderlands/La Frontera: The New Mestiza.* San Francisco: Aunt Lute Books, 1987. Print.

---. "Haciendo Caras, Una Entrada." *Making Face, Making Soul/Haciendo Caras: Creative and Critical Perspectives by Women of Color.* Ed. Gloria Anzaldúa. San Francisco: Aunt Lute, 1990. xv-xxviii. Print.

---. *Light in the Dark/Luz en lo Oscuro: Rewriting Identity, Spirituality, Reality.* Ed. AnaLouise Keating. Durham: Duke University Press, 2015. Print.

---. "now let us shift...the path of conocimiento...inner work, public acts." *This Bridge We Call Home.* Eds. Gloria E. Anzaldúa and AnaLouise Keating. New York: Routledge, 2002. Print.

Keating, AnaLouise. "From Borderlands and New Mestizas to Nepantlas and Nepantleras: Anzaldúan Theories for Social Change." *Human Architecture: Journal of the Sociology of Self-Knowledge* 4.3 (2006): 5-16. Print.

Krogstad, Jens Manuel, and Richard Fry. "Dept. of Ed. Projects Public Schools Will Be 'Majority-Minority' This Fall." Pew Hispanic Center. Pew Research Center, 18 Aug. 2014. Web. 12 Oct. 2015. <http://www.pewresearch.org/fact-tank/2014/08/18/u-s-public-schools-expected-to-be-majority-minority-starting-this-fall>

Moraga, Cherríe. "Entering the Lives of Others: Theory in the Flesh." *This Bridge Called My Back: Writings by Radical Women of Color.* Eds. Cherríe Moraga and Gloria Anzaldúa. New York: Kitchen Table Women of Color Press, 1981. 23. Print.

REIMAGINING K–12 EDUCATION WITH/ THROUGH GLORIA E. ANZALDÚA

SYLVIA MENDOZA AVIÑA

In the first semester of a visiting scholar position, I was graciously invited to guest lecture in a bilingual education class on the topic of critical pedagogy. The faculty member who invited me to lecture shared with me a PowerPoint presentation prepared for that particular class discussion. In it, the usual critical pedagogy heavy hitters were mentioned: Paulo Freire and Henry Giroux. In fact, a quick search online draws the same key players, to include John Dewey, Michael Apple, and Peter McLaren. At the heart of critical pedagogy and the work of these undoubtedly stellar scholars is a reimagining of education in ways that are transformative, social justice oriented, and critically conscious. However, this kind of inquiry has existed, specifically by indigenous and women of color, in multiple settings and contexts before the field of critical pedagogy emerged.

Dolores Delgado Bernal explored this in her seminal piece, *Using a Chicana Feminist Epistemology in Educational Research.* Drawing from black feminist thought and indigenous scholars, Delgado Bernal identifies what she terms a Chicana feminist epistemology that Chicana scholars bring into the research and writing process. In it, she outlines how Chicanas cultivate and embody their own systems of thought to navigate their multiple oppressions in the research process, within institutions of higher education, and in society overall. In this way, Chicanas and other women of color have engaged in their own theories of teaching, learning, researching, knowing, and being.

Knowing this, as a Tejana/Chicana feminist and Anzaldúan scholar, I have often wondered why the go-to for discussions of critical pedagogy within education colleges and departments remains Paulo Freire and other men. In this theoretical paper, then, in line with Dolores Delgado Bernal and the women of color scholars she draws from, I argue for a recentering of critical pedagogy and discourses of transformative education through the knowledges and pedagogies of women of color scholars, in particular Gloria E. Anzaldúa. This is not to argue for the sole use of certain scholars over others, but rather to problematize the continued privileging of white and male scholars within education colleges and departments, while women of color and other marginalized communities have been in an historic and continued struggle for educational equity and can contribute theoretically, pedagogically, methodologically, and epistemologically to conversations and research on critical and transformative education.

As such, this paper explores the following key questions: What would it mean to include Anzaldúa as a staple scholar within education departments and colleges? What does Anzaldúa offer pedagogically, curriculum-wise, and holistically in regards to transforming colonizing K–12 schooling institutions and engaging with young people, particularly marginalized youth? In this paper, I first introduce the work of Anzaldúa before engaging a discussion of the ways in which educational researchers have taken up her work to transform education, particularly within institutions of higher education. I then engage a discussion of what it could look like to extend the work of Anzaldúa to K–12 schooling institutions.

GLORIA ANZALDÚA

Anzaldúa painfully and honestly describes what it means to live within a borderland, referring not only to the literal and geopolitical landscape that exists at the U.S.-Mexico border, but the metaphysical impact of borders on human lives and subject positions—essentially what borders *do* to people spiritually, physically, psychologically, materially. Anzaldúa argues that borders impact women of color and queer women through traumatic histories and painful memories as a result of colonization and economic exploitation that are prevalent along the border. She offers that borders contribute to contradictory subject positions as a result of displacement and forced migration, while, at the same time, contributing to the development of complex, beautiful, emergent positionalities.

Because of these traumatic histories, Anzaldúa recognizes that there is no one nor easy way to *be* a queer woman of color, and that subject positions are complex, divergent, and fluid. Anzaldúa offers that, as a result of this amalgamation of histories, wounds, and cultures, comes a unique consciousness that provides a lens in which to view and understand the self and the world through a prism of intersectionalities that accounts for Chicanas' diverse and fluid experiences and positionalities. In her oft-cited book co-edited with AnaLouise Keating titled *This Bridge We Call Home: Radical Visions for Transformation*, Anzaldúa expands on this consciousness she refers to as nepantla. She explains:

> Bridges span liminal (threshold) spaces between worlds, spaces I call nepantla, a Nahuatl word meaning tierra entre medio. Transformations occur in this in-between space, an unstable, unpredictable, precarious, always-in-transition space lacking clear boundaries. Nepantla es tierra desconocida, and living in this liminal zone means being in a constant state of displacement—an uncomfortable, even alarming feeling. Most of us dwell in nepantla so much of the time it's become a sort of "home." Though this state links us to other ideas, people, and worlds, we feel threatened by these new connections and the change they engender. (1)

Nepantla, for Anzaldúa, not only reflects the ways in which borders have contributed to colonizing constructions of women of color and presented these constructions as universal truths but also highlights the process of Tejanas/Chicanas actively resisting and undoing these colonizing dominant narratives. This process of undoing coloniality, of learning to see beneath the surface of dominant narratives of white supremacy and patriarchy, is both painful and liberating. It is liberating for women of color and queer people of color to shed social constructions that do not serve their interests as these constructions work in the service of coloniality. However, this process is also painful, resulting in feelings of liminality, as marginalized communities must continue to live, love, work, and function within a white supremacist and patriarchal society in the U.S. and thus find themselves in a constant state of in between: in between an imagined world that desires social justice and in between an existing social order that oppresses queer people and women of color. Anzaldúa offers this constant state of nepantla is potentially transformative as this process entails intense self-reflection and coalition building, which can lead to social change. However, she recognizes that nepantla is also potentially debilitating, confusing, and painful because of the contradictions, tensions and messiness that exist as a result of living as a threshold person in a constant state of in between.

Anzaldúa's discussion of nepantla, applied to marginalized youth and certainly all school-aged students, recognizes them as nepantleras/os who embody colonizing constructions as a result of their positionalities as young people who desire liberation from social constructions. Understanding students as nepantleras/os not only helps to situate their contemporary realities within a borderlands history, recognizing how their material realities are bound up in the history of colonization, but also helps to recognize the agency and penchant for activism young people embody. Nepantleras/os possess the ability to cultivate what Anzaldúa refers to as facultad, or embodied and inherited knowledge that provides insight and forewarning to oppression. As a result, nepantleras/os, through their facultad, are able to see beneath the surface of colonizing constructions of themselves and the world, and possess the desire and knowledge to undo coloniality, moving toward a world that is anti-oppressive and socially just. When applied within traditional schooling institutions, understanding students as nepantleras/os helps to locate and utilize the unique perspectives, facultad, and agency of youth to transform colonizing curricula and larger society.

As such, Anzaldúan philosophy can transform traditional school curricula and pedagogical praxis through humanizing approaches to engaging and learning with and from young people, enhancing not only how students experience their education, but also how they understand and view themselves, one another, and the world. As such, Anzaldúa is significant to discussions of critical and transformative education, particularly K–12, because of her recognition of borderlands experiences and resulting nepantlera/o worldviews. The next section explores the work of Chicana/Latina feminist scholars who have bridged Anzaldúa's work with educational research.

ANZALDÚA AND EDUCATION

Chicana/Latina feminist educational researchers have argued that educators need to be aware of the various epistemologies present in their classrooms and teach in a way that recognizes, validates, and incorporates these various worldviews and systems of thought. Since we exist in different subject positions with different histories and different realities, Chicana feminists offer that we also come to and produce knowledge in a multitude of ways. In this section, I discuss how Chicana/Latina feminist scholars have taken up Anzaldúa to reveal how pedagogy occurs and functions—outside of schooling institutions; in nontraditional ways such as culturally relevant practices, as opposed to solely standardized curricula; and within youth spaces and women of color spaces, or what C. Alejandra Elenes refers to as borderlands spaces (15).

Through a discussion of these Chicana feminist and border pedagogies, it becomes evident that people of color engage in pedagogical practices that are "nontraditional" in that they are informed by all parts of the self, "bodymind-spirit," to include the following: the home, family, parents, land, other mujeres, community members, place, body, spirituality, and sexuality. I argue that, at the heart of many of these Chicana feminist and border pedagogies, is Anzaldúan thought. The Chicana/Latina feminist scholars featured in this section draw from what I refer to as Anzaldúan pedagogies—those concepts and theoretical tools offered by Anzaldúa in her scholarship that are taken up and used by Chicana/Latinas as praxis in the classroom.

Delgado Bernal offers her conceptualization of pedagogies of the home developed out of the necessity to include the epistemologies, pedagogies, and knowledge of Latina/o homes that are typically left out of schooling institutions. This knowledge includes wisdom passed down through oral history practices such as storytelling, legends, and corridos. Pedagogies of the home serve as a form of informal education, or the everyday schooling Latina/o students receive at home from parents/guardians and family members that, when incorporated into schooling institutions, transforms and enhances Latina/o students' educational experiences.

Elenes, Francisca E. Gonzalez, Delgado Bernal, and Sofia Villenas argue that Chicanas/Mexicanas embody "pedagogies that recognize knowledge, power, and politics as central to all teaching and learning" (95). Specifically, they examine the Chicana/Mexicana/Latina feminist pedagogies of consejos, respeto, and educación in the everyday lives of these mujeres to offer new ways of thinking about teaching, learning, and education as a whole. The authors examine pedagogy from the position that pedagogical practices are not restricted to formal learning spaces such as schooling institutions, but rather occur within community spaces and in the home through everyday cultural practices. They cite Ruth Trinidad Galvan's conception of pedagogical formation, arguing that, for women of color, pedagogy is directly tied to women's ways of knowing and their everyday ways of being in the world.[1]

María Fránquiz and María del Carmen Salazar add to this with their ethnographic study of Mexicano and Chicano high school youth, finding that the pedagogical formations of consejos (advice), confianza (trust), and buen ejemplos (good role models) contribute to students' academic achievement. This broadened understanding of pedagogy looks toward women's everyday spaces—the home, communities, community centers, churches, tiendas, the outdoors—as spaces where theory and pedagogical practices that could transform the educational experiences of women of color emerge (596).

Anita Tijerina Revilla identifies a muxerista pedagogy cultivated by undergraduate Chicana activists involved in an organization titled Raza Womyn at the University of California in Los Angeles. Through this space, their relationships with each other, and critical reflection and dialogue, Tijerina Revilla found that these mujeres cultivated a loving pedagogical praxis rooted in their shared and divergent experiences as women of color. A muxerista pedagogy centers Chicana/Latina realities; involves dialogue, praxis (theory and action), and dialectical exchange; and is motivated by "a commitment to creating social change through Chicana/Latina resistance to subordination" (84). The mujeres shared their personal experiences, expressed their thoughts on global politics and social justice issues, discussed their health and other intimate details of their lives, and, as a result, developed deep relationships with one another that helped them navigate the White, patriarchal, and heteronormative space of the university. In this way, the mujeres in this group learned from each other relationally and produced their own pedagogical praxis using their own experiences, theories, and knowledges.

Like Tijerina Revilla, Elenes engages in a process of identifying pedagogical formations that occur within spaces Chicanas/os occupy. Informed by borderlands theory, Elenes argues Chicanas/os inhabit multiple spaces in between—in between cultures, ethnicities, languages, sexualities, genders, and classes. She contends that "the discourse of the borderlands speaks a language of fluidity, migration, postcolonialism, and displacement: of subaltern identities. The borderland is the discourse of people who live between different worlds" (11). As a result of this borderland discourse, Elenes argues there are border/transformative pedagogies that speak to the realities and cultural practices of borderland students that can transform their educational experience.

She uses elements of Chicana/o popular culture as examples of border/transformative pedagogies, revealing how icons such as la Virgen de Guadalupe, Malintzin/Malinche, and La Llorona convey epistemological and pedagogical meanings to Chicanas. Elenes explores how these icons traditionally teach women of color patriarchal ideas around femininity, motherhood, and religion. She offers that these traditional and dominant narratives can be disrupted and changed into transformative pedagogies through counter-narratives that highlight these icons' multiple oppressions, their strategic responses to their oppression, and, as a result, their strength and feminism.

Border/transformative pedagogies not only function to help Chicanas reimagine cultural icons and, as a result, locate alternative histories that highlight women of color and their feminisms, but can also transform pedagogical praxis cross-culturally. In her article highlighting the experiences of Chicana faculty teaching in predominantly White, middle-class university classrooms, Elenes offers that border/transformative pedagogies provide a way to build bridges to meet one another across divergent life experiences and ideologies. Through Anzaldúa, Elenes focuses on disrupting dualistic thinking in these classroom spaces, offering, "My pedagogical efforts are to try and get us all to the 'same side of the river' or, at least, to agree that there is a river" ("Transformando fronteras" 693).

Border/transformative pedagogies in these types of classrooms help to dismantle "commonsensical" thinking by revealing the various ways people come to knowledge through their divergent experiences. Elenes offers that the predominantly White women in class were able to understand this through their experiences with gender, but struggled to understand racial oppression. Through disputing what she refers to as commonsensical thinking steeped in Eurocentric epistemology, Elenes, using Anzaldúan thought, aims "to dilute any notion that there is one exclusive Truth, denaturalizing the hegemony of dominant discourses" ("Transformando fronteras" 695). She offers,

> Gloria Anzaldúa's mestiza consciousness can help us all—Chicanas/os and non-Chicanas/os—learn to deal with differences in a productive way. Her conceptualization and my notions of border/transformative pedagogy are not intended to reproduce forms of oppression, or to sanitize classroom practices. On the contrary, this methodology offers ways in which we can all bring our different, contradictory, and oppositional points of view for discussion. ("Tranformando fronteras" 700)

Through Anzaldúa, Elenes develops her own pedagogical praxis informed by borderlands theory to engage in teaching and learning with university students from diverse backgrounds, highlighting how Anzaldúan thought functions pedagogically. Similarly, Linda Prieto and Sofia A. Villenas discuss how Anzaldúan thought informed their praxis in teacher educator classrooms. Using nepantla as a framework, Prieto and Villenas share their testimonios as women of color faculty in a predominantly White institution to develop themes around cultural dissonance, conciencia con compromiso, and cariño as distinct Chicana feminist pedagogies that "highlight processes of self-healing, resilience, and transformation" in the classroom (413). In reflecting on and naming these Chicana feminist pedagogies as part of their praxis, Prieto and Villenas argue that women of colors' "teaching practices, which emerge from our diverse cultural experiences and memory, are invaluable to the university classroom" (413–414). Nepantla provides a lens in which to understand uncomfortable moments, uncertain terrain, shifting consciousness, and fluid positionalities in the classroom. For the authors,

> Pedagogies of nepantla rooted in cariño engage students who enact racism, classism, sexism, homophobia, or anti-immigrant sentiments, not as individual racists, sexists, or nativists, but as cultural beings who are tapping into vast epistemological systems that support hierarchies of dominance. (426)

Important within these Chicana feminist and border pedagogies is the underlying theme outlined by Anzaldúa in her borderlands theory: Chicanas embody their own systems of thought that inform how they understand and produce knowledge in the world—a nepantlera subjectivity. As evidenced in this literature review, this nepantlera subject position produces knowledges that can transform schooling institutions, pedagogical praxis, and function cross-culturally, recognizing and validating the various ways people come to and embody knowledge.

As such, Anzaldúa's borderlands theory provides to the field of education theoretical concepts to name the varied, complex, and beautiful experiences, histories, and subject positions of students in K–12 schooling institutions. This is significant not only as an ontological project, but an epistemological and pedagogical project as well. As evidenced by the work of these mujeres, Anzaldúa's borderlands theory, utilized within educational spaces, transforms schooling institutions, curricula, and praxis through this recognition and validation of other ways of being, thus transforming how adults and educators learn/teach/engage in the classroom, particularly with young people.

Chicana feminist and border pedagogies, informed by Anzaldúan thought, possess the potential to transform the educational experiences of all students who embody their own theories in the flesh and express a desire for recognition of their complex positionalities, within and outside of schooling institutions. In this way, Anzaldúa in education contributes to an overall reimagining of education, of other ways of teaching and learning, and, further, of other worlds where the marginalized can exist free from coloniality. The next section explores Anzaldúa's concept of El Mundo Zurdo and how this construct helps to imagine other ways of engaging in education with youth.

REIMAGINING EDUCATION THROUGH ANZALDÚA'S EL MUNDO ZURDO

> We are the queer groups, the people that don't belong anywhere, not in the dominant world nor completely within our own respective cultures. Combined we cover so many oppressions. But the overwhelming oppression is the collective fact that we do not fit, and because we do not fit we are a threat. Not all of us have the same oppressions, but we empathize and identify with each other's oppressions. We do not have the same ideology, nor do we derive similar solutions. Some of us are leftists, some of us practitioners of magic. Some of us are both. But these different affinities are not opposed to each other. In El Mundo Zurdo I with my own affinities and my people with theirs can live together and transform the planet.
>
> *Moraga and Anzaldúa, This Bridge Called My Back 209*

El Mundo Zurdo within the field of education presents an opportunity to reimagine youth, classroom spaces, curricula, praxis, relationships, and education as a whole. In doing so, educational researchers and practitioners can begin to imagine new, humanizing curricula that welcome the whole student with their complex nepantlera/o positionalities, divergent life experiences, and embodied knowledges. This re-imagining of transformational educational spaces comes as a response to realities of colonizing schooling practices and curricula.

Paul Issahaku recognizes "the North American public education system as a colonizing industry" and uses the work of Frantz Fanon to explore possibilities for the disruption and transformation of these colonizing practices (29). Specifically, Issahaku envisions a "transformed system and structure where minoritized students feel liberated and empowered to pursue the type of schooling that satisfies their material and spiritual hopes and aspirations" (32). For Issahaku, racism, classism, sexism, capitalism, and gender disadvantage represent colonizing social processes in need of transformation. Rather than reproduce these -isms, public schools can instead serve as sites of social justice and healing by discussing and highlighting the existence of these structures of oppression in society and moving towards transforming them. Issahaku, like Anzaldúa and her concept of El Mundo Zurdo, imagines the possibilities of an education that acknowledges students of color holistically, recognizing their complete selves: academically, physically, emotionally, spiritually, and relationally.

For this reason, Anzaldúa's El Mundo Zurdo becomes an important concept not only to imagine new curricula and relationships with/for students but also to provide an opportunity for young people to engage in processes of healing from the violence they have endured. That El Mundo Zurdo must even be imagined comes as a result of the reality and existence of coloniality and its impact on borderlanders, which includes young people and youth of color in particular. Presently, young people are not allowed to engage in questions around sex/sexuality, cuss, talk about their desires, shout or scream, talk about things that happen to them outside of school, or talk in class, period. They are not allowed to express themselves in schools.

Instead, they are socialized via schooling institutions, the family, and larger society to act "appropriately": speaking only when spoken to, without exhibiting too much energy or wildness, without raising their voices, without speaking against authority, or expressing their true thoughts and ideas. Students and youth of color specifically, then, are denied basic human rights and are dehumanized within and outside of school daily. Anzaldúa's El Mundo Zurdo highlights and connects the shared frustration and coraje of two marginalized groups: Chicana/Latina feminists and young people who feel dehumanized, silenced, erased, forgotten, and multiply oppressed. Because of this, proponents of ethnic studies and Chicana/o studies in K–12 schooling argue that the sooner students can center their education around their lived experiences, the better. By centering their material realities within a borderlands and recognizing their nepantlera/o positionalities, students can begin to imagine new possibilities for their education and their lives. By learning early on the language to name their oppression through reflecting on and examining their lived experiences, students can cultivate their nepantlera/o subject positions to transform how they understand themselves, others, and structures of power.

In my work as a co-creator and co-instructor of an after school Introduction to Chicana/o Studies class with fifth- and sixth-grade Chicana/o youth in Utah, I used Anzaldúa's concept of El Mundo Zurdo to have students reflect on their educational experiences. The students immediately began to share their negative experiences; their stories included unfair schooling practices, such as not being able to speak in class, not being able to leave their seats, and teachers embarrassing them or treating them poorly. I then asked the students to reimagine and recreate their own school, to recreate the kind of educational experience they desired as a way to come up with positive solutions regarding the type of relationships, teaching, and learning they wanted in school. As such, El Mundo Zurdo became a transformational tool for students to engage in critical thinking and develop problem-solving skills, as well as to improve their writing by focusing on a societal issue and figuring out ways to improve their current situation.

The following is an excerpt from this assignment, completed by David,[2] a fifth-grade student:

> I don't like math.
>
> I like science because we do a lot of projects.
>
> I don't like math because it's kinda boring. I would have games for math so it could be fun.
>
> I wish we didn't have any uniforms and we could wear whatever we want cause I don't like [our] colored uniforms. And I would convince the principal for us to have free choice.

Through El Mundo Zurdo, this fifth-grade student reimagines education. In his version of education, academics would involve hands-on projects and activities that are fun and allow for him to engage in learning in ways different from the existing dominant practices that do not meet his educational needs. He shares that he does not like math, listing this twice, and offering that math is "boring." He imagines that math could be fun through the incorporation of games or different activities that would engage him better. He laments over having to wear uniforms in school. He imagines an education in which he can express these concerns directly to the principal, who would not only genuinely listen to him, but also take his recommendations into consideration and change the school dress code policy. Essentially, this fifth-grade student reimagines an education in which he has agency, is supported in exercising his agency over his education, and is allowed to make decisions and voice his ideas about the best way that he learns.

For me, introducing Anzaldúa into education colleges and departments and K–12 schools is not only about providing alternative histories and recognizing alternative embodied knowledges, but is also about healing through the (re) clamation, (re)membering, and (re)telling of individual stories and life histories. This is why Anzaldúa and other Chicana/Latina feminist scholars have much to contribute to education. By infusing Anzaldua and Chicana/Latina feminisms into pedagogical praxis and curriculum development and viewing and approaching students holistically—bodymindspirit—educators can thus create classroom spaces where youth feel comfortable opening up, speaking, sharing, listening, and, as a result, healing from the historical and persisting wounds of colonialism, White supremacy, and patriarchy.

Incorporating and centering Anzaldúa and other Chicana/Latina feminist scholars within education departments and colleges helps to recognize the borderland experiences of students; understands young people as nepantleras/os who understand the material realities they are positioned within and desire social change; acknowledges the responses and approaches to social change through youths' paradigms and informed by young peoples' experiences at the intersections of multiple oppressions, including age, race/ethnicity, gender, social class, and sexuality; and reflects the development of a transgenerational community committed to collaboratively working toward social change. Anzaldúa within education allows for students, educators, families, and communities to develop *otro mundos* within schooling institutions, worlds where students feel they fit, free from colonizing schooling practices and curricula, and in line with their lived experiences and embodied knowledges.

NOTES

1 Ruth Trinidad Galvan's work focuses on what she refers to as the every day and "mundane" womanist pedagogies of Central Mexican rural women, who engaged in teaching and learning together through spirituality, convivencia, and well-being in their work in campesinas (603–621).

2 Pseudonyms are used to protect the youth as part of the study. Interviews and student work were collected and analyzed as part of data collection for my dissertation research during the 2013–2014 academic school year.

WORKS CITED

Anzaldúa, Gloria. *Borderlands/La Frontera: The New Mestiza*. San Francisco: Spinsters/Aunt Lute Books, 1987. Print.

Anzaldúa, Gloria and AnaLouise Keating, eds. *this bridge we call home: radical visions for transformation*. New York: Routledge, 2002. Print.

Chabram-Dernersesian, Angie, and Adela de la Torre, eds. *Speaking from the Body: Latinas on Health and Culture*. Tucson: University of Arizona Press, 2008. Print.

Delgado Bernal, Dolores. "Learning and living pedagogies of the home: The mestiza consciousness of Chicana students." *International Journal of Qualitative Studies in Education*, 14.5 (2001): 623–639. Print.

Elenes, C. Alejandra. "Transformando fronteras: Chicana feminist transformative pedagogies." *International Journal of Qualitative Studies in Education,* 14.5 (2001): 689–702. Print.

—. *Transforming Borders: Chicana/o Popular Culture and Pedagogy*. United Kingdom: Lexington Books, 2011. Print.

—. Elenes, C. Alejandra, Francisca E. Gonzalez, Dolores Delgado Bernal, and Sofia Villenas. "Introduction: Chicana/Mexicana feminist pedagogies: *Consejos, respeto, y educación* in everyday life." *International Journal of Qualitative Studies in Education*, 14.5 (2001): 595–602. Print.

Fránquiz, María and María del Carmen Salazar. "The transformative potential of humanizing pedagogy: Addressing the diverse needs of Chicano/Mexicano students." *The High School Journal*, 87.4 (2004): 36–53. Print.

Galvan, Ruth Trinidad. "Portraits of *Mujeres Desjuiciadas*: Womanist pedagogies of the everyday, the mundane and the ordinary." *International Journal of Qualitative Studies in Education*, 14.5 (2001): 603–621. Print.

Issahaku, Paul. "Decolonizing the Euro-American public education system: A transgressive revisiting of Fanon." *Fanon and the Counterinsurgency of Education*. Ed. George J. Sefa Dei. Rotterdam: Sense Publishers, 2010. Print.

Moraga, Cherríe and Gloria Anzaldúa. Eds. *This Bridge Called My Back: Writings by Radical Women of Color*. Watertown, MA: Persephone Press, 1981. Print.

Prieto, Linda, and Sofia Villenas. "Pedagogies from Nepantla: Testimonio, Chicana/Latina Feminisms and Teacher Educator Classrooms." *Equity & Excellence in Education,* 45.3 (2012): 411–429. Print.

Revilla, Anita Tijerina. "MUXERISTA PEDAGOGY: Raza Womyn Teaching Social Justice Through Student Activism." *The High School Journal*, 87.4 (2004): 80–94. Print.

LOCALIZING THE BODY FOR PRACTITIONERS IN WRITING STUDIES

YNDALECIO ISAAC HINOJOSA

Bordered, my body begins here. ¿Pero, qué es el lugar aquí? What compels my body to write? My conscious body emerges from rhetorical practices Chicanas engage with, and I lie in-between the lines of such conversations. Rhetorical practices by Chicana feminist writers "mark a consciousness of resistance to the repression of language and culture, a recognition of a 'third space' located within intersecting structures of power in which women construct claims to human agency" (Arredondo et al. 5). As Chela Sandoval explains, these "feminists of color exist in the interstices between normalized social categories" (45.6) and thus articulate a "theory of difference" (46.7). Emma Pérez, who brings attention "to that third space where agency is enacted through third space feminism," calls Sandoval's differential mode of consciousness a "third space feminist practice" (xvi). Rhetorically, these feminist practices go on to create spaces of representation that Lisa A. Flores argues reveal "ethnicity" through a rhetoric of difference, "repudiating mainstream discourse and espousing self- and group-created discourse" (145). Chicana discourse "reject[s] dominant definitions and create[s] internal definitions [that] will reflect the historical circumstances and nature of the oppression of the group," claims Flores (146). As a third space feminist practice, my attraction here to Chicana rhetoricians involves, then, how

I emerge from their conversations (rhetoric) as a conscious body, fully aware of the limitation that male subjectivity within a feminist discourse presents.

Male subjectivity will set me apart from any female perspective. I cannot transgress the identity politic my gender assigns nor my sexuality partiality against a feminist theoretical perspective, especially a Chicana subject expressivity grounded in specific social and historical frameworks. However, my sexuality can provide me with a relational voice to Chicana rhetoricians like lesbian-feminist Gloria Anzaldúa and others. My *relational understanding* connects to knowledge "*always grounded in bodily existence*, recognized as interpretive, and acknowledged as always being partial" [Emphasis in original](Shapiro 41). From this position, my sexuality, which up until now has remained unspoken or unwritten, so to speak, becomes a bodily layer that I speak into existence in order to locate my body with and in a particular context, or rather a particular place. Anzaldúa claims that while writing *Borderlands* she had a "lesbian perspective," but a perspective that "had not evolved to the place" where "you realize that you like women" (*Interviews* 167). Her admission demonstrates how she occupied the interstitial space between *knowing* and *becoming* a homosexual. As a gay, Chicano writer, I too occupy a similar position now with and in this article, for although I have lived my life as a homosexual, this *is* the first time that I write to publicly voice that I am gay.[1] By breaking my silence, I hope to transgress that border concerning my sexuality, the border between knowing I am gay and becoming characterized as a gay writer. I reveal my sexual difference in part to expose, as Anzaldúa indicates, "*las caras por dentro*" because "[to] make face is to have face—dignity and self-respect" [Emphasis in original]("Haciendo Caras" xxvii). Anzaldúa draws this notion from ancient nahuas whose belief suggests, "one was put on earth to create one's 'face' (body) and 'heart' (soul)" (xvi). Consciously, I compel my body to write so that I may spatialize what my soul speaks at this time.

The spatialization of bodies is a process of not only causing something to occupy space, but also of placing that something into a specific context. As such, writers, especially marginalized writers, produce artifacts (writings) that not only respond directly to the sociocultural contexts of a place, but also create a literate body as the byproduct of relations in and of such a place. My literate body is a byproduct of Chicana third space feminist practices. For me, a Chicano scholar in Writing Studies, to theorize about writing instruction or pedagogies is to also theorize about the body in relation to place(s), especially for bordered subjectivities. Unlike border subjects that represent the inhabitants of a border area that co-construct a border culture, *bordered subjectivities* represent individuals that highlight the embodiment of borders or bordered cultures into a spatial body. A spatial body's "material character," as either corporeal or discursive, manifests from a particular space, "from the energy that is deployed and put to use there" (Lefebvre 195). I propose that by studying Chicana rhetoricians, like Gloria Anzaldúa, practitioners in Writing Studies can learn to understand how writers localize a "spatial body" into a specific context, the places felt. As bordered subjectivities, Chicana rhetoricians spatialize their body into existence discursively and localize that body into a particular sociocultural context. It is through and in the act of writing that they engender a *distinctive place-identity*, meaningful aspects of identity linked to places felt.

When it comes to places felt, vivid Chicana accounts draw upon a conscious familiarity. Chicanas and I share a similar sangre caliente, a similar experience to pain and harsh conditions, specifically with the physical realities or alienation we face individually. Like Chicana rhetoricians, specifically Anzaldúa, my experience with writing involves being bordered by many fronteras. My body is caught in-between cultural gaps, especially when my body inhabits an area like the borderland between the United States and Mexico. These gaps are the intersticios that situate my body not only in-between, but also against borders. Para mi cuerpo, the act of writing exemplifies, therefore, a situated lived experience. The words and phrases I use will have "situated meanings" because they are "rooted in [my] embodied experience" (Gee 164).

Cuerpo,
respiré profundamente y nací.
Nací adentro de los intersticios aquí.
Soy un cuerpo situado entre las fronteras
sobre el pecho de mí madre, Gloria.[2]
De entre las manos de mí padre, soy
un cuerpo situado dentro de los márgenes.
Ten cuidado, cuerpo mío.
Cuidado.

My poem points to intersticios because I learned such spaces compel my body to write, and a *body writing* I am. Anzaldúa says the act of writing for her felt like she was "carving bone" and how in that act she was "creating [her] own face, [her] own heart" (*Borderlands* 95). Her words speak to my cuerpo because I create my words on this page from flesh and blood experiences too, so writing then, like for Anzaldúa, is my act of placing pieces of my flesh onto the page, and as a result, my *writing body* speaks, "Ten cuidado, cuerpo mío. Cuidado."

Writing is "radically contingent" and "radically situational," according to Gary Olson (9). Therefore, it's important for practitioners in Writing Studies to understand how the body and writing intersect with places felt. In an interview with Andrea A. Lunsford, Anzaldúa compares the act of composing to a compustura (seamstress): "seaming together fragments to make a garment which you wear, which represents you, your identity and reality in the world" (43). By using sewing as a metaphor for the act of writing, Anzaldúa contextualizes her body to a specific sociocultural place because the act of a compustura places her squarely within the Chicana/o literary tradition as well as within indigenous Native American traditions of the southwest. Also, as an independent, yet essential, item that extends what a body signifies, a garment provides the body with a specific felt experience relative to its context and use. Thus, Anzaldúa's perspective begins to highlight the interdependent relationship that exists, somehow, between acts of writing and a body localized *with* and *in* a lived space. She demonstrates this relationship in *Borderlands* when she localizes her body to the places felt by her *mestizo* body: "The U.S.-Mexican border *es una herida abierta* where the Third World grates against the first and bleeds" (25). Chicana rhetoricians, like Anzaldúa, examine and deal with space and materiality in relation to bodies with and in places, especially over how bodies and place(s) intersect. Their rhetorics highlight how bodies exist relative to place and symbolize an *embodied discourse*, discursive practices that underscore how physicality and lived experience fuse. This discursive practice is radically contingent on space and radically situational in materiality, and as a result, from that position Chicanas engage rhetorical practices to re-present the physical realities lived by the Othered.

This notion of identity linked to a felt place came to me when I came into contact with Chicana rhetoric, which spread within my body like semillas, seedlings of knowledge.

Scatter semillas,
y con el tiempo volverán
a crecer.
La Chicanita breaks dry, caked soil, vigorously
sprouts generation lines and overgrows him quickly.
Man trims her invention back, naturally
prunes away at that unattainable essence she holds
to grow and to spread wildly. Like a budding Mexican Plum,
however, she blossoms Aztlán,
ripens faith, and seeds the sight of her
uncovered fertile form. Crafted instinctively
as she may be, she sows thin layers of herstory,
grows high to bask amid silenced tongues, bare
before a sweltering sun that radiantly reaps

her rooted cuerpo. Embarazada
de nepantlas, ella es
el conocimiento conceived,
so strategically conceived in wild tongues
that therein lies the beauty of what
comes from scattering semillas.

Coming from remediation and sexual difference, I felt marginalized as a practitioner in Writing Studies. I felt different entering the field because I saw myself still as a basic writer, "learn[ing] by making mistakes," as Mina Shaughnessy suggests in her landmark book *Errors and Expectations* (5). Moreover, as a practitioner I remained silent about my sexuality because I was gay within a field that needed a "better understanding of how heteronormativity operates in society at large" or "in our classrooms" (Alexander and Wallace 301). Chicana rhetoric offered me not only personal inspiration, but also a possible space to grow as a practitioner and to develop theories in writing instruction and pedagogies.

As a first generation Chicano scholar, I was concerned about the experience most Chicana/o bodies have within writing classrooms. As most Chicanas or Chicanos can attest to, marginalized bodies experience suppression from conventional, hegemonic social practices prevalent across writing classrooms, especially with(in) the borderland area (Newman, Kells, Mejía, Villanueva, Anzaldúa, Rendón). Writing instruction or pedagogies set on conventional, hegemonic social practices make "the body irrelevant to the words the body produces" (Yagelski 45). To demonstrate, Laura I. Rendón, who grew up in Laredo, Texas, reflects about an experience where her body is irrelevant:

> When I was a schoolgirl, I rarely had assignments that asked me to reflect on the meaning and purpose of what I was learning. No one asked me to write about what I knew best—*mi familia, mi barrio*, my life experiences and what I had learned from them. Instead, I attended classrooms with teachers who seemed so far removed from what I represented, teachers who had been socialized to not get too close to their students, to teach the basics, day in and day out, to maintain discipline and order, and to teach a content that was foreign to me. [Italics in original](3)

Rendón, who represents a body marginalized due to the marginalization of her ethnic background, describes writing instruction pedagogy suppressing her identity, sociocultural background, or any subjective interpretation. She also describes pedagogies that alienate her body. Her body is irrelevant, then, toward any literacy practices or the locations that involve formal education with(in) this borderland context.

Based on my flesh and blood experiences, both as student and composition instructor, theories and pedagogies of writing instruction are in need of an alternate perspective or approach that includes "Otherness" as well as lived spaces, particularly for bodies on the border. According to education scholars Dora Ramírez-Dhoore and Rebecca Jones, beliefs about pedagogy and difference directly affect the work that takes place with(in) a classroom:

> Our teaching practices and our students' differences and especially our beliefs about these things matter when they affect the outcome of work in a class. Just being of a different race, gender, or culture does not necessarily make teaching or learning different. Instead, we [practitioners] must examine the particular things within a political and educational space that necessitate differences in practice and theory. (68)

Ramírez-Dhoore and Jones urge practitioners to look beyond the surface for what constitutes difference and to examine further social practices that take place with(in) the sociocultural political and educational contexts.

To prove a point, "no pedagogical approach in composition," claims Jaime Mejía, "takes a Texas Mexican student's ethnicity into account" (44). Why? How could Mejía make such a claim in 2004, especially when notions about situated literacies permeated the field of Writing Studies? Most practitioners, including myself, have adopted the notion that literacies as social practices are situated, but Mejía's observation about disregarding Texas Mexican student's ethnicity in the classroom becomes relevant, especially when "literacies are positioned in relation to the social institutions and power relations which sustain them" (Barton et al. 1). Under such conditions, practitioners probably overlook the impact sociocultural contexts imprint on bodies, especially when those bodies and their literacies are put in a hierarchy within hegemonic social institutions. Damián Baca argues for "new ways of thinking about writing today, based on material and corporeal practices that have shifted across time" (*Mestiz@ Scripts* xvi). Speaking about Anzaldúa's *Borderlands*, Baca suggests that practitioners "shift from merely 'talking about' Anzaldúa's fragmented Chicana identity to 'inventing and writing from' her conceptual borderlands in order to contemplate how Western rhetorical knowledge can be revised by learning from Mestiz@s who are living in and thinking from colonial legacies" (*Mestiz@ Scripts* 122). This approach would situate Anzaldúa as a colonized subject who is engaged in literacy practices that reflect her own subjugated sociocultural context because "Anzaldúa's border thinking is a distinct articulation that emerges from the underside of colonization, from the perspectives of the subjugated and silenced" ("Damián Baca" 3). This perspective includes how marginal bodies exist, Othered bodies in particular, and includes their lived spaces, or what Moraga and Anzaldúa identify as the "physical realities" of bordered subjects, "our skin color, the land or concrete we grew up on, our sexual longings" (23).

THE SPATIAL BODY

Practitioners in Writing Studies who seek to localize bodies can find support in Chicana rhetoric associated with Chicana Third Space Feminism, especially with the idea of a theory in the flesh, which attempts to "use flesh and blood experiences to concretize a vision" (Moraga and Anzaldúa 23). The flesh contributes to "[t]heoretically infused writing practices" that inscribe "a different register," according to Norma Alarcón, "the register of women of color" (113). In *Borderlands*, Anzaldúa introduces an enfleshed borderland intermingling the corporeality and materiality of colonized subjects with the spatiality of a border culture. As an embodied discourse, Chicana rhetoric exemplifies a symbolic action that represents a body spatialized in a way that is localized in relation to place(s) or multiple ecologies. Ecologies are significant because they aid in constructing discourses, both in their "ideological contents" as well as in "shaping their reception," and how a body exists relative to place(s) is both complex, generating embodied meanings as the effect of literacy practices from and with that place, as well as interactive, responding rhetorically from a felt experience (Alexander 75). Like Anzaldúa, what Chicana rhetoric showcases is a literate body, or rather a situated literacy practice, which reveals embodied knowledge, that is to say, "knowledge grounded in situated practices," about localizing bodies to place(s) (Prior and Shipka 230). Chicanas, especially Anzaldúa, express a realization that articulates the situated nature of their *body writing* (act) as well as their *writing body* (discourse) relative to place(s), where place(s) and bodies intercept. They interactively engage corporeality and materiality rhetorically to signify a spatial body—a body that constitutes a bordered corporeality as a distinctive place-identity. This spatial body is a rhetorical counterpart to the corporeal body that is shaped from an embodied discourse, or with what I call an embodied rhetoric, where writers inextricably link their body to specific places and physical realities. The spatial body manifests from what I call interactive rhetorical actions; discursive formations not only contextualized from the body and connected with a specific place, but also actions inextricably linked, thus, with the ecological setting in which such acts of writing manifest.

To conclude, Chicanas "look in nontraditional places" for theories, maintains Saldívar-Hull, because hegemonic discourses construct "cultural modes of production" that marginalizes and devalues bodies of color or sexual difference (46). In similar fashion, as a result of being culturally marginalized by hegemonic discourses, I looked toward my experiences with writing as a nontraditional place for theorizing writing instruction and pedagogies that underscore the body in relation to place(s). My experiences with writing (or reading) have led me as a practitioner in Writing Studies to become emotionally invested in order to understand how the literate body manifests and how literacy practices are affected as a result of that manifestation. In that, I found Anzaldúa and Chicana rhetoric instrumental as it profoundly examines issues dealing with space and materiality in relation to bodies with(in) place(s).

NOTES

1 I consider my sexuality a private matter. As a writer, I did not want to "come out," so to speak. My family understands that I am gay, but to this day, there has been no dialogue between us on this matter.

2 Gloria refers not only to my biological mother Gloria S. Hinojosa, but also to Gloria E. Anzaldúa, whose text *Borderlands/La Frontera* has been a major influence in my life and graduate studies.

WORKS CITED

Alarcón, Norma. "Anzaldúa's Frontera: Inscribing Gynetics." *Decolonial Voices: Chicana and Chicano Cultural Studies in the 21st Century.* Eds. Arturo J. Aldama and Naomi H. Quiñonez. Bloomington: Indiana UP, 2002. 113–26. Print.

Alexander, Jonathan. *Literacy, Sexuality, Pedagogy: Theory and Practice for Composition Studies.* Logan, Utah: Utah State UP, 2008. Print.

Alexander, Jonathan, and David Wallace. "The Queer Turn in Composition Studies: Reviewing and Assessing an Emerging Scholarship." *CCC: College Composition and Communication* 61.1 (2009): 300–20. Print.

Anzaldúa, Gloria. *Borderlands/La Frontera: The New Mestiza.* 2nd ed. San Francisco: Aunt Lute Books, 1999. Print.

---. Interview by Andrea A. Lunsford. *Crossing Borderlands: Composition and Postcolonial Studies.* Eds. Andrea A. Lunsford and Lahoucine Ouzgane. Pittsburgh: U of Pittsburgh P, 2004. 33–66. Print.

---. "Haciendo Caras, Una Entrada." *Making Face, Making Soul/Haciendo Caras: Creative and Critical Perspectives by Feminists of Color.* Ed. Gloria Anzaldúa. San Francisco: Aunt Lute Books, 1990. xv–xxviii. Print.

---. *Interviews/Entrevistas.* Ed. AnaLouise Keating. New York: Routledge, 2000. Print.

Arredondo, Gabriela F., et al. "Chicana Feminisms at the Crossroads: Disruptions in Dialogue." Introduction. *Chicana Feminisms: A Critical Reader.* Eds. Arredondo, et al. Durham: Duke UP, 2003. 1–18. Print.

Baca, Damián. "Damián Baca, Scripts for Liberation." Interview by Lisa Alvarado. *La Bloga.* Blogger, 15 Jan. 2009. Web. 20 June 2014. <http://labloga.blogspot.com/2009/01/damian-baca-scripts-for-liberation.html>.

---. *Mestiz@ Scripts, Digital Migrations, and The Territories of Writing.* New York: Palgrave Macmillan, 2008. Print.

Barton, David, Mary Hamilton, and Roz Ivanic, eds. *Situated Literacies: Reading and Writing in Context.* London: Routledge, 2000. Print.

Flores, Lisa A. "Creating Discursive Space Through a Rhetoric of Difference: Chicana Feminists Craft a Homeland." *Quarterly Journal of Speech* 82 (May 1996): 142-56. Print.

Gee, James Paul. "Literacies, Identities, and Discourses." *Developing Advanced Literacy in First and Second Languages: Meaning with Power.* Eds. Mary J. Schleppegrell and M. Cecilia Colombi. New York: Routledge, 2002. 159–75. Print.

Lefebvre, Henri. *The Production of Space*. Trans. Donald Nicholson-Smith. Malden: Blackwell Publishing, 2007. Print.

Mejía, Jaime. "Bridging Rhetoric and Composition Studies with Chicano and Chicana Studies: A Turn to Critical Pedagogy." *Latino/a Discourses: On Language, Identity and Literacy Education*. Eds. Michelle Hall Kells, Valerie Balester, and Victor Villanueva. Portsmouth: Boynton/Cook, 2004. 40–56. Print.

Moraga, Cherríe, and Gloria Anzaldúa, eds. *This Bridge Called My Back: Writings by Radical Women of Color*. 2nd ed. New York: Kitchen Table: Women of Color Press, 1983. Print.

Olson, Gary A. "Toward a Post-Process Composition: Abandoning the Rhetoric of Assertion." *Post-Process Theory: Beyond the Writing-Process Paradigm*. Ed. Thomas Kent. Carbondale: Southern Illinois UP, 1999. 7–15. Print.

Pérez, Emma. *The Decolonial Imaginary: Writing Chicanas into History*. Bloomington: Indiana UP, 1999. Print.

Prior, Paul, and Jody Shipka. "Chronotopic Lamination: Tracing the Contours of Literate Activity." *Writing Selves / Writing Societies: Research from Activity Perspectives*. Eds. Charles Bazerman and David R. Russell. Fort Collins, Colorado: The WAC Clearinghouse and Mind, Culture, and Activity, 2003. 180–238. *The WAC Clearinghouse*. Web. 18 Jan. 2015. <http://colostate.edu>.

Ramírez-Dhoore, Dora, and Rebecca Jones. "Discovering a 'Proper Pedagogy': The Geography of Writing at the University of Texas-Pan American." *Teaching Writing with Latino/a Students: Lessons Learned at Hispanic-Serving Institutions*. Eds. Cristina Kirklighter, Diana Cárdenas, and Susan Wolff Murphy. New York: State U of New York P, 2007. 63–86. Print.

Rendón, Laura I. *Sentipensante Pedagogy: Educating for Wholeness, Social Justice and Liberation*. Sterling: Stylus, 2009. Print.

Saldívar-Hull, Sonia. *Feminism on the Border: Chicana Gender Politics and Literature*. Berkeley: U of California P, 2000. Print.

Sandoval, Chela. *Methodology of the Oppressed*. Minneapolis: U of Minnesota P, 2000. Print.

Shapiro, Sherry B. *Pedagogy and The Politics of the Body: A Critical Praxis*. New York: Garland Publishing, Inc., 1999. Print.

Shaughnessy, Mina P. *Errors and Expectations: A Guide for the Teacher of Basic Writing*. New York: Oxford UP, 1977. Print.

Yagelski, Robert P. *Writing as a Way of Being: Writing Instruction, Nonduality, and the Crisis of Sustainability*. New York: Hampton, 2011. Print.

EPISTEMOLOGIES OF THE BODY/MIND/SPIRIT

THE LIMINAL, THE LUMINOUS & THE DARK

THE PATH OF CONOCIMIENTO AND THE DARK NIGHT OF THE SOUL

CARLA WILSON

This essay embodies what Anzaldúa refers to in the preface to *This Bridge We Call Home* as a personal, political, and spiritual intimacy (3); therefore, rather than form an argument that can often feel oppositional and rigid, I'm seeking to open a dialogue that will hopefully continue to grow and take on a life long after the "El Mundo Zurdo 2015: Memoria y Conocimiento, Interdisciplinary Anzaldúan Studies—Archive, Legacy, and Thought" conference. I invite your openness while I explore my thoughts as I have no solid questions, only my imagination and my desire. Neither do I have definitive answers, only my intuition and ideas. However, I am certain of one thing, I have a calling to enter and explore "uncomfortable," or as Gloria Anzaldúa refers to as, "(Un) safe spaces," inclusive of feelings of isolation, alienation, conflict, tension, ambiguity, uncertainty, vulnerability, grief, sadness, and anger, alongside faith, hope, yearning, desire, imagination, possibilities, and potential. As Anzaldúa so courageously shared in the preface, "(Un)natural bridges, (Un)safe spaces":

> But there are no safe spaces. "Home" can be unsafe and dangerous because it bears the likelihood of intimacy and thus thinner boundaries. Staying "home" and not venturing out from our own group comes from woundedness, and stagnates our growth...To step across the threshold is

> to be stripped of the illusion of safety because it moves us into unfamiliar territory and does not grant safe passage. To bridge is to attempt community, and for that we must risk being open to personal, political, and spiritual intimacy, to risk being wounded. (3)

She warns us that in order to heal, grow, and transform, not only ourselves, but also the world, we must take risks. These risks are not "safe" nor are they familiar, and they require vulnerability. Anzaldúa reminds us that in order to heal and transform, we must step into unknown territory, let go of our habitual patterns of thinking, and be willing to get hurt again and again. I like to think of her words in relation to growing pains, we cannot grow and change without some sort of pain and suffering. Fear of uncertainty and a lack of guaranteed safety are what prohibits many of us from leaving our comfort zones; however, I do believe it is crucial to move out of these spaces of false comfort and "risk" ourselves in these (Un)safe spaces Anzaldúa speaks of: it is time.

My exploration of the intersection between St. John of the Cross'ss dark night of the soul and Anzaldúan thought is just that, an adventure into the unknown without a road map. My research process has been a bit elusive, fluid, and abstract. As soon as I feel I'm on to something, that something swiftly slips away. My thinking and writing processes are similar to how Anzaldúa describes nepantla: non-linear, ambiguous, and fluid yet also full of potential. My interest in dark spaces and depression originates from a twenty-year obsession with St. John of the Cross'ss concept of the dark night of the soul. Many friends and family members, myself included, have suffered or still suffer from depression in one form or another. I've always struggled to find a way to see my own depression as both useful as a catalyst and a point of departure for personal change and transformation. Who wouldn't want to end their own suffering? However, I never saw the connection between my suffering and the suffering in others and in the world.

When I was first introduced to Anzaldúa's work, like many others, I immediately felt a strange sense of familiarity. Her honesty and vulnerability immediately drew me in and I felt as though she was sharing some of my very own personal feelings and doubts. Her words resonated with me on an extremely deep level. I was particularly drawn to her essay "now let us shift...the path of conocimiento...inner work, public acts" because it is here that I felt she unapologetically wrote about her dark feelings of depression and hopelessness and her vulnerability and honesty provided me with courage and a sense of hope. For the first time, I was not alone. When feeling overwhelmed and hopeless, both elements of depression, I saw spiritual activism as a tool to utilize the "(Un)safe spaces" I often found myself in throughout my life. In all that I'd read about the dark night of the soul, I was never introduced to a vision or tools, to imagine how practical "(Un)safe spaces" could be in my own personal and social activism work. To this day, Anzaldúa's writing provides me with hope and vision to see "(Un)safe spaces" such as the experience of depression as transformational spaces.

While making connections between Cross'ss dark night of the soul and Anzaldúa's "now let us shift..." I discovered how Anzaldúa not only provides examples for how we might personally navigate liminal spaces within nepantla through her personal narrative, she also offers a vision that can inspire us to use our own narratives to re-envision a future where social injustice no longer exists. She provides practical tools through the sharing of her personal experiences for how we might exploit dark spaces and extend beyond a relationship between the personal and the spiritual world. By creating bridges from the self out into the world, our personal changes can contribute to societal transformation. After revisiting St. John of the Cross'ss work on the dark night of the soul, I propose that Anzaldúa's theory of spiritual activism expands on the concept moving beyond a relationship between an individual and God and into a planetary relationship inclusive of all that exists in the physical, mental, and spiritual worlds. An expansion beyond the self is vital if we are to dismantle cultural norms that construct identities and ultimately lead to forms of subjugation based not only on social categories such as race, class, gender, sexuality, age, ability, and many others but also on systemic oppression overall.

First I will share definitions of concepts I refer to throughout this essay. The concept of liminal and liminality is seen throughout Anzaldúa's work. She speaks of the liminality of nepantla when she describes bridges in the preface of *This Bridge We Call Home*:

> Bridges span liminal (threshold) spaces between worlds, spaces I call nepantla [...] Transformations occur in this in-between space, an unstable, unpredictable, precarious, always-in-transition space lacking clear boundaries. Nepantla es tierra desconocida, and living in this liminal zone means being in a constant state of displacement—an uncomfortable, even alarming feeling. (1)

Liminality is an important concept that speaks to the capacity her work has in occupying multiple spaces of transformation. An ability to move and transform is an asset in personal and social change work. The ability to think beyond rigid status-quo narratives is necessary if we are to begin to do the work of sustainable social change.

Another important concept I see throughout Anzaldúa's work is luminosity or luminous. Her work is indeed luminous in that it creates awareness, or conocimiento, where there is unawareness, or desconocimiento. In the introduction of *Light in the Dark/Luz En Lo Oscuro: Rewriting Identity, Spirituality, Reality*, Keating writes, "Anzaldúa redefines the term [conocimiento], incorporating imaginal, spiritual-activist, and ontological dimensions. An intensely personal, fully embodied process that gathers information from context" (xxvii). From this, I conceive desconocimiento to be a lack of these imaginal, spiritual-activist, and ontological dimensions. I conceive it to be unawareness, and on occasion, a willed ignorance. In researching the term luminous, I searched specifically for a definition that I felt did justice to Anzaldúa's work. I found one such definition in the Oxford English Dictionary from 1877 where in describing his invention of a certain chemical process invoked from an invention of his, W. H. Balmain defined luminous as:

> My invention relates to a method of rendering paints, varnishes, white-washings, and temperings luminous, and consists in the introduction into ordinary paints, varnishes, or washes of a phosphorescent substance, by which means the object to which the paint, or varnish, or wash is applied is made visible in the dark and more or less capable of imparting light to other objects. ("luminous")

Just as the chemical process Balmain describes illuminates objects, I propose Anzaldúa's theory of spiritual activism illuminates St John of the Cross'ss concept of the dark night of the soul, extending it from a relationship between an individual and God and transforming it into an interconnected planetary relationship between all that exists in the physical, mental, and spiritual worlds.

I acknowledge there are unfortunate implications that the language around darkness can have on a black and white binary. In thinking about what this could mean for my research on the dark night of the soul and the dark and shadow language in Anzaldúa's work, I came across María DeGuzmán's work in *Buenas Noches, American Culture: Latina/o Aesthetics of Night*. She asserts, "Anzaldúa's shadow darkness presents a decolonizing challenge to some of the most fundamental assumptions within the binaries 'dark/light' and 'absence/presence' in dominant Western epistemology" (33). DeGuzmán continues by saying shadow darkness is actually decolonizing in that it frees darkness from the reservation of shame to which it has been bound and creates a way for us to identify with what has been historically devalued, demonized, and persecuted (33). Instead of stigmatizing or pathologizing it, it allows us to see darkness as enlightening. My hope is through theorizing the "(Un)safe spaces" in Anzaldúa's work, there will be further exploration into the many ways in which Anzaldúa's work illuminates the possibilities for transformation within darkness. By revisiting the ways darkness is portrayed in Cross's dark night of the soul, it becomes evident how Anzaldúa's work in "now let us shift..." is illuminating, transformative, and extends the dark night of the soul beyond the individual journey.

The concept of the dark night of the soul has been theorized and referred to throughout history. I've traced it to the mid-16th century and to the writings of

St. John of the Cross. He is attributed with being the originator of the concept and language of the dark night of the soul. He was born in 1542 and died in 1591. He was a major figure of the Counter-Reformation, a Spanish mystic, a Roman Catholic saint, a Carmelite friar, and a priest. He was also a reformer of the Carmelite Order and is considered, along with Saint Teresa of Ávila, a founder of the Discalced Carmelites. St. John of the Cross'ss primary concern within his writings was with a mystical quest for the reality of God. The most enduring of his work is that of the poem "The Dark Night of the Soul" written in 1578 while he was imprisoned. The poem narrates the journey of the soul from its physical or bodily home to its reconnection with God. In the poem, darkness represents the hardships, difficulties, impasse, and detachment to the world that the soul meets as it searches and eventually reaches the light of the union with God (King).

Anzaldúa describes a similar journey when she introduces us to the seven stages of conocimiento in her essay "now let us shift..." It is in this essay that we see and feel the confusion, pain, and suffering on the path of conocimiento. The term conocimiento is derived from a Latin verb *cognoscera* meaning "to know," and it is also the Spanish word for knowledge and skill. Anzaldúa uses the term as an aspect of consciousness urging us to act on the knowledge gained on the path of conocimiento. She explains, "intuitive knowing, unmediated by mental constructs—what inner eye, heart, and gut tell you—is the closest you come to direct knowledge of the world and this experience of reality is partial too" (Anzaldúa 542). Conocimiento involves a search for alternative forms of knowledge and transformation all the while recognizing all knowledge as partial and contextual.

In this essay, I theorize the intersection of St. John of the Cross's dark night of the soul and the stages within Anzaldúa's path of conocimiento. I am primarily interested in the second and third stages on the path: nepantla and the Coatlicue state. The concept of nepantla refers to the second stage on the path of conocimiento and is a liminal, transitional space, suspended between shifts where you are two people, split between before and after. Nepantla is a zone of possibility, fluid, expanding and contracting where you are able to access knowledge coming from inner feelings, imaginal states, and external events (Anzaldúa 544).

It is an in-between space extending beyond borders, imaginary or real, into multiple perceptions and belief systems. Anzaldúa writes, "In this liminal, transitional space, suspended between shifts, you're two people, split between before and after. Nepantla, where the outer boundaries of the mind's inner life meet the outer world of reality, is a zone of possibility" (544). It is in here in "now let us shift..." that I began to see the common language used to describe the spaces inhabited by the dark night of the soul, nepantla, and the Coatlicue state.

In *dark night spirituality*, Peter King quotes Belden C. Lane in reference to the impasse one finds oneself in when inhabiting the space of the dark night of the soul:

> In a genuine impasse one's accustomed way of acting and living is brought to a standstill. The left side of the brain, with its usual application of linear, analytical, conventional thinking is ground to a halt. The impasse forces us to start all over again, driving us to contemplation. On the other hand the impasse provides a challenge and a concrete focus for contemplation…It forces the right side of the brain into gear, seeking intuitive, symbolic, unconventional answers, so that action can be renewed eventually with greater purpose. (5)

As seen here, there are many similarities between Anzaldúa's description of nepantla, the Coatlicue state, and Lane's description of the dark night of the soul. For example, spaces of impasse are described in both the dark night of the soul and nepantla.

Feeling torn between opposing realities, an illumination of the ability to exist in more than one space opens you up to the third stage of the path of conocimiento, the Coatlicue state. In this state you come to the realization that you cannot change reality but you can change the meaning you've ascribed to it. Although this space includes feelings of anger, despair, depression, and pain, it is also the stage on the path with the highest potential to "realize that it's the negative thoughts (your reactions to events) that rouse the beast and not something 'real' or unchangeable out there in the outer world" and acknowledge your capacity and ability to change your thoughts and confront your past traumas and inner shadow or demons (Anzaldúa 553).

Initially I was drawn to the many commonalities between the dark night of the soul, Anzaldúa's nepantla, and the Coatlicue State. Within these liminal spaces are feelings of depression, isolation, confusion, chaos, ambiguity, uncertainty, pain, suffering, and loneliness. However, it wasn't long before I began to imagine: what was next? Once we recognize these commonalities and acknowledge what these spaces contain, how can we use this awareness, or conocimiento, to move through these "(Un)safe spaces"? This led me to wonder about the differences between the dark night of the soul and the path of conocimiento. Through the act of paying attention to the differences, we allow and create more space for the imaginal and intuitive ways of knowing that Anzaldúa refers to in her definition of conocimiento. These are the ways in which we can transform the personal experience of the dark night of the soul into a more relational experience.

Although I'm sure there are many differences between St. John of the Cross'ss dark night of the soul and Anzaldúa's stages of conocimiento, in this essay I choose to focus on three areas where Anzaldúa expands on the dark night that I believe will create a space for sustainable personal and planetary transformation. First, St. John of the Cross's concept of the dark night of the soul focuses on an individual's journey to spiritual enlightenment culminating in a reunification with God, whereas Anzaldúa's focus on the path of conocimiento is more relational and expands on the dark night of the soul's individual journey by way of a planetary citizenship. Second, Anzaldúa's work emphasizes the capacity of dark feelings experienced within nepantla, particularly depression, to be transformative on both a personal and a systemic level. And finally, I failed to find a connection to socio-political and cultural effects in regards to suffering experienced within the space of the dark night of the soul, whereas Anzaldúa claims cultural norms and expectations as well as the cultural constructs and categories continue to oppress and exploit subjects yet they can also serve as a catalyst to entering the path of conocimiento. These three areas of expansion, although not exhaustive, speak most to how Anzaldúan thought broadens Cross's concept of the dark night of the soul, moving it beyond the individual and into a relational and transformational experience.

Unlike Anzaldúa's path of conocimiento, St. John of the Cross'ss dark night of the soul primarily focuses on the relationship between the self and God. There is little, if any, mention about society or culture and their effects on an individual's journey into darkness. The poem narrates the journey of the soul from its physical or bodily home to its integration and reconnection with God. The focus on an individual body is noted by Peter King in ***dark night spirituality***, "For St. John of the Cross, the dark night was a profoundly personal and individual experience. It was a stage on one's journey towards God. For us it has become a social and corporate reality, embodied in our society, our culture and our history" (2). The individualistic perspective has not gone unnoticed and is described by the Got Questions Ministries organization as follows: "This eight-stanza poem outlines the soul's journey from the distractions and entanglements of the world to the perfect peace and harmony of union with God" ("What is a 'dark night of the soul'?"). Although St. John of the Cross'ss perspective was very individualistic, others have built on his work and consider the socio-political implications within the dark night of the soul.

One such voice is that of Trappist Monk Thomas Merton. He expands on Cross's work and writes predominantly on what it is to live the life of a contemplative. It is worth noting that Merton is mentioned in Anzaldúa's essay "now let us shift…" in relation to those critical points of transformation that inspire an individual to adopt the work of spiritual activism. She refers to, "a pervasive form of modern violence that Thomas Merton attributes to the rush of continual doing" (Anzaldúa 572). In writing about the journey of exploration into what it meant to be a contemplative in the modern world, Merton extended St. John of the Cross'ss concept of the dark night of the soul in his later work when he began to include the events of world history and social and political affairs within the scope of his writings. I find it significant that in my research on the intersections between the dark night of the soul and Anzaldúan thought, I found Merton to be an important bridge connecting the two theorists.

Another voice is that of Eckhart Tolle. He describes the dark night of the soul as a "collapse of perceived or conceptual meaning in life…an eruption into your life of a deep sense of meaninglessness" and claims it is very close to what is conveniently called depression where nothing makes sense anymore and all sense of hope and purpose is lost (Tolle). Tolle talks about the dark night in reference to the death of the egoic sense of self, an illusory identity. He claims that once you pass through the dark night of the soul you look upon events and people with a deep sense of aliveness through your own sense of aliveness without trying to fit your experience into a pre-conceived conceptual framework anymore. Likewise, Kim Hutchinson describes the dark night of the soul as a phenomenon many seekers experience on their journey to re-enlightenment. Although painful and frightening, it can also be liberating and empowering. She divides the process into three stages: Ego Death, Existential Crisis, and the final stage of Purification by Fire which entails emptying yourself of ego and fear allowing more room for your soul's love, light, wisdom, beauty, and joy (Hutchinson). Although many voices speak of the dark night of the soul beyond an individual's relationship with God, I've found Anzaldúa's work to be more expansive in extending Cross's concept of the dark night of the soul both beyond the individual and into the relational as well as bridging the concept into areas of identity and social constructs that enact experiences of oppression and injustice on a personal and social level. I propose that Anzaldúa does this work by way of dissecting the root causes of some experiences of depression. Instead of pathologizing depression and viewing it as something to be fixed or eliminated, she emphasizes the transformative capacity of depression. We can use her work to destigmatize depression, explicitly in the third stage of the path of conocimiento, the Coatlicue state.

Anzaldúa describes the Coatlicue state as being "overwhelmed by the chaos felt by living between multiple identities and/or stories, in the nepantla stage, one descends into the Coatlicue State. It is a space inclusive of despair, self-loathing, hopelessness, anger, fear, depression, and inadequacy" (569).

In the Coatlicue state, depression can be seen as an opportunity to expand consciousness, therefore destigmatizing the mental, physical, emotional, and spiritual experience, "by seeing your symptoms not as signs of sickness and dis-integration but as signals of growth, you're able to rise from depression's slow suicide. By using these feelings as tools or grist for the mill, you move through fear, anxiety, anger, and blast into another reality (Anzaldúa 552). Not only does Anzaldúa see depression as a means to transform, she speaks specifically to the problem of medicalization in particular when she says:

> Though modern therapies exhort you to act against your passions (compulsions), claiming health and integration lie in that direction, you've learned that delving more fully into your pain, anger, despair, depression will move you through to the other side, where you can use their energy to heal. Depression is useful—it signals that you need to make changes in your life, it challenges your tendency to withdraw, it reminds you to take action. (553)

We are once again invited to enter into these "(Un)safe spaces" to be challenged, to seek answers, and to take action that will enable us and empower us to make necessary changes in our life and in our world.

Similarly, in the article, "What a Shaman Sees in a Mental Hospital," according to Malidoma Patrice Somé, mental illness signals "the birth of a healer" (Marohn). He claims that mental disorders are actually spiritual emergencies. When Somé visited a fellow student in an American mental hospital, he was shocked at how the symptoms were pathologized. This was in complete opposition to the way his culture viewed such a situation. He inquired, "So this is how the healers who are attempting to be born are treated in this culture. What a loss! What a loss that a person who is finally being aligned with a power from the other world is just being wasted" (Marohn). Anzaldúa's view on depression is in alignment with Somé's perspective. It is worth considering that there is a purpose for depression and what society considers mental illness beyond that of sickness and medicalization that goes unacknowledged and is purposefully ignored in our society. Within depression exists a capacity to transform and to heal one's self and the world.

I want to discuss one of many ways Anzaldúa's work can lead us out of the dark night of the soul and into spaces of transformation. In *The Hidden Ground of Love,* Thomas Merton wrote in a letter to the Indian poet and philosopher, Amiya Chakravarty:

> The reality that is present to us and in us: call it Being, call it Atman, call it Pneuma...or Silence. And the simple fact that by being attentive, by learning to listen (or recovering the natural capacity to listen which cannot be learned any more than breathing), we can find ourself engulfed in such happiness that it cannot be explained: the happiness of being at one with everything in the hidden ground of Love for which there can be no explanations. (Merton 21)

The capacity to listen, the practice of compassionate listening in particular, can be considered a form of spiritual activism. I've traced the practice of compassionate listening to Gene Knudsen Hoffman, international peacemaker, founder of the US/USSR Reconciliation program for the Fellowship of Reconciliation, and student of Vietnamese Buddhist Monk, Thich Nhat Hanh. In the introduction to *Listening with the Heart,* Hoffman describes compassionate listening as follows: "I'm not talking about listening with the 'human ear.' I am talking about discerning. To discern means to perceive something hidden or obscure. We must listen with our 'spiritual ear.' This is very different from deciding in advance who is right and who is wrong, and then seeking to rectify it" (xiii).

Compassionate listening is predominantly defined, discussed, and practiced within the bounds of communication between two or more people. I invite you to reimagine the definition, discourse, and practice including listening compassionately to one's self. Compassionate listening consists of specific behaviors such as staying present, being gentle with yourself, allowing silence, witnessing your judgments, not trying to fix anything, and listening with your heart instead of your head. These behaviors can be practiced with one's self and ultimately should begin with one's self in order to be present for others. I propose the practice of compassionate listening with ourselves as a form of spiritual activism while traveling the path of conocimiento, particularly during the third stage, the Coatlicue state, in order to illuminate the signs hidden within the shadows of the dark night of the soul. These signs are messages that can be utilized in mapping out the liminal spaces of nepantla enabling us to imagine new territories as well as transforming habitual feelings that no longer serve us.

Just as Anzaldúa spoke of a need to "append new growth" to things that have reached their zenith when she introduced the intent behind *This Bridge We Call Home,* my hope is that the exploration of the intersection between Cross's dark night of the soul and Anzaldúan thought will expand on the current discourse on the dark in her work. The "intense pain" and woundedness in "Borderlands" and "mestiza consciousness" are deserving of further exploration. In "Gloria Anzaldúa's Mestiza Pain: Mexican Sacrifice, Chicana Embodiment, and Feminist Politics," Suzanne Bost warns us how "celebrating this chaos risks romanticizing sites of continued oppression, such as the borderlands" (9). I refuse to simplify or romanticize Anzaldúa's experience or writing on depression, as tempting as it may be at times, as it would overlook the need we have to continue to theorize and imagine a future that does not yet exist, one without social injustice in all of its manifestations. Just as King describes the work of contemplation:

> Yet contemplation is no passive exercise. Piercing through to the reality of God leads to action. It leads to action in regard to oneself, to the world, and to one's faith in God. Contemplation leads to change and transformation in oneself, in religious communities, and in the world at large. It leads to commitment to work to bring things closer to the vision

> of reality that one has glimpsed. This is contemplation – and yet it is not. In the end, contemplation defies formulation and description. It remains elusive and open, awaiting a specific human life in a particular context to give it content. (10)

My desire to continuously grow and strengthen my own contemplative practices and discover new ways to include these practices in my pedagogy combined with my desire to imagine ways to see the transformative ability of the spaces we often try to avoid, "(Un)safe spaces," spaces filled with conflict, tension, ambiguity, uncertainty, vulnerability, grief, sadness, and anger, inspire me to redefine the dark, see it in a new light, as transformative. The work of redefining, reimagining, and re-envisioning is vital in order to make the personal and social transformations needed on multiple levels. Just as Anzaldúa's work continues to invite us into "(Un)safe spaces," I am inviting you, will you join me?

WORKS CITED

Anzaldúa, Gloria E. "now let us shift…the path of conocimiento…inner work, public acts." In *This Bridge We Call Home: Radical Visions for Transformation,* Eds. Gloria E. Anzaldúa and AnaLouise Keating. New York: Routledge, 2002. 540-78. Print.

Belden C. Lane. "Spirituality and Political Commitment: Notes on a Liberation Theology of Non Violence." *America* 144:10 (1981): 197-202. Print.

Bost, Suzanne. "Gloria Anzaldúa's Mestiza Pain: Mexican Sacrifice, Chicana Embodiment, and Feminist Politics." *Aztlán* 30:2 (2005): 5-34. Print.

DeGuzmán, María. *Buenas Noches, American Culture: Latina/o Aesthetics of Night.* Bloomington: Indiana University Press, 2012. Print.

Fitzgerald, Constance. "From Impasse to Prophetic Hope: Crisis of Memory." *CTSA Proceedings* 64 (2009): 21-42. Print.

Hoffman, Gene K. *Compassionate Listening and Other Writings*. Portland: Friends Bulletin, 2003. Print.

Hwoschinsky, Carol. *Listening With the Heart: A Guide for Compassionate Listening.* Indianola: The Compassionate Listening Project, 2001. Print.

Hutchinson, Kim. "The Light Side of the Dark Night of the Soul." *The Mind Unleashed, Inc.* n.p. Web. 15 May 2015.

Keating, AnaLouise. "From Borderlands and New Mestizas to Nepantlas and Nepantleras: Anzaldúan Theories for Social Change." *Human Architecture: Journal of the Sociology of Self-Knowledge* IV, Special Issue (2006): 5-16. Print.

King, Peter. *dark night spirituality.* London: Holy Trinity Church, 1995. Print.

Lanzetta, Beverly J. *Radical Wisdom: A Feminist Mystical Theology*. Minneapolis: Fortress, 2005. Print.

"luminous, adj." *OED Online.* Oxford University Press, September 2015. Web. 23 October 2015.

Marohn, Stephanie. "What a Shaman Sees in a Mental Hospital." *Earth We Are One.* n.p. 12 June 2014. Web. 22 May 2015.

Merton, Thomas. *The Hidden Ground of Love: The Letters of Thomas Merton on Religious Experience and Social Concerns.* New York: Farrar, Straus, Giroux, 1985. Print.

---. "The Mystic Life Lesson #28 Dark Night of the Soul." *The Mystic World Fellowship.* n.p. 2001. Web. 12 May 2015.

Solnit, Rebecca. "Woolf's Darkness: Embracing the Inexplicable." *The New Yorker.* Apr. 2014. Web. 13 May 2015.

Tolle, Eckhart. "Eckhart on the Dark Night of the Soul." *Eckhart Teachings Inc.* Oct. 2011. Web. 13 May 2015.

"What is a 'dark night of the soul'?" *Got Questions Ministries.* GotQuestions.org, n.d. Web. May 2015.

DREAMING OF ADELITA

A SWAPA ON SPIRITUAL ACTIVISM IN THE WAKE OF CHILD LOSS

NICHOLAS CENTINO

ON SWAPA

A ritual, a performance, a method, an art, and an exchange, the practice of Spoken Wor(l)d Art Performance Activism, or SWAPA, is rooted in the theory and politics of US Third World feminisms. Developed by Chela Sandoval, SWAPA is a method that challenges passive consumption of text and performance and calls upon artist and audience alike to draw upon a mestiza consciousness and be willing to be an active witness. As Sandoval observes, "When you stand and deliver, sharing those connections with us, you transform from passive-witness members of the audience into active witnesses. As you speak you are transformed and transformer" (Jamakani and Troka 6).

The following SWAPA was performed at SSGA's 2015 El Mundo Zurdo Conference. In the SWAPA method, each piece is written in reaction to key moments in Anzaldúa's work that called out to me. Just as I bear witness to the ways in which the text has moved and inspired new ways of thinking, creating, and being for me, SWAPA calls upon the audience to witness and reflect and share their own reactions to the ritual/performance.

I was initially hesitant to deliver this piece as a SWAPA instead of as a traditional spoken word performance or conference presentation. A multifaceted method, SWAPA can be an effective tool in organizing, facilitation, and in the classroom as a form of what Eddy Francisco Alvarez Jr. calls jotería pedagogy (218). However, in conversations with Sandoval, we both feared that SWAPA could be stripped of its political teeth and liberatory practice and dismissed as solely a form of therapy. While this piece does follow my own path of healing and conocimiento, it also engages in the highly political task of decolonizing the ways in which we mourn, grieve, and process loss. Since its performance, "Dreaming of Adelita" has provided me with an instrument to engage others working through their own forms of loss and bereavement. As such, I encourage you to share your own witnessing to this piece with me. If you yourself are bereaved, I also extend an open hand and an open ear.

. . .

My daughter Adelita's short and intense time in this world was the most tiring, amazing, and exhilarating three days of my life. Looking back on it, it felt like a dream. I was physically exhausted, drifting between sleep and awake, yet every second I could spend with my little girl lifted my spirits. The night that we came home, with Ana, my wife, trying to get some sleep, I held Adelita in my arms. We rocked in the glider, nursery versions of The Cure and Michael Jackson playing on the stereo. We swayed and I danced her to sleep. Every time I tried to sing to her, I couldn't—I got choked up and couldn't get the words out. I tried humming and that helped.

She passed over to the spirit world three days after she was born. It is hard for me to try and remember what happened. My wife nursed Adelita and the baby went to sleep; when she did not awake, we called 9-1-1. The hospital staff tried to save her, but it was her time. Ana pleaded with the hospital staff to keep going. Adelita squeezed my wife's hand as if to say goodbye. I held her body and somewhere in my head the song "Dream a Little Dream" came to me. I tried to sing it to her through my tears. I wailed. My little girl left her earthly form.

We were interviewed by different people, a sheriff deputy, a detective, and then, the coroner investigator. Finally, at three in the morning, we made it home to an empty house. I was devastated and cried and cried and cried. I let our loved ones know what had happened and I finally made it to the bedroom to sleep. As I dozed off, I could swear that I could smell her—that raw organic smell of blood and amniotic fluid she carried when she was first born. I caught it, and then it was gone.

In the year following my daughter's passing, I have strived to remain on a path of conocimiento, as envisioned by Gloria Anzaldúa. I find the strength each morning to live in honor of my daughter and invest the spiritual labor to heal my own inner wounds of trauma in order to complete each day in a good way. In all honesty, I found little solace in mainstream ways of conceptualizing grief, both Anglo and Latina/o. The Kübler-Ross model of grief did little for me: I was never in denial, nor did I ever feel particularly angry. Nor did dichos or sugar-skulled platitudes on death being a natural part of life offer any solace. Children should bury parents, and not the other way around. My daughter's passing was a violation of the life cycle, not a natural result of it. Anzaldúa's seven stages of conocimiento not only provided me with a narrative that I could relate to but it did more than call me to accept what had happened: it reminded me that I had an ethical and moral mandate to be a better person because of it.

While the path to conocimiento provided a model for healing, I turned to words and movement as tools to work through my grief. As Audre Lorde reminded Black women in "Poetry is not a Luxury," "Poetry is the way we help give name to the nameless so it can be thought. The farthest external horizons of our hopes and fears are cobbled by our poems, carved from the rock experiences of our daily lives" (36). Following my daughter's passing I drifted in and out of spirit world and writing became a way to re-ground myself in the world in which I belonged. What began as little scribbles on gas station receipts evolved into some of the pieces featured in this paper. Slowly, random thoughts and flashes of images grew, coalesced, and formed into SWAPA, Spoken Wor(l)d Art Performance Activism, as introduced to me through the work of Chela Sandoval. In turn, SWAPA became a way for me to pray and commune with my child. It allowed me to speak aloud the words no one else could or would understand.

In "now let us shift," Anzaldúa describes the Path of Conocimineto as a non-linear trail snaking through seven spaces: the arrebato, nepantla, the coatlicue state, the call to action, putting coyolxauqui back together, the blow-up, and spiritual activism. The Path of Conocimiento provided me the equivalent of a ship's manifest, a document detailing a vessel's often treacherous journey, and the cargo lost and gained along the way. Ultimately, it provided me a model from which I could develop a language to narrate my own path, and detail my own journey.

This paper is crafted as a personal shaman-witness ceremony. In revisiting *Borderlands/La Frontera* and "now let us shift," certain words, passages, and quotes spoke to me at moment when I needed them most. I bear witness and honor these words through SWAPA and poetry. Some of the pieces are ones I've carried since the dawn of my grief, others crafted specifically for this paper. After each SWAPA, I share a small autohistoria as a way to reflect and share moments on my own path. In the tradition of my talking circle, I offer no advice, no consejos, no counsel. However, my only wish is that whatever speaks to you in my words provides you or someone you know with the medicine I found in those of Gloria Anzaldúa.

THE ARREBATO & THE COATLICUE STATE: LLORONA/LLORÓN

> "... if I escape conscious awareness, escape 'knowing,' I won't be moving. [...] 'Knowing' is painful because after 'it' [*the arrebato*] happens I can't stay in the same place and be comfortable. I am no longer the same person I was before."
> (Anzaldúa, *Borderlands/La Frontera* 70)

When I was 13 years old I saw her

Northbound on the 285 somewhere outside of Romeo

Clear as day there she was

Dona Sebastiana and her black cart.

She came back, y'know?

With my child on one hand,

Cracked leather reigns in the other, she rode off slowly.

Frozen, I watched the cart slowly disappear into the horizon.

Alone I stood, 13 years old again.

Northbound side of the 285

somewhere outside of Romeo.

One of the cruel ironies of losing a baby is just how quickly life goes back to being normal. For the past nine months, I had endured constant prompting about how much my life was going to change. Yet after the condolence cards stopped coming, after family went home, and after the funeral was over, my life largely returned to the way it was before, albeit excruciatingly more banal. The trash still had to be taken out, the bills still had to be paid, the dogs still had to be walked and so forth. The fact that life went on as it had before, to me, was the sickest joke imaginable. *My* world had crumbled; I was fundamentally a different and broken person, and ***the*** world went on as if nothing had happened. Anzaldúa writes of addiction as an escape for those not yet ready to face the schism of who they were before and after the arrebato. Although not quite an addiction, I dove into my work as a graduate student, grading exam papers hours after my daughter stopped breathing. I was months from filing my dissertation and leaving UC Santa Barbara as a doctor in Chicana and Chicano Studies, and no matter how hard I tried to move on just as the world had, I couldn't. I couldn't eat, or I ate too much. I couldn't sleep, and even when I did sleep, I never got rest. Caught in nepantla, the walls separating realms spiritual, physical, and those in between, faltered for about 200 days after Adelita's passing. In my dreams I wandered spirit world in search of my daughter, a desperate llorón wailing.

I met her y'know,
the real llorona?
Plain as I see you people, plain as I saw Dona Sebastiana.
She whispered a secret in my ear.
She told me
I know why we cry.
And it ain't 'cause we lost our kids.
It's 'cause we're afraid our kids lost us. Or even worse,
that they never wanted us at all.

THE CALL & PUTTING COYOLXAUHQUI TOGETHER: FLAPPER DRESS

> "Having only partial knowledge of the consequences of crossing, you offer La Llorona [...] a token. You pray, repeat affirmations, take a deep breath, and step through the gate. Immediately a knowing cracks the façade of your former self and its entrenched beliefs: you are not alone; those of the invisible realm walk with you; there are ghosts on every bridge."
> (Anzaldúa, *this bridge we call home* 557)

Still as beautiful as the day she wore it
Grandma Isabel's beaded wedding gown hangs proudly on the wall,
A jazz age reminder that the roaring 20s did in fact make it to tiny San Acacio, Colorado. Population 25 counting the cats and dogs.
I stare at the intricate lacing, each individual bead catching the overhead lighting,
The gown casts a soft iridescent shine
the kind that gives me a little glare in my glasses.
"Where's the gown?"
I hear my mother's voice ask my great aunt Margaret across the room.
"That's the overlay, but where's my grandma's gown?" Mom repeated.
"You didn't know?" whispers aunt Margaret, hoping I don't hear.
"She used the gown to bury the daughters she lost."

I learned that, like many others, I didn't have an etiquette around discussing death openly and honestly, but instead with compassion and mindfulness. Sometimes my words were too blunt, at other times, too evasive. Friends and acquaintances would often trip over the words in their condolences, or even worst of all act as if we didn't have a daughter at all.

Yet, what surprised me most was just how many people we knew had lost children but never talked about it. Like Grandma Isabel, they suffered silently as many never allowed themselves the time and space to properly grieve. One of the few places we could speak honestly and openly was with our support group of bereaved parents. Not a círculo in the traditional sense, The Compassionate Friends became a circle to us, of people bound by a shared reality, bereavement. As nepantleras we suffer the misfortune of knowing too much. That the time on Earth of any loved one, in our case, that of our children, goes completely unpromised. Outsiders in our places of work, and even amongst our own families, the shared experience of bereavement allowed us to forge lines of solidarity across borders of race, class, gender, and geography. We recognize that although we all grieve differently, we long for nothing more but to hold our lost ones one more time.

My daughter began to call me to heal on the first Holy Saturday following her death. With the gracious support of our friends and family, we had been able to bury her in accordance with our values, meaning no chemicals and no cement grave liner separating her from Mother Earth. We were able to invest the money left over in our own healing. We went to ceremony, were able to compensate elders for limpias and counsel, traveled, reconnected with family, and got back involved with our own healing and talking circles. In my case, it was with the Los Compadres National Network, a Chicano/Native network of men's talking circle I had been involved in since 2001.

For many men of color, healthy ways to heal, to weep, to speak openly about emotional and spiritual pain, fall far outside the bounds of traditional gender norms. While patriarchy has done its greatest damage against women, it has also constrained the agency of men to heal in ways that allow them their full humanity, to express a full range of emotions, or even to express emotion at all. I speak openly about the difficulties I have faced with the passing of my daughter, and sadness, pain, and tears in a frank, honest, and sober manner, precisely because many men of color have been socialized to swallow their pain and sorrow, or to only express those feelings while under the influence of alcohol, or worse, to channel that pain into the violence they commit on others, usually domestic partners and children.

On August 31st, my wife and I performed a showcase routine in memory of our first child, at what would be the equivalent of an international conference for swing dance. As swing dancers, we felt it was a fitting tribute: for nine months our daughter was our consistent third dance partner, bouncing along to the music she could hear and feel from the womb.

In all honesty, I was not sure how people would react to such a simple and melancholy routine. I expected some polite applause and little more. This simplicity is in stark contrast to the other showcase routines that many had worked on months in advance to perfect complicated rhythms and sequences. Furthermore, Lindy Hop is a joyous and celebratory dance, one hardly associated with grief. Frankly, the tremendous response we actually got was rather overwhelming. While cathartic, performing this routine taxed me immensely. In those three to four minutes, the memories I carry of her brief but intense life came flooding back. Leaving the floor I felt drained—physically, emotionally, and psychologically.

What made it all worth it was talking to people, many of them complete strangers, and hearing their reactions. A handful of parents confided in me that the routine reminded them of just how precious their own children are to them. Some people reflected on their own loved ones who have passed away. Others called or emailed loved ones who had lost children themselves to check in and see how they were doing. I even was able to refer a couple of families dealing with child and sibling loss to The Compassionate Friends. A friend who faced potentially terminal cancer confided in us that she wasn't afraid of dying, knowing that our daughter was on the other side to greet her. The routine had allowed us to build bridges with people who I would never consider allies, in the political or activist sense. We had grown accustomed to dismissing and bemoaning the myriad of dancers we encountered with radically different cultural and political values than our own, many with the most hateful of views. However, through the playfulness of dance, we invited them to become what Maria Lugones calls world travelers (395), to allow us to enter their lives, and they briefly into ours and see the humanity in each other. Their love and expressions of solidarity forced me to re-evaluate exactly who I take for granted as the other.

THE BLOW UP AND SPIRITUAL ACTIVISM: FREEDOM PRAYER

> "Although all your cultures reject the idea that you can know the other, you believe that besides love, pain might open this closed passage by reaching through the wound to connect. Wounds cause you to shift consciousness- they either open you to the greater reality normally blocked, by your habitual point of view or else shut you down, pushing your body into desconocimiento [...] Excessive dwelling on your wounds means leaving your body to live in your thoughts, where you re-enact your past hurts [...] As victim you don't have to take responsibility for making changes. But the cost of victimhood is that nothing in your life changes."
> (Anzaldúa, *this bridge we call home* 572)

I pulled the plug on my daughter.
I didn't call 9-1-1 fast enough.

I didn't know CPR.
Words of pain
Words of regret
I went back to work the day after she was born
I traded a third of her life for a 2-hour commute and 47 exam books.
I graded those exam books the day after she died.
Words of pain
Words of regret
I release you to the fire
I speak you and I release you
Words of guilt, regret, anguish, fear,
trauma
You unfairly tether my daughter's spirit
You bind her feet, her arms, her legs, her wings.
And so I release you
I release you
So Adelita Susana
May fly free.

As 2014 came to a close, upon the advice of a curandera, we refashioned Adelita's altar in all-white to symbolize her freedom, and our willingness to un-tether her from our own pain and anguish. The consistent message we got from elders and medicine people was that she has work to do. That she has work to accomplish, but as a dutiful daughter, she will stay with us, in our home, in her nursery for as long as we need. Yet, for every moment she stays, her work goes unfinished. We had to let her go.

Yet I couldn't. For months, we had no resolution for her death. She wasn't a victim of SIDS, wasn't sickly, and had been seen by a medical professional almost every day of her life. If she had died of police brutality like Eric Garner or Michael Brown, or of an unjust war like Casey Sheehan, or due to inadequate access to quality health care as a working-class child of color, I could let her go, and honor her memory by working on these issues and dedicating my life to those struggle. But she didn't. She just died, and as an activist and an educator who organizes against seemingly insurmountable issues of racism and other systems of oppression, no amount of mobilization, political pressure, or education was going to bring her back. Her passage had left such a void, that each day, all I wanted was for her to stay the next, and the next, and the next.

Yet what of her agency? Even after death, was I going to bind my child to my own expectations, desires, wishes, pain? Was I truly comfortable being the family patriarch demanding piety even from those beyond the grave? What of her desires? Her wishes? Her work? Who was I to impede the spiritual activism, of an activist spirit?

After four weeks we rebuilt her altar, this time replete with the rich spring colors that had decorated it before. I ceased mourning. I still grieve. I will be forever bereaved. I would be lying to you now if I told you I had it together, that I am healed, that I am whole. To be sure, my facultad is sharper, and feelings of compassion and patience certainly come easier. Yet I still grapple with desconocimiento, with the cargas of guilt, shame, and aguish that I have yet to leave in the pyre. Yet every so often as I drift off to sleep, I catch it. I catch that raw organic smell of blood and amniotic fluid as I journey to dream world. I catch it,

I turn

and I look.

and I see her smile.

WORKS CITED

Alvarez, Eddy Francisco Jr. "Jotería Pedagogy, SWAPA, and Sandovalian Approaches to Liberation" *Aztlán: A Journal of Chicano Studies* 39:1 Spring 2014. Print

Anzaldúa, Gloria. *Borderlands/La Frontera: The New Mestiza.* San Francisco: Aunt Lute. 1987. Print.

---. "now let us shift . . . the path of conocimiento . . . inner work, public acts." In *This Bridge We Call Home: Radical Visions for Transformation,* edited by Gloria Anzaldúa and AnaLouise Keating, 540–79. New York: Routledge. 2002. Print

Jarmakani, Amira, and Donna Troka. "Critical Moments: A Dialogue Toward Survival and Transformation". *Carribbean Review of Gender Studies* (April 2007): 1:24. Print.

Lorde, Audre. *Sister Outsider: Essays and Speeches.* Berkeley: Crossing Press, 1985. 36. Print

Lugones, Maria. "Playfulness, 'World' Traveling, and Loving Perception" *Hypatia: A Journal of Feminist Philosophy* 2(2). 1987. Print.

Sandoval, Chela. "Critical Moments: A Dialogue toward Survival and Transformation," keynote panel dialog, Emory University, March 29, edited by Amira Jarmakani and Donna Troka. *Caribbean Review of Gender Studies*, no. 1, April 1–24. 2007. Print.

PARALLEL LIVES

SETH, PSYCHIC DEVELOPMENT, SRI AUROBINDO, AND GLORIA'S SOUL-MAKING

DAVID HATFIELD SPARKS

Through our close friendship of thirty years, and our mutual study of esoteric literature, I learned that Gloria Anzaldúa was deeply influenced by spiritual ideas attributed to New Age thought, transcendental and metaphysical philosophies, and spiritualism. From Blavatsky and Cayce, she learned to explore other realities; from Aurobindo and the Mother, she learned of the necessity of "soul-making;" from spiritualism, how to communicate with spirits; and from New Age thought, how to structure her life esoterically, as by way of the chakras. The works of Jane Roberts (1929-1984), who channeled the entity Seth, deeply influenced Anzaldúa's life and work. Anzaldúa believed, like Roberts, that messages might be delivered by way of channeling or mediumship. From Roberts and from our mutual study of psychic practices with Tamara Diaghilev in the early 1980s, Gloria came to believe that the self is not monolithic, but is a gestalt, a weaving or quilt, of various selves into a complex, ever-shifting pattern; and that this complex multi-self is linked to "parallel lives," a view of reincarnation which suggests that so-called "past lives" are being lived out simultaneously as we inhabit our present existence.

Gloria remarked in a 1983 interview, "The work I see myself doing is being a channel" (Anzaldúa 120). I'd like to share with you some personal memories

I have of Gloria and several spiritual teachers who influenced her life and work. I'll focus here on the realms of the mystical and psychic, as opposed to the earth-centered, elements of her spirituality. Gloria, Randy, and I were avid readers of esoteric literature, our bookshelves brimming over with works by Evelyn Underhill, Madame Blavatsky, Aleister Crowley, Edgar Cayce, Joan Grant, Jean Houston, and many others. We were also drawn to the Ouija board and convinced of the reality of spirits and the possibility of spirit communication.

In 1982, Gloria spoke of reading Jane Roberts's *Seth Speaks* in early 1974. "She's a medium," Gloria explained to the interviewer, "and Seth's voice speaks through her, the voice of a future self [. . .] [Seth] talks about the history of the earth [. . .] race, [and] sexuality" (Anzaldúa 49). Roberts, born in 1929, channeled the entity Seth for a number of years before her death in 1984. Many who have by now read this interview may not realize just how significant a role Seth and Roberts played in the formation of Gloria's spirituality. We were fascinated with Seth's innovative—in those days, radical—ideas regarding spirituality. I recall when Randy laid in bed, very ill, grappling with hepatitis, Gloria and I took turns reading Roberts's novel *Oversoul Seven* to him.

Gloria was deeply influenced by Seth's notion that the self is not monolithic, but instead is a continuum, a gestalt, of various selves inhabiting various realities. Especially in her poetry, and particularly in those poems that were to be included in *Tres Lenguas del Fuego*,[1] Gloria called upon her own spiritualist skills to write of other selves, other lifetimes. Like the ancient sibyl of Cumae, prophesying from her tripod, Gloria deployed her mediumistic gift, bringing forth poems of a priestess of Hecate, a young Christian woman in love with a Moor in medieval Spain, a lesbian nun obsessed with a witch, two Basque female witches who loved one another during the period of the Inquisition, and an Aztec noblewoman forced to translate for the *conquistador* who would destroy her civilization. What many do not know is that these were not mere historical poems incorporating fanciful metaphors; they were, in Gloria's belief system, narratives of other lives she had lived, or *was living*, or was aware of in some profound way. She was convinced not only of the certainty of reincarnation but of Seth's highly innovative conception of reincarnation, if one can call it that. According to Seth, our so-called "past lives" are being lived out simultaneously in other epochs and cultures as well as in other dimensions.

Gloria was also drawn to Seth's notions concerning gender and sexuality. At a time when occult or esoteric literature, together with the literature of the emerging New Age movement, was decidedly hetero-centric, if not blatantly homophobic, as well as transgender-phobic, Seth offered an alternative, then very radical, vision. "The psyche is not male or female," Seth insists the "psyche is male and female, female and male" (Roberts 63-64). Roberts continues with a radical notion, "What you think of as lesbian or homosexual activity is quite natural [as a form of] sexual expression" (72) and "[…] it is as natural for a man to love a man, and for a woman to love a woman, as it is to show love for the opposite sex" (Roberts 75). In Seth's view, it is in fact "more natural to be bisexual. Such," he argues, "is the 'natural' nature of the species" (Roberts 75). Further, Seth relates that this newfound understanding of gender and sexuality "will allow [us] to glimpse the nature of the reality of the gods [we] have recognized throughout the ages. You will no longer need to clothe them in limited sexual guises" (Roberts 101). If one accepts the reality of multiple selves and multiple incarnations or "parallel lives," then diversity and fluidity of gender and sexuality make psychic sense (Roberts 101). For Gloria, as someone who thought of herself as gender-diverse and bisexual—this is what she means when she says she has "chosen" lesbian self-identification and not that meaning often assigned to her by constructionist academics—Seth's privileging of both gender fluidity and bisexuality provided validation and nurturance. In her construction of spiritual *mestizaje*, Gloria would utilize what she had learned from Jane Roberts and Seth in connecting psychic wisdom to gender and sexual diversity and fluidity in her concept of *la facultad*, a sort of psychic sense she attributed to LGBTQ/Queer persons.

Together, in the early 1980s, Randy, Gloria, and I studied psychic development with Tamara Diaghilev, a Russian-American relative of Sergei Diaghilev, the famous impresario of the *Ballets Russes*, the Russian Ballet. Gloria spoke of these classes in a 1983 interview with Christine Weiland (Anzaldúa 107). From Tamara, we learned how to better understand and "clean" our chakras, the seven psychic centers in the body in Hindu and especially in Tantric philosophy. The chakras are comprised of the anal chakra, which focuses on survival; the genital chakra, which focuses on sexuality and desires; the stomach or solar plexus chakra, which focuses on strength and power; the heart chakra, which expresses love and compassion; the throat chakra, that of communication, including by writing; the third eye chakra, which speaks to psychic abilities; and the seventh chakra, that at the top of the head, which brings cosmic consciousness. Tamara taught us to view the chakras as plates that were at first stationary and dirty, and to see them become clean as we washed them. Now rinsed of negativity, they spun rapidly, glittering with healing energy and purity. Tamara also offered us techniques for remote viewing and out-of-body travel (visiting someone in one's spirit or astral body, an exercise that involved our describing friends of hers whose houses we visited) and lucid dreaming (knowing that one is dreaming and taking an active role in the dream, sometimes meeting collectively with others in dreams). I recall experiencing the latter at least twice with Gloria and Randy when we lived at 948 Noe in San Francisco. In one of these, we met in a dream café with prints of paintings by the writer and artist Hermann Hesse, author of *Steppenwolf*, *The Glass Bead Game*, and other works. Another was a terrifying dream of nuclear holocaust. Tamara also instructed us in learning more about past or parallel lives. Each of us held a candle in a darkened room, gazing together into a mirror. In this way, we learned of other lives we'd spent, or were spending, together, including a lifetime we had shared in Spain during the Inquisition.

In speaking of yoga and related subjects with Christine Weiland in 1983, Gloria spoke of commencing to read works by Sri Aurobindo and the Mother. Mirra Alfassa [was] a half-Turkish, half-Egyptian woman born in France. She

> died in 1973. She has these books called *The Mother's Agenda*. She was connected with Sri Aurobindo. . .[H]e was educated in England [but later returned to India] . . . He became a self-realized person by plugging into [the] Oversoul . . . [H]e met the Mother around 1926. . . They became part of the same consciousness. Some people think he was the last avatar. . . The ideas I had already were very similar to his, so I did a meditation. I said, "OK. Did I get these ideas from him?" I had never read or heard of this man. And this whole bunch of stuff came through. (Anzaldúa 100)

Later in the interview, she remarked on the concepts she shared with Aurobindo: "They're not my ideas. . . I thought they were mine, until I started reading Sri Aurobindo" (Anzaldúa 120). "[He's] a spirit," she added, "He's a teacher. He can come and teach you through dreams or through meditation. [He is an] enlightened sou[l]" (Anzaldúa 125). Indeed, Gloria believed, as she wrote in a copy of Satprem's *Sri Aurobindo, or, The Adventure of Consciousness* she sent to Randy in June 1983, that she had already begun to be "inhabited" by the spirit of Aurobindo. She explained to the interviewer that when she meditated on the commonalities she and Aurobindo shared, she was told to read the Mother's writings. Of the Mother, Gloria added, "[W]hen she became a realized woman [...] she had everything at her command [...] she knew what people were thinking. She knew what they needed. She knew that she was total consciousness. . . She was everything, this little skinny woman" (Anzaldúa 125).

What first attracted Gloria to the mystic couple was their belief that "the seeker must understand that he is being born to another life [. . .] It is [. . .] a passage to a new consciousness [. . .]" (Satprem 37). She also found their affirmative view of literature and the arts welcoming. "Poetry is the most convenient means of explaining what th[e] higher planes of consciousness are," they asserted (Satprem 209). Gloria found in Sri Aurobindo and the Mother support for her belief that writing is a sacred act and that it has the potential to deepen and transform consciousness.

Gloria admired Aurobindo and the Mother because, in contrast to many mystics, they did not believe in "rejecting all worldly activities in order to plunge into the exquisite quest of the soul" (Satprem 105). Instead, they explained, "[...]we have embraced everything in our search" (Satprem 105). Nor did they disparage the earth in their quest for the transcendent. They took to heart the poetic lines found in the *Atharva Veda XII.1*: "I am a son of earth, the soil is my mother" (Satprem 267). Amala Levine, in "Champion of the Spirit: Anzaldúa's Critique of Rationalist Epistemology," explains that this encouraged Gloria to "formulat[e] a 'yoga of the body' that unites mind and spirit with body" (Keating 175).

Gloria was also intrigued, despite her belief in the soul as manifold, by their linked beliefs in an individual's psychic center and reincarnation. "Only the psychic [...] is eternal," they insisted; "Our experience of reincarnation depends [. . .] on the discovery of [our psychic] Centre [...] and on the degree of our psychic development [...] [The] psychic Master [...] carries his memories from one life to another" (Satprem 99). Gloria's conceptions of the Shadow-Beast and the Coatlicue state may have also been inspired in part by Aurobindo and the Mother's belief in "adverse forces," which they referred to by various names, including "the dark half of the truth" (Satprem 252), and "the shadow of our light" (Satprem 249). These are "very conscious forces whose sole aim [...] is to discourage the seeker or turn him from the path he has chosen [...] (Satprem 75). [M]ore often they bring about a state of depression [...] They have a thousand ways of attacking us [...] " (Satprem 76). As Gloria would discover, Aurobindo and the Mother cautioned that the "clearer the goal becomes, the stronger becomes the shadow" (Satprem 250). However, Gloria also learned that "[i]nstead of taking these brutal [attacks] as a sort of fatality, the seeker [can] make them the basis of his work" (Satprem 246).

From Sri Aurobindo and the Mother, as well as from other texts on yoga and Tantra, Gloria learned more about the chakras (Satprem 56-57), assimilating and eventually transforming the path of the chakras, led up the spine by the invisible Kundalini serpent goddess, into her own seven stages of *conocimiento*. Although her stages do not directly follow the system of chakras, she nevertheless writes in "now let us shift" that they "symbolize *los siete 'ojos de luz'* or seven chakras of the energetic dreambody" (Anzaldúa and Keating 540). She begins by describing an encounter with a serpent, echoing her encounter in Borderlands, here, describing a "glistening black ribbon undulat[ing] in the grass, crossing [her] path...The snake," she tells us, clearly thinking of the Kundalini serpent, "is a symbol of awakening consciousness" (Anzaldúa and Keating 540). The first, the so-called "anal" chakra, stresses survival. For Gloria, this chakra is expressed by her surviving a devastating earthquake in 1989 (Anzaldúa and Keating 543-44).

She veers away from traditional significations in regard to her second and third, as well as the sixth and stage, but returns to more traditional ones with stages four, five, and seven. The fourth chakra, known as the "heart" chakra, signifies or embodies life-affirming emotions, especially love. For Gloria, this stage of *conocimiento* commences with "the pounding of [one's] heart," and moves on to speak of recognizing one's "core passion" (Anzaldúa and Keating 554-557). "Your passion," Gloria imparts, "motivates you to discover resources within yourself." At this stage, one also discovers "self-respect and love" (Anzaldúa and Keating 557). Moreover,

> Love swells in your body and shoots out of your heart chakra, linking you to everyone [and] everything – the aboriginals in Australia, the crows in the forest, the vast Pacific Ocean. . .This *conocimiento* motivates you to work actively to see that no harm comes to people, animals, ocean – to take up spiritual activism and the work of healing (Anzaldúa, Keating 558).

The fifth, or "throat" chakra, focuses on communication, including written communication. For Gloria, the fifth stage of *conocimiento* emphasizes "sift[ing and] sort[ing] [through one's] experiences," finding personal symbols, and "scan[ning one's] inner landscape, books, movies, philosophies, mythologies, and the modern sciences for bits of lore you can patch together to create a new narrative articulating your personal reality" (Anzaldúa and Keating 545). In Goddess-centered terminology, Gloria suggests, "you re-member Coyolxauhqui in a new composition" (Anzaldúa and Keating 562). Although perhaps not as imposing as Aurobindo's linking of the seventh chakra to "*supra*mental" consciousness, one of "[g]lobal vision, undivided vision [...] eternal vision [...] link[ing] past, present and future in their indivisible connections [...] " (Satprem 268), Gloria evokes, in certain respects, Aurobindo's vision in speaking of this seventh stage of *conocimiento* as "the critical turning point of transformation," embracing the "shift[ing of] realities. . . holistic alliances," and "acts of love. . . giveaways to the cosmos" (Anzaldúa, Keating 574).

Gloria's study of Sri Aurobindo and the Mother's rather unusual attitude among mystics toward sociopolitical action—rather than non-involvement, as in Gandhi's case, they took the side of the Allies in World War II—may have seeded her concept of spiritual activism. For Aurobindo and the Mother, "It is self-evident that in the actual life of man, intellectual, social, political, moral, we can make no real step forward without a struggle [. . .] Therefore, so far as the problem of the individual's action goes, his abstention from strife [. . .] may help his own moral being, but it leaves the Slayer of creatures unabolished" (Satprem 146-47). Moreover, they held that "[i]f we want 'to transform [. . .] the world' [. . .] [we must] work [on our] own individual bod[ies] without escaping into the beyond [. . .] [and we must] discover that principle of consciousness which will have the power to transform Matter" (Satprem 182).

Gloria insisted that her vision was not a finite one. According to Sri Aurobindo and the Mother, "We are at the beginning of the 'Vast' which will always be vaster [. . .] [A] new curve is taken in the eternal Becoming [. . .] Each time the Mage in us turns over his kaleidoscope [. . .] all is unexpected" (Satprem 368-69). "[. . .] [I]t is only the very small beginning of another voyage . . . in an even vaster consciousness [. . .]" (106). In Gloria's words, "You realize that 'home' is [the] bridge, the [. . .] place of . . . constant transition [. . .] [Y] ou don't build bridges to safe and familiar territories, you have to risk making *un mundo nuevo*, have to risk the uncertainty of change [. . .]" (Anzaldúa and Keating 574). She urges us on, "We are ready for change. . .*vámonos*" (Anzaldúa and Keating 576).

NOTE

1 A collection of poems which Gloria hoped to publish during her lifetime and was not able to do so, but which will be published in the near future.

WORKS CITED

Anzaldúa, Gloria E. *Interviews/Entrevistas*. Edited by AnaLouise Keating. New York, NY: Routledge, 2000.

Anzaldúa, Gloria E., and AnaLouise Keating, eds. *This Bridge We Call Home: Radical Visions for Transformation*. New York, NY: Routledge, 2002.

Keating, AnaLouise, ed. *Entre Mundos/Among Worlds: New Perspectives on Gloria Anzaldúa.* New York, NY: Palgrave Macmillan, 2008.

Roberts, Jane. *The Nature of the Psyche*. 1979. New York, NY: Bantam, 1984.

Satprem. *Sri Aurobindo: or, The Adventure of Consciousness*. Trans. by Tehmi. New York, NY: Harper and Row, 1968.

DOS CELIAS

RACE, GENDER, AND PSYCHOPATHOLOGY IN A CRITICAL APPROACH TO *"ATAQUE DE NERVIOS"*

SONIA HART SUÁREZ

La encrucijada/ The Crossroads
A chicken is being sacrificed
At a crossroads, a simple mound of earth
a mud shrine for Eshu,
Yoruba god of indeterminacy,
who blesses her choice of path.
She begins her journey.

Su cuerpo es una bocacalle. La mestiza has gone from being the sacrificial goat to becoming the officiating priestess at the crossroads.
-Borderlands/La Frontera: The New Mestiza, Gloria Anzaldúa (102)

At the core of ecologies of knowledges is the idea that different types of knowledge are incomplete in different ways and that raising the consciousness of such reciprocal incompleteness (rather than looking for completeness) will be a precondition for achieving cognitive justice.
-Epistemologies of the South: Justice Against Epistemicide by Boaventura de Sousa Santos (212)

The *Diagnostic Statistical Manual of Mental Disorders*, or DSM, is regarded colloquially as the psychiatric "bible." This colloquialism is significant because it reflects the compelling power of this text in conceiving mental illness, including its ubiquitous presence in modern healthcare. In the desk reference casebook to one edition of this text, the DSM-IV, the first chapter introduces the case of a young woman named Celia: "Celia Vega is a 21-year-old woman, born in Puerto Rico, who is brought, by the police, to the emergency room of a city hospital in handcuffs and leg chains" (Spitzer et al. 1). This bleak description's language offers a glimpse into the stigma and criminalization that emerge from the meeting points between psychiatry and women of color. However, the text does not intend to stigmatize or criminalize anyone, at least not outright. Specifically, the casebook is designed to provide a reference for US diagnostic concepts in psychology at the beginning of the twenty-first century (xii). They intend to help doctors help their patients through proper psychiatric diagnosis.

After Celia's initial introduction, the authors narrate her psychopathology as "nervous" (5). Clinicians in this case study waver over the proper diagnosis for Celia, unsure of what to make of Celia's *nervios* and are puzzled by her amnestic, violent, and self-injurious episodes. They ask her, "What do you call these attacks or spells that keep happening to you?" (1). In response, Celia attributes her psychiatric emergency to *brujería* (translated in the text uncritically from Spanish as "witchcraft") imparted from her former mother-in-law. [1] Though the discussion never addresses this detail, it is salient enough to be included in the write-up and, in fact, to merit the title of this case called simply *"Brujeria."* Standard procedures of differential diagnosis make it clear why attending psychiatrists diagnose Celia Vega, albeit hesitantly, with Post-Traumatic Stress Disorder. Thus my central question is, why are Celia's "attacks" and *brujería* so prominent in this case?

In approaching this question, I draw from my undergraduate and early graduate training in applied psychology, my current graduate studies in comparative ethnic studies, and my positionality as a Chicanx and practitioner of non-Western spirituality who has experienced both mental illness and Western mental healthcare. In this narrative, I invite you to problematize how (Afro)Latinx/Chicanx women like Celia Vega are represented in the psychiatric literature, and by consequence, how we are treated in clinical and social settings every day. [2] While not necessarily everyone knows a woman who has complained of nervous *brujería* attacks, though many do, certainly everyone has been exposed to the stigmatizing and humiliating stereotype of the overly dramatic, semi-crazed, non-rational, and superstitious black or brown woman. Some of us may have even been exposed as one! Those moments are dehumanizing and unjust and I suggest that a different reality is possible for people who occupy these intersections of race, gender, and mental illness.[3]

Inspired by the story of Celia Vega, I turn our attention to race and gender in scientific studies of people who exhibit a biomedical diagnosis called *Ataque de Nervios* (or *Nervios*). *Nervios* is not an official psychiatric disease, but rather it is a psychiatric category used primarily to diagnose (Afro)Caribbean/Latinx/Chicanx individuals who present symptoms that are similar in etiology to those of Panic Disorder and Post-Traumatic Stress Disorder (PTSD). In the most recent edition of the DSM, it is classified as a culture-bound syndrome, or set of symptoms more common in some cultures than others that are shaped by cultural context and expressed through local "idioms of distress," for example, nerves or attacks (American Psychiatric Association 758; United States Center for Mental Health 11). The *Nervios* label carries an important but often misunderstood function in the far-reaching literature on culture and psychopathology. In order to demonstrate this function, I draw out methods, narrative, theoretical assumptions, and institutional context from existing psychiatric literature. This essay focuses exclusively on the case study of Celia Vega in order to evaluate how experts of applied biomedicine may circulate ideas about women of color and their worldviews. Then, I consider possible non-Western responses and alternatives to existing literature on *Nervios.* Finally, I rebut the conventional depiction of women of color through *Nervios* by introducing another woman, coincidentally also named Celia, who is portrayed as an agent of both knowledge production and healing for mind, body, and spirit.

Eshu, who Gloria Anzaldúa introduces in the epigraph as the Yoruba god of indeterminacy that lives at the crossroads, is also a trickster, often two-faced, who is adept at testing people and every side of a situation or interaction. I construe *Nervios* as an Eshu/Janus-faced site of knowledge production that offers two divergent opportunities to conceptualize race, gender, and mental illness. The first of these illuminates how biomedical psychopathology racializes and genders women of color who experience mental illness. A woman of color feminist rereading of biomedical literature on *Nervios* exposes hierarchical relationships between Western doctors and (Afro)Latinx/Chicanx patients, as well as those between Western and non-Western epistemologies of mental health. I find that as *Nervios* is characterized through such power hierarchies, the category acts to silence the knowledge that women of color carry about their own bodies. I aim to think beyond the traditional approach to *Nervios,* which focuses on discussions of cross-cultural translation, by evaluating how psychiatric research is influential in transmitting harmful racialized and gendered ideas about women of color.

In the second conceptualization, I analyze *Nervios* through the theoretical frames of intersectionality and embodied knowledge to resituate *Nervios* as an opportunity to consider alternative epistemologies of mind, body, and spirit. To account for *other* possible understandings of *Nervios,* Anzaldúan concepts show how border women like those pathologized through *Nervios* in the biomedical system are always grounded in indigenous and diasporic connections, which inspire *movimientos de rebeldía,* rebellion (Anzaldúa, *Borderlands* 37). I take these forms of *rebeldía*, or rather embodied knowledge and resistance, seriously within my analytical approach to *Nervios.* With these two directions in mind, let us explore how physical, psychological, and metaphorical "borderlands" shape US women of color to inhabit liminal spaces like messy diagnostic of *Nervios,* in which women of color embody and know distinct worlds across the raced and sexed boundaries that divide psychopathology from *brujería.*

The causes and psychopathology of culture-bound syndromes have been widely explored in cross-cultural psychiatry, and there are many kinds of culture-bound syndromes associated with populations from non-Western, non-White cultures. Some examples are 'fallin' out' in African-American cultures (Hunter, Hunter, and Kessler 231) or 'brain fag' in West African cultures (Ayonrinde and Bhugra 237). Appearing consistently in the literature on culture in psychology and epidemiology since 1955 (Fernández-Marina 79), *Ataque de Nervios* is one of the more salient culture-bound syndromes associated with US Latinxs of all races. Originally called "the Puerto Rican Syndrome," it is distinguished from a panic attack by bouts of anger and rage, expressed through somatic, psychotic, and/or violent behavior (ibid). Much of the literature emerging from the study of this syndrome pores over the linguistic and cultural meanings and translations of *ataques, nervios,* and the magical beliefs and practices of people who display these and other related symptoms.

While *ataque de nervios* translates to English as either "nerve attack" or "attack of nerves," among its many nuanced and highly variable meanings, Spanish speakers often think of an *ataque de nervios* as a nervous breakdown or panic attack.[4] Critical medical anthropologist Mark Nichter has explored some of the underlying linguistic and idiomatic subtleties of culture-bound syndromes since the 1980s ("Idioms of Distress" 379-408). His influential research on idioms of distress, relating in part to *Nervios*, has helped subsequent researchers to assess "patients' social relational, as well as 'cultural,' context and adaptive/maladaptive strategies for coping within these nested contexts" (Nichter, "Idioms of Distress Revisited" 408). Reading further into these social exchanges, Nichter adds that idioms of distress can help identify a group's response to social injustice and discrimination (404). Such explorations of cross-cultural assessment and diagnosis reveal how the process of categorizing health is fundamentally an exchange between doctors, researchers, patients, and publics (Trostle 85). For example, *Nervos* emerged in poor, northeastern Bahia, Brazil when its inhabitants needed to express to their doctors that the hunger caused by structural inequality had psychosocial effects in addition to, or as Nancy Scheper-Hughes shows, in lieu, of the physiological/material effects of hunger (169). The result of these interrogations of *Nervios* and other cultural concepts and idioms of distress has been a more robust and nuanced approach to the psychology of people of color in the US and internationally (Nichter, "Idioms of Distress Revisited" 412).[5] However, even this helpful work falls short of providing holistic, contextualized, and empowering depictions of the people who experience non-Western symptoms and disorders like *Nervios.* Often, these studies conflate or otherwise uncritically subsume racial and gender categories within the realm of culture as they wrestle with the incongruence between their patients' experiences of illness on the one hand, and Westernized concepts of psychiatry and medicine on the other (e.g. Korht, et al 365).[6] Questions and experiences of race, gender, and sexuality are rarely if ever used to conceptualize the contours of the disorder.

Intent on doing this work using a woman of color feminist intervention to address these omissions, I ask a new set of questions because the story of Celia on page one of the DSM casebook did not sit well with me. I ask three questions in my reading of this example of biomedical literature in psychiatry that features *Nervios*. In order to find textual evidence of racialized, gendered, and sexualized representations, I ask: How are race, gender, and sexuality represented in the stories and uses of *Nervios?* In order to map *Nervios*' appearances in the literature, I ask: Is there evidence of circulation of this disease category? And finally, in order to locate structural and institutional structures of power, I ask: Where can we identify hierarchies between expert and patient, science and superstition?

In the case of Celia Vega, her diagnosis of PTSD rests on a history of childhood sexual assault, gathered from several stages of interviewing by a social worker, psychiatrists, and a group of psychiatry residents. Notably, Ms. Vega is not and cannot be diagnosed with *Nervios,* because it is not an official disorder. Her case is exemplary and useful as a clinical resource because it brings to bear the many complications that arise in the patient/doctor encounter in real life contexts of a diagnosis. For example, the opening sentence of Celia's case study indicates potential complicating variables to producing a psychiatric diagnosis, like language, age, gender, race/ethnicity, and immigration, medical, and criminal history. The patient's name, Celia Vega, has Spanish origins; she is identified as a young adult, woman, US citizen, born outside of the US; and she is in some type of medical or psychiatric emergency. Furthermore, she has been implicated in criminal behavior, as indicated by the presence of police and the use of arm and leg restraints, and it may be inferred that she is poor, due to her admission into a city hospital. Note that we can read these categorizations through one simple opening sentence, though these complications are substantiated sporadically throughout the narrative. When asked if her "attacks/spells" are related to her history of sexual trauma, she retorts, "embarrassed, that they are called brujeria (witchcraft)." This highlights the barrier posed by Spanish-language idioms as conceptualized by Nichter and others, like her nerves, attacks, and accusations of witchcraft. Indeed, the authors concede that Ms. Vega's condition is not fully captured by the label of PTSD. A typical analysis of Celia's case would focus on obstacles to diagnosis, like culture, language, education, and class. I choose instead to highlight how the social and structural categorizations of race and gender shape psychiatric depictions of *Nervios.*

First I ask, how are race, gender, and sexuality represented in this story? Ms. Vega is given a Spanish-name and identified as Puerto Rican-born, though the case lacks any detail about her immigration history and language ability. Issues of translation appear in the story when clinicians ask her to clarify what she means by "attacks" and "spells." They also struggle to translate the meaning of her "nervous" feelings. Her gender and sexuality are prominent in the case. She is described as seductive and having displayed "wild" behavior. Her depression was exacerbated by a recent abortion. She is unemployed, financially dependent, and cohabitates with her boyfriend out of wedlock. She had been married and had two children as a teenager. Her ex-husband was a drug dealer and the case explains that Ms. Vega does not enjoy sex and can only engage in intercourse if she is under the influence of drugs. She lost custody of her two children to the woman who Ms. Vega claims did *brujería* to her, and the case describes that it is unclear why she cannot care for her children but that she gets "nervous" around them. Lastly, her psychopathology is fundamentally linked to her history of child rape(s) and incest.

Then I ask, is there evidence of circulation of the disease category? The chapter is titled "Brujeria," which the preface explains was chosen to make the case "easier to refer to." This style of cheeky naming for psychological case studies is described, in the text, as "[f]ollowing Freud's example," (Spitzer et al. xi). The casebook's audience is clinicians, teachers and students in psychology-related fields, medical professionals, and attorneys. The preface states that the purpose of casebook and treatment companion is "applying the principles of differential diagnosis to a wide range of patients," also indicating that it is made for use in clinical and forensic practice (ibid). It is also intended for use as study guide for specialty examinations, like psychiatry boards, as well as assessment of clinical staff expertise and reliability. It serves as a mediator between the formal DSM-IV and the clinical applications because it "brings the DSM diagnostic criteria to life" and it is "based on actual patients." Finally, the casebook also functions as a historical reference of US diagnostic cases and concepts, past and present (xii).

Lastly, I ask where can we identify hierarchies between expert/patient, science/superstition? The casebook is published through the certifying authority on mental health, the American Psychiatric Association. The pages leading up to the first chapter of the casebook, where we meet Celia Vega, list its authorship by "well-known experts" in administrative, teaching, and research positions of major east coast US research and learning institutions (vii-xiii). In the case's text, Ms. Vega's request for a private interview is denied, and she is interviewed about her childhood rape in a room of eight clinicians. She is even asked if she "understands how fortunate she is to be in a famous teaching hospital" (2). The clinicians are generally portrayed in a positive light. For example, a psychiatric resident and social worker follow-up with Ms. Vega at her home; this is in contrast to the patient, who does not keep her follow-up appointments. Ms. Vega's interpretation of *brujería* as the underlying cause of her *Nervios* is completely ignored in the clinical interview. We may infer that the clinicians did not pursue the topic of *brujería* because it does not translate into the biomedical concepts and diagnostic framework of official psychiatric disorders, like PTSD. Ironically then, her beliefs in witchcraft are highlighted in the case's title.

With these initial questions, I have begun to map out how *Nervios* imparts assumptions about Latina women that reproduce racist and sexist forms of discrimination. As I look for moments of resistance and alternative sources of knowledge within the examples I study, I find it important to draw from critical frameworks. For example, Anzaldúa's borderlands theories, the Combahee Collective's Black Feminist Statement of the 1980s, and many others more recently have established that the intersections of race, gender, sexuality, and class are rendered invisible through uncritical and generalizing categorizations, e.g. "culture." An approach like that of biomedical *Nervios*-related literature, which merely describes social categories, names identities, and adopts a politically correct identity politics, is inadequate because it does not untangle underlying intersections and structures of power. Kimberlé Crenshaw offers this analysis "to suggest that…[t]okenistic, objectifying, voyeuristic inclusion [of women of color] is at least as dis-empowering as complete exclusion" (10). While not excluded, (Afro)Latinx/Chicanx figures are few and far between in the majority of psychiatric scholarship, making Celia Vega's appearance as the first example of adult mental disorders seem tokenistic. Celia also stands out for the way she is objectified within the racialized and sexualized particularities of her case, including her belief in *brujería.* Furthermore, and especially as her sexuality and history of sexual violence become the central causal elements of her psychological disorder, many points in Celia's story indeed verge on voyeuristic.

In response to similar trends in her field of critical legal studies, Crenshaw looks at gender violence specifically through a lens that acknowledges simultaneous interactions between racism and patriarchy (3). This response is particularly relevant in the context of *Nervios* because of its comorbidity with PTSD and somaticizing disorders, which are often related to domestic violence and/or sexual trauma. The psychopathologists discussing the case of *Brujeria,* for example, overcome the quandary of differential diagnosis posed by the *Nervios* presentation by ignoring Celia's own explanations and instead pursuing her history of child sexual abuse. However, even as its authors highlight non-normative expressions of disease and stereotypical assumptions of culture, they fail to identify and examine underlying structures of race, gender, and sexual oppression. [7] Again, a new question emerges: What underlying structures remain invisible if we focus singularly on Ms. Vega's sexual trauma and do not account for other intersections that may contribute to, produce, or give meaning to her *Nervios?*

Sandra Harding establishes the stakes of invisibilizing intersections in research and knowledge production in scientific traditions, like those of the psychological science which have produced culture-bound syndromes and *Nervios.* She explains, "culturewide assumptions that have not been criticized within the scientific research process are transported into the results of research" [italics in original](Harding 57). Harding also notes that scientific method provides no rules, procedures, or techniques for identifying and eliminating social interests and values, and that in general the "scientific worldview" reflects that of dominant groups in Western societies (57).[8] But how can we account for racism and patriarchy in ways that humanize the experiences of women of color and digress from the traditional culture/patient focused approach to *Nervios?*

Harding heralds standpoint epistemologies rooted in embodied knowledge in her response to the existing, inadequate standards for objectivity that permeate the sciences. She describes how feminist knowledge from the bottom of social hierarchies arranged according to race, ethnicity, class, gender, sexuality, and other such politics "can provide starting points for thought—for *everyone's* research and scholarship—from which human' relations with each other and the natural world can become visible" [italics in original](Harding 24). Like Anzaldúa, Chela Sandoval, M. Jaqui Alexander, Audre Lorde, Patricia Hill-Collins, and other forbearers of non-Western and US women of color feminist thought, Harding agrees that women's experiences are the authoritative foundation of feminist knowledge even in the context of science and objectivity.

Because feminist knowledge is multiple, collective, heterogeneous, and even contradictory, bringing women's lives to light requires that knowledge production start from multiple women's lives (Harding 66-68). Using this as a jumping off point from which to rethink the narratives surrounding *Nervios* and Celia Vega, I turn to Anzaldúa's conceptualization of Chicanx knowing, of *conocimiento*, she writes:

> Before rewriting the disintegrating, often destructive "stories" of self constructed by psychology, sociology, anthropology, biology, and religion you must first recognize their faulty pronouncements, scrutinize the fruit they've borne, and then ritually disengage from them. [...] Knowing the beliefs and directives your spiritual self generates, empowers you to shift perceptions, te capacita a soñar otros modos of conducting your life, revise the scripts of your various identities, and use these new narratives to intervene in the cultures' existing dehumanizing stories. (Anzaldúa, "now let us shift" 559)

I see *Nervios* as one of those stories constructed by sanctioned representatives from the very disciplines that Anzaldúa cites above. This passage reflects the fundamental approach that I argue will expand the story of *Nervios* from one that unwittingly dehumanizes (Afro)Latinxs/Chicanxs into one that allows us to dream up other modes of conducting research and knowledge production. Anzaldúa's vision of knowledge enables me, from my position as both a Chicanx and researcher, to apply a new narrative to existing *Nervios* research. Anzaldúa writes, "When you're in the place between worldviews (nepantla) you're able to slip between realities to a neutral perception" (569). Unlike a conventional biomedical "knowledge," *conocimiento* represents a new kind of neutral objectivity.

Thus, I turn to work that transgresses disciplinary boundaries, from a standpoint of people of color in the global south and US third world. I find it productive to think about Nervios using knowledge produced by women of color healers and authors who are disciplinary *nepantleras*. For example, *curandera* and registered psychiatric nurse Elena Avila is a *nepantlera* who engages conventional medicine directly. She elaborates many complementarities between *curanderismo* and modern healthcare, but finds that partnership across these disciplines is only possible if "the modern doctor is able to have a genuine attitude of respect toward folk healing and genuine interest in its healing modalities" (308). Given reciprocity and validation of this kind, non-Western knowledge can broaden our views of medicine. *Curanderismo,* just one of the many traditions that have been accused of and referred to as *brujería*, represents a non-Western discipline that understands disease as caused by biological factors in addition to emotional and soul factors (182). The implications of these "alternative" perspectives from other knowledge systems are vast.

I will leave you with a final example to contrast with the case of Brujeria. This case is authored by *curandera* and PhD, Patrisia Gonzales and narrates the origin story of an Apache-Chicana elder and grandmother of the Mexican Sun Dance at Teotihuacan, Mexico. Whereas Celia Vega is a pseudonym for an anonymous Latinx psychiatric patient, this story describes a Latinx/Chicanx woman whose real name is Celia Perez-Boothe:

> Grandmother Celia finds Spider near her hair, her long white hair, not yet braided for the day. She saves Spider and goes to shake it outside, where Wind takes it. Sun Dance Grandmother goes back to her braiding and in her mirror she sees lots of little spiders in her white strands. Spider mother had had some babies on white hair woman, lots of little baby spiders clinging to her white strands. Grandmother Celia goes to Mexico to sacrifice. In the Mexican Sun Dance circle not far from the Teotihuacan Spiderwoman, where spiders hang from her hair, Grandmother Celia sees a circle of light, a web of light—Spiderwoman's woven tress of prayers. At the tree of life, she saw strands of light attached to everyone in the Sun Dance circle and attaching to everyone. "They were knitting a web. These *hilos* (threads) just kept attaching to everyone. That is how I became godmother to the spiders." The web of life, the circle of life, spun out this story. (Gonzales 188)

I offer this story as a new starting point to think about woman of color psychology because this real-life Celia portrays a very different view of (Afro) Latinx/Chicanx knowledge than what I have found through *Ataque de Nervios.* This Celia interacts with the web of life as if it were a process of communication between her and other celestial beings (i.e. Sun, spiders, other people). She listens to Spider's message, with Spider's babies clinging to Grandmother Celia's hair, and takes action. She goes to sacrifice and be prayerful. In her travels, she witnesses the movement of light/life up from within the buried roots of the tree of life. Taking the shape of her prayers, the light travels out to the Sun Dancers, who are her grandchildren and who dance to receive their grandmother's prayers, her light. This Celia's experiences and visions are taken seriously, her families are varied and distinct, but they gather in spiritual practice and become interconnected through Grandmother Celia's powerful relationships to the cosmos, her *brujería,* if you will. In this process, by which her prayers and interactions with the divine produce light/life, she learns to understand life in terms of a web. Celia explains to Gonzales, "[in] my time of quaking changes and cycles ending, she tells me: You stand alone at the center of the web. Spin out. All women are Spider-woman" (188). This Celia conceives her world in terms of a pre-Colombian Mesoamerican system of knowing the cosmos, which allows her visions to carry meaning and, as her prayers are answered, enables her spiritual practice to produce healing for herself and her loved ones, as they connect through her engagement with the realm of spirit. Grandmother Celia's teachings, as are Gonzales' on Indigenous medicinal practices, show people and their experiences in terms of the principles and properties of a relational (as opposed to individualized), cyclical (as opposed to linear), and living (as opposed to static) cosmos (e.g. 190). This luminous and prescient Celia teaches that every woman may participate in divine healing by recognizing her position at the center of a web and then recognizing her ability to spin away from this web when it becomes unstable or disordered.

In *Borderlands,* Anzaldúa conceptualizes moments of instability or blocks in life as the Coatlicue State. *Coatlicue* is the depths, patterns, and internal whirlwinds of the psyche (Anzaldúa, *Borderlands* 68). She both gives and takes life, but these processes exist in relationship to pain and suffering, which we either face and give voice to, or hide from, deny, and allow to stagnate. When we experience movement from spaces of light within the cycle of life, through *Coatlicue,* to blockages, darkness, and *mictlán,* the underworld (70), we also access the properties of *Coatlicue* that allow us, as Grandmother Celia teaches, to spin away from the now constricting, painful web of life, to create new threads and new webs. Anzaldúa describes these forms of creative, life-making acts and adds, "It is this learning to live with la *Coatlicue* that transforms living in the Borderlands from a nightmare to a numinous experience" (95). Reconsidered through the teachings of these outsider experts, I begin to gain a new sense of how to understand the nightmarish, traumatic episodes of *ataques de nervios* plaguing our younger, psychologically pathologized Celia. While I do not mean to imply that *Nervios* represents a positive experience (indeed, anyone who has experienced *Nervios* would agree that it is scary and undesirable), like *Coatlicue,* perhaps something empowering and healing can come from learning to live with and understand the connections between *Nervios* and *brujería* by invoking non-Western knowledge of *brujería.* In the case of *"Brujeria,"* Celia's prognosis is grim, she does not continue psychotherapy and her mental health remains mostly untreated. What might have transpired had Celia's worries of *brujería* been considered seriously? *Nervios* represents an invisible friction between the visions, experiences, and knowledge of (Afro)Latinxs/Chicanxs and the beliefs and sciences of psychiatric biomedicine that "encourage fear and distrust of life and of the body" and "encourage a split between the body and the spirit and totally ignore the soul" (59). This friction produces a complex crossroads and a confrontation with a *Coatlicue* State that forces us to discern a new path for *Nervios* and other culture-bound syndromes.

The opening epigraph to this essay describes such a crossroads, at which Anzaldúa's *La Mestiza,* who knows and inhabits the borderlands of two worlds, has transformed from a sacrificial goat to the officiating priestess at the crossroads. In this tale of two Celias, the first pseudonymous Celia of psychiatry who is plagued by her episodes of trauma, unreasonableness, and *brujería,* is the sacrificial goat and through my rereading of *Nervios,* I have argued for the introduction of a second, real-life Celia, who is the officiating priestess at the crossroads. The juxtaposition of the Celia of *brujería* and *Nervios* alongside a new Celia places the figure of the (Afro)Latinx/Chicanx in a position of power and expertise where she has access to new ways of interpreting and addressing her pains and instabilities, and also providing new options and futures for understanding the experiences of *Ataques de Nervios.*

NOTES

1 The term *brujería* has a range of connotations and meanings, ranging from traditional or indigenous herbal medicine to the realms of the metaphysical and psychosocial.

2 In this essay, I position (Afro) in parentheses to signify the ubiquitous presence of African influence and ancestry among the range of Latinx and Chicanx populations and their experiences of Latinidad. I use the terms Latinx and Chicanx to reflect the unquantifiable range of expressions of gender and sexuality among our communities.

3 Critical engagement with questions of race and science have produced an understanding of race as biosocial, a variable that is mutually constitutive of biology and sociality (e.g. Montoya 96; Gravlee 47). This framework shifts the decades-long debates of nature vs. nurture by embracing a non-dichotomous approach. For example, in epidemiologist Nancy Krieger's ecosocial theory, racial/ethnic, gender, and class inequality organize multiple pathways of embodiment, health, and disease (Krieger 214). This framework enables us to abandon dichotomous models of disease/health and instead link disease to its source by tracing connections along multiple paths and levels. The guiding question, then, becomes: where on multiple pathways can you intervene to alter the path of exposure to social and material deprivations, hazards, and trauma along categorizations of race, gender, and class? (214)

4 My mother, a bilingual, first-generation, US-born Mexican-American Chicana, insists that I translate ataque de *nervios* as a panic attack when I explain this research. Though some researchers would disagree (e.g., Keough, Timpano, & Schmidt 16-21), recommendations for the DSM-V by Lewis Fernandez et al. back up my mother's claim (212-229). I would also add that in addition to bilingual and Spanish speakers, English-speaking clinicians of medicine and psychology (doctors, nurses, pharmacists, therapists), and experts in cross-cultural psychology and critical epidemiology, all hold nuanced understandings of the similarities between *Nervios* and panic attacks. From my experience, these conceptualizations are often kept behind the scenes of published literature, which favors more literal translations of the term in order to distinguish it from an official panic attack. Bowker and Star share a telling example that speaks to this discordance between what people know versus what makes it into the classification and literature itself, noting "psychiatrists increasingly use the language of the DSM to communicate with each other and their accounting departments, although they frequently do not believe in the categories they are using" (60).

5 For a broader, more thorough analysis showing how conversations surrounding cultural concepts play out on the scale of global health, see Nichter's book called Global health: Why cultural perceptions, social representations, and biopolitics matter.

6 The meta-analysis by Kort, et al. documents a representative sample of studies on these concepts and disorders.

7 For example, in one near exception, the 2010 study by Guarnaccia, et al. highlights the correlation between *Nervios* and a construct the authors identify as social vulnerability. Though they explicitly define social vulnerability as "...contextual factors (e.g., gender relations; racial discrimination; and political and economic circumstances, including poverty) that differentially and adversely impact various populations," this study does not critically engage these variables outside of this definition (Guarnaccia, et al 298).

8 A 2009 article in American Psychologist introduces an intersectional approach to psychology that offers ways to integrate black feminist thought into mainstream psychology (Cole 170-1). However, the author overemphasizes social categories when she applies women of color thought to her analysis. I would also disagree with the author who concludes, "To translate the theoretical insights of intersectionality into psychological research does not require the adoption of a new set of methods; rather, it requires a reconceptualization of the meaning and consequences of social categories" (178-9). Cole does not distinguish social categories from structural hierarchies, in this case, nor are they contextualized in terms of power and history, e.g., between patient and doctor. Furthermore, critical writing on race and science shows a pressing need to reconceptualize methods and shows a long history of racist and sexist problems at the level of data collection and methods (e.g. Harding; Tallbear; Washington; and Bolnick).

WORKS CITED

American Psychiatric Association. Diagnostic and Statistical Manual of Mental Disorders: Dsm-5. Washington, D.c: American Psychiatric Association, 2013.

Anzaldúa, Gloria. Borderlands / La Frontera: The New Mestiza. 4Th Ed. San Francisco: Aunt Lute Books, 1987/2012.

Anzaldúa, Gloria. now let us shift ... the path of conocimiento ... inner work, public acts. In Anzaldúa, Gloria & Keating, Ana Louise, Eds. This Bridge We Call Home: Radical Visions For Transformation. New York: Routledge, 2002.

Avila, Elena, And Parker, Joy. Woman Who Glows in the Dark: A Curandera Reveals Traditional Aztec Secrets Of Physical And Spiritual Health. New York: J.P. Tarcher/ Putnam, 1999.

Ayonrinde, Deji & Bhugra, Dinesh. "Culture Bound Syndromes." In Troublesome Disguises: Managing Challenging Disorders in Psychiatry. 2nd Ed. Eds. Bhugra, D., & Malhi, G. S. Chichester. West Sussex, UK & Ames, Iowa: John Wiley & Sons Inc, 2015.

Bolnick, Deborah A. "Individual Ancestry Inference and the Reification of Race as a Biological Phenomenon." In Revisiting Race in a Genomic Age. Eds. Koenig B, Lee S, Richardson S. New Brunswick: Rutgers University Press, 2008, 77-85.

Bowker, Geoffrey C., and Star, Susan L. Sorting Things Out: Classification and its Consequences. Cambridge, Mass: Mit Press, 1999.

Cole, Elizabeth R. "Intersectionality and Research in Psychology." American Psychologist. 64, 3 (2009): 170-180.

Crenshaw, Kimberlé. "Mapping the Margins: Intersectionality, Identity Politics, and Violence Against Women Of Color." In Critical Race Theory: The Key Writings That Formed The Movement. Eds. Crenshaw, K., Gotanda, N., Peller, G., & Thomas, K. New York: New Press, 1995.

Gonzales, Patrisia. Red Medicine: Traditional Indigenous Rites of Birthing and Healing. Tucson: University Of Arizona Press, 2012.

Gravlee, Clarence C. "How Race Becomes Biology: Embodiment of Social Inequality." American Journal Of Physical Anthropology 139 (2009): 47-57.

Guarnaccia, P. J., Lewis-Fernandez, R., Martinez, P. I., Shrout, P., Guo, J., Torres, M., Canino, G., & Alegria, M. "Ataque de Nervios as a Marker of Social and Psychiatric Vulnerability: Results from the NlAAS." The International Journal of Social Psychiatry, 56, 3 (2010): 298-309.

Harding, Sandra. "Rethinking Standpoint Epistemology: "What is Strong Objectivity"?" In

Feminist Epistemologies. Eds. Alcoff, L., & Potter, E. New York: Routledge, 1993.

Hunter, Christine M, Hunter, Christopher L, and Kessler, Rodger. Handbook of Clinical Psychology in Medical Settings: Evidence-Based Assessment and Intervention. New York: Springer, 2014.

Keough, Meghan E., Timpano, Kiara R., & Schmidt, Norman B. "Ataques De Nervios: Culturally Bound and Distinct From Panic Attacks?" Depression and Anxiety, 26, 1 (2009): 16-21.

Krieger, Nancy. Epidemiology and the People's Health: Theory and Context. Oxford: Oxford University Press, 2011.

Lewis-Fernández, R., Hinton, D. E., Laria, A. J., Patterson, E. H., Hofmann, S. G., Craske, M. G., Stein, D. J., & Liao, B. "Culture and the Anxiety Disorders: Recommendations for DSM-V." Depression and Anxiety, 27, 2 (2010): 212-29.

Montoya, Michael J. "Bioethnic Conscription: Genes, Race, And Mexicana/o Ethnicity in Diabetes Research." Cultural Anthropology 22, 1 (2007): 94-128.

Nichter, Mark. "Idioms of Distress: Alternatives in the Expression Of Psychosocial Distress: A Case Study From South India." Culture, Medicine and Psychiatry: An International Journal of Comparative Cross-Cultural Research, 5, 4 (1981): 379-408.

---. Global Health: Why Cultural Perceptions, Social Representations, and Biopolitics Matter. Tucson: University Of Arizona Press, 2008.

---. "Idioms of Distress Revisited." Culture, Medicine, and Psychiatry: An International Journal of Cross-Cultural Health Research, 34, 2 (2010): 401-416.

Santos, Boaventura De Sousa. Epistemologies of the South: Justice Against Epistemicide. Herndon, VA: Paradigm Publishers, 2014.

Scheper-Hughes, Nancy. Death Without Weeping: The Violence Of Everyday Life In Brazil. Berkeley: University Of California Press, 1992.

Spitzer, R. L., Gibbon, M., Skodol, A.E., Williams, J. B. W., & First, M. B. DSM-IV-TR Casebook: A Learning Companion to the Diagnostic and Statistical Manual of Mental Disorders, 4th Ed., Text Revision. Washington, DC: American Psychiatric Publishing, 2002.

Tallbear, Kimberley. "Chapter 1, Racial Science, Blood, And Dna" And "Chapter 2, The Dna-Com: Selling Ancestry." Native American Dna: Tribal Belonging and the False Promise of Genetic Science. Minneapolis: University of Minnesota Press, 2013, 31-103.

Trostle, James A. Epidemiology and Culture. Cambridge, UK: Cambridge University Press,

2005.

United States Center For Mental Health Services. Mental Health: Culture, Race, and Ethnicity: A Supplement to Mental Health: A Report of the Surgeon General. Rockville, Md: Dept. Of Health and Human Services, U.S. Public Health Service, 2001.

Washington, H. A. Medical Apartheid: The Dark History of Medical Experimentation on Black Americans from Colonial Times to the Present. New York: Doubleday, 2006.

EPISTEMOLOGIES OF EMOTION

EXPLORATIONS OF GLORIA ANZALDÚA'S LA FACULTAD AND JANE BENNETT'S ENCHANTMENT

SARA ISHII

> During her menses she feels fragile, expansive, the limits of her body stretched beyond her skin, she flows out like a sheet, encompassing, covering trees, people, everything around her.
>
> *Gloria Anzaldúa "El paisano is a bird of good omen" (51–2)*

Through the imagery of a body pulled beyond its physical corporeality to extend to others, human and nonhuman, Gloria Anzaldúa crafts a narrative that bridges fiction and theory, illuminating the connection between the body, emotion, and knowledge. Anzaldúa presents a form of knowledge creation that runs contrary to dominant Western epistemology, which is heavily influenced by a Cartesian framework. Descartes presents a form of knowledge production that privileges the mind over the body, constructing a dualism that remains deeply ingrained in contemporary thought. As Elizabeth Grosz notes, "Descartes instituted a dualism which three centuries of philosophical thought have attempted to overcome or reconcile" (6). Anzaldúan theory, which problematizes the body/mind dualism, works to break down binary thought and demonstrates the interdependence of the mind and body in knowledge creation. The above passage from Anzaldúa's short story "El paisano is a bird of good omen" relates the experiences of the protagonist, Andrea, who is able to access alternative modes of perception related to her embodied and emotional experiences. The importance of materiality and emotion runs through much of Anzaldúa's work, both fictional and academic. One such Anzaldúan theory, la facultad, relies heavily on bodily experience and emotion to prompt a shift in perception. In a similar manner, political scientist Jane Bennett posits a theory of enchantment that also discusses a change in one's perception as a result of experiencing strong emotions.

The following analysis focuses on Anzaldúa's theory of la facultad as an alternative epistemology to Cartesian thought. In addition, I examine Bennett's theory of enchantment and discuss the commonalities between Anzaldúa's and Bennett's theories. I posit that Anzaldúa's theory of la facultad and Bennett's enchantment demonstrate similar avenues for alternative knowledge creation that challenge Western paradigms of knowledge production. Ultimately, I argue that a reading of Bennett's concepts through the lens of la facultad reveals areas of potential development to the theory of enchantment, namely a closer examination of the role of the body and spirituality[1] as related to one's change in perspective, and, conversely, the application of vital materialist thought to Anzaldúa's theory of la facultad can extend to shifts in perception regarding nonhumans.

LA FACULTAD

The breadth of Anzaldúa's work can be connected to multiple academic fields, such as feminism, queer theory, border theory, and postmodernism, and addresses a number of social issues, including gender, race, sexuality, colonization, and citizenship (Mah y Busch 139). Similar to Anzaldúa's complex notion of identity,[2] her theories are equally multifaceted. However, Anzaldúa's identity and theories have been dissected and adopted piecemeal in some academic research.[3] A narrow engagement with Anzaldúa's scholarship is problematic because this approach obscures the interaction between her multiple theories and identities and, thus, limits the potential contribution of Anzaldúan theorizing across academic fields. As the current analysis focuses on specific aspects of Anzaldúa's theory, I acknowledge that her work is not and cannot be limited to the parameters of the current discussion. Nevertheless, the insight Anzaldúa offers in her theory of la facultad has important epistemological implications that have the potential to inform academic fields that have yet to fully explore Anzaldúan theorizing, specifically vital materialism.

Anzaldúa describes la facultad as a "deeper sensing" born from intense emotions (*Borderlands* 61). La facultad is a lens to view the world that is oftentimes developed as a tool for survival. Anzaldúa posits that intense emotions, such as fear and pain, can develop the acute sense of la facultad (*Borderlands* 61). As such, la facultad is more readily developed in marginalized peoples; however, Anzaldúa notes that this sensitivity is a quality latent in all people (*Borderlands* 61; "Within the Crossroads" 122). Everyone, then, has the potential to connect with this underlying faculty. In accessing la facultad, one can see beyond the exterior to reveal the "deep structure below the surface" (Anzaldúa, *Borderlands* 61). The cultivation of la facultad allows one not only to explore a sense of self but also to perceive the underlying social systems (Mah y Busch 152). In developing la facultad, one is more sensitive to one's own body, emotions, and the surrounding world.

Just as la facultad emerges from emotional and embodied experience, the effects of an internal sensing present themselves in visceral and physical feelings. For example, Anzaldúa states, "I feel a tingling on my skin when someone is staring at me or thinking about me. I can tell how others feel by the way they smell, where others are by the air pressure on my skin" (*Borderlands* 61). The evocation of other physical senses (touch and smell) demonstrates the collaboration of the body and mind in the expressions of la facultad. However, the theory of la facultad offers more than a heightened sensing: it is a vehicle for an alternative consciousness. Anzaldúa conceptualizes la facultad as that which prompts a shift in awareness, which "deepens the way we see concrete objects and people" (*Borderlands* 61). The result of this shift is a development of one's inner sense of "Self" and one's connection to others (*Borderlands* 61). As AnaLouise Keating and Gloria González-López assert, Anzaldúa's focus on self-experience enables her to develop new insight and draw connections with others, which can prompt social change (2).

"THE FLESH SINGS":[4] THE EPISTEMOLOGY OF LA FACULTAD

One such form of social change is Anzaldúa's presentation of an alternative understanding of knowledge production. Much of Anzaldúan theorizing critiques Western dichotomies; for instance, subject/object, mind/body, and theory/autobiography splits (Torres 198). Within a Cartesian framework of knowledge production, there are certain Truths that can be known to everyone solely through the mind. Recalling the Cartesian quote "Cogito ergo sum" (I think, therefore I am), the mind is established as the source of knowledge production. Following this line of thought, the body is not valued as a knowledge source because only the mind can access truth. In effect, the body and mind are placed in a hierarchical dualism (Grosz 3). The body does not contribute to gains in knowledge: rather, senses and emotions can mask the truth (Descartes). However, Anzaldúa explores the notion of knowledge as multiple truths that can be created, particularly through the dissolution of the body/mind split. For example, Monica Torres posits that Anzaldúa's theory of the mestizaje offers an alternative to Manichean structures; a mestiza is "suspicious of those [Western] rigid epistemological assumptions embedded in our perspectives and our social structures" (198). Torres notes that the language Anzaldúa uses to describe a mestizaje epistemology, such as "shifting," "sustaining contradictions," and "transcending," signifies a movement or mobility necessary in an alternative knowledge creation (198). As Torres argues, the mestiza consciousness bridges the mind/body split articulated by Cartesian thinking (198).

Building on Torres's argument, I posit that Anzaldúa's theory of la facultad also breaks down binaries to embrace multiple sites of knowledge construction. Through a reliance on emotional and embodied experiences to access a deeper sense of Self, the theory of la facultad articulates a shift in perception that flattens the hierarchical dualism through bridging the body and mind. For example, Anzaldúa notes, "I can spot the love or greed or generosity lodged in the tissues of another" (*Borderlands* 61). In recognizing physical manifestations of emotional characteristics, the one who senses through la facultad relies on both the body and mind to interpret the actions and feelings of others. In addition, just as la facultad challenges the Western system of knowledge through an equal estimation of the body and mind, the notion of a shift in perception posits multiple modes of knowledge creation. Thus, Anzaldúa's theories demonstrate that "how we know deeply influences how we act" and indicate a shift in awareness that impacts one's actions and ability to effectuate change (Torres 199).

ENCHANTMENT

The concept of social change emerging from a shift in perspective runs parallel to Jane Bennett's theory of enchantment. Situated within a vital materialist philosophical viewpoint, one of Bennett's primary concerns is challenging Western notions of a human/nonhuman binary. Vital materialism, according to Jane Bennett, advocates for the recognition of nonhumans as actants through a critique of anthropocentrism, the re-examination of nonhumans as actants, and the questioning of ontological hierarchies of matter that privilege humans over nonhumans. In *Vibrant Matter: A Political Ecology of Things*, Bennett argues that nonhumans play a role beyond that of a product of human design: rather, things possess an active role in public life (2). One way Bennett aims to illuminate nonhumans as actants is to challenge the notion of a modern "disenchanted" world. The concept of a "disenchanted" world can be described as a mode of thought that "discourages affective attachments" in our world (Bennett, *Enchantment* 3). Derived from an Enlightenment viewpoint, the story of disenchantment divides existence into two separate and distinct spheres: the natural world and the social world (Latour 13). The modern split between the two realms is asymmetrically aligned. The citizens of the social world, humans, are viewed as possessing life and the ability to act, whereas the inhabitants of the natural world, nonhumans, are passive objects or tools for human use (Latour 13; Bennett, *Vibrant Matter* 3). In *The Enchantment of Modern Life: Attachments, Crossings, and Ethics*, Bennett discusses one such method she calls "enchantment," which allows humans to see beyond the human/nonhuman divide to perceive nonhuman subjectivity.

According to Bennett, enchantment is a strong emotional feeling: one is in a "state of wonder [...] [I]t is to be transfixed, spellbound" (*Enchantment* 5). Upon arriving at an enchanted state, one is immersed in a "condition of exhilaration or acute sensory activity," a heightened state in which one's faculties are finely attuned (5). Once the senses are intensified by enchantment, one's perception may shift. Similar to la facultad, which allows one to see beyond the exterior, enchantment prompts a shift in how nonhumans are perceived. Through enchantment, the ordinary becomes extraordinary (4). Bennett's goal is to locate moments of enchantment in order to explore the "possibility that the affective force of those moments might be deployed to propel ethical generosity" (3). Such a move is valuable in fostering attitudes of interconnectivity and renegotiating human/nonhuman relations.

INTERACTIONS BETWEEN LA FACULTAD AND ENCHANTMENT

In discussing both Anzaldúa's la facultad and Bennett's enchantment, I view multiple commonalities held by both theories. Through identifying these common points I aim to further emphasize the potential for an alternative to Cartesian thought. Furthermore, the commonalities between la facultad and enchantment create a path of fluidity between the theories. In other words, I identify the potential for each of the theories to inform the other. Specifically, la facultad's emphasis on the body and spirituality may address points in Bennett's enchantment that can be further developed. Likewise, the vital materialist position Bennett advocates has potential to expand Anzaldúa's theory to address how a shift in perception as a result of la facultad may impact one's understanding of nonhumans.

COMMONALITIES

Descartes presents the mind as the epicenter of knowledge production; however, in privileging the mind over material and emotional experience, one is not able to access additional levels of awareness. La facultad and enchantment present the possibility of a deep sense of knowing accessed through emotional experiences. Though the emotions Anzaldúa and Bennett often attribute to their respective theories differ, both note the intense quality of these feelings. On one hand, Anzaldúa notes that la facultad can emerge as a survival technique; for example, "material such as depression, illness, death and the violations [sometimes the product of oppression]" can be emotions fueling the formation of la facultad (*Borderlands* 61). On the other hand, Bennett focuses on the emotions of exuberance and elation to describe the feelings associated with enchantment. Bennett states, "the overall effect of enchantment is a mood of fullness, plentitude, or liveliness, a sense of having had one's nerves or circulation or concentration powers tuned up or recharged—a shot in the arm, a fleeting return to childlike excitement about life" (*Enchantment* 5). Though Anzaldúa and Bennett evoke different emotions, I do not posit a binary between these sets of feelings. Instead, I aim to highlight the range of powerful emotions, which present evidence that a felt sense is an effective tool for knowledge creation.

In what could be described as epistemologies of emotion, la facultad and enchantment possess an element of creativity. For example, Anzaldúa remarks that those possessing la facultad "have this radar, and it's connected to the same thing, the creative life force. It's creative. It's connected to creativity" ("Within the Crossroads" 123). Likewise, enchantment is "not simply an experience to be received but something to be made, a technical or cultured effect" (Bennett, *Enchantment* 51). In other words, enchantment can be created or cultivated, as well as be a creative action. One such act of creation is the shaping of an altered perspective. La facultad and enchantment enable one to peel back the layers of everyday experiences to reveal complexities that lie beneath. For Anzaldúa, la facultad cultivates an awareness that "tears the fabric of our everyday mode of consciousness and that thrusts us into a less literal and more psychic sense of reality" (*Borderlands* 61). Similarly, Bennett asserts that enchantment is a feeling of being "struck and shaken by the extraordinary that lives amid the familiar and the everyday" (*Enchantment* 4). In sum, emotions can be an effective means of knowledge creation.

POSSIBILITIES IN THE DIFFERENCES

Though the epistemologies of la facultad and enchantment share a number of commonalities, I also view the differences in their positions as equally informative. I argue that, in parsing these differences, there is potential to further develop Anzaldúa's and Bennett's theories. For example, Anzaldúa's discussion of la facultad is more heavily invested in the body when accessing this sense. In reference to materiality, Anzaldúa states, "We are taught that the body is an ignorant animal; intelligence dwells only in the head. But the body is smart. It does not discern between external stimuli and stimuli from the imagination. It reacts equally viscerally to events from the imagination as it does to 'real' events" (*Borderlands* 59–60). Thus, Anzaldúa refuses the mind/body binary that positions the mind as the only source of knowledge. Rather, the mind is in many ways reliant on the body in creating knowledge. Anzaldúa states, "For me esta hoya is the **body**. I have to inhabit the body, discover its sensitivity and intelligence" [bolded in original] ("Speaking Across the Divide" 292). In Anzaldúa's discussion of la facultad, she asserts, "[t]hose who are pounced on [oppressed] the most have it [la facultad] the strongest—the females, the homosexuals of all races, the darkskinned, the outcast, the persecuted, the marginalized, the foreign" (*Borderlands* 60). The physical bodies of the marginalized peoples listed often contribute to their identity as, for example, a woman or a person of color. Thus, the body one inhabits shapes one's interactions and experiences, which contribute to knowledge creation.

The role of the body is also discussed in Bennett's conceptualization of enchantment, though to a lesser extent as compared to Anzaldúa's la facultad. Bennett discusses the effects of enchantment on the body, stating, "[O]ne of the distinctions of this state [enchantment] is the temporary suspension of chronological time and bodily movement. To be enchanted, then, is to participate in a momentary immobilizing encounter" (*Enchantment* 5). Therefore, Bennett recognizes the role of the body within a state of enchantment but not in relation to the body's role in cultivating enchantment. In other words, how might a person's embodied experiences affect their potential to become enchanted? Considering Anzaldúa's assertion that marginalized persons may be more likely to develop a heightened sense, those possessing la facultad may also have a greater potential to foster enchantment. If la facultad is "an instant 'sensing,' a quick perception arrived at without conscious reasoning [in which] [t]he one possessing this sensitivity is excruciatingly alive to the world," then this sense of being "alive" may lend itself to the vibrancy of enchantment (Anzaldúa, *Borderlands* 60).

In addition to further considerations of embodiment, Anzaldúa's theories also suggest a spiritual component that offers potential development to Bennett's consideration of human/nonhuman interconnection. In the foreword to *Cassell's Encyclopedia of Queer Myth, Symbol and Spirit*, Anzaldúa defines spirituality as a means to connect many forms of life, humans, animals, and nature, in a way that "transforms our perception of 'ordinary' life and our relationships with others, but also invites encounters with other realities, other worlds" (229). Spirituality allows one to see underneath the surface of the everyday to realize new potential for relations among beings. Anzaldúa discusses the importance of spirituality in a chapter in her unpublished autohistoria, *La Serpiente Que Se Come Su Cola: The Death and Rebirth Rites-of-Passage of a Chicana Lesbian*: "She attributed most of her ills to the separation of the flesh from the spirit" ("Dream of the Double-

Faced Woman" 71). For Anzaldúa, the spirit and body are closely connected: one cannot be removed from the other without severe negative consequences. Though I am not arguing that Bennett removes the spirit from the body, I do posit that a deeper consideration of the spirit within her notion of enchantment can aid in further articulating the connection between humans and nonhumans. For example, Bennett's aim in calling for a cultivation of enchantment is to enable humans to perceive nature, animals, and things in a new light in order to forge stronger connections with nonhumans. "The ethical aim," according to Bennett, is to "distribute value more generously, to bodies as such"; thus, humans may be able to sense stronger connections to nonhumans if both have a more equitable sense of being (13). By considering a spiritual connection between humans and nonhumans, Bennett's notion of enchantment could potentially be considered a shift in perception that allows one access to these spiritual networks.

Just as the intermingling of Anzaldúa's and Bennett's theories can potentially benefit the depth and breadth of the theory of enchantment, vital materialist concerns may also be influential to readings and applications of Anzaldúa's theories. The concept of human/nonhuman connection has been articulated in a number of Anzaldúa's writings.[5] In an interview with Linda Smuckler, she states, "I'm concerned with why people differentiate animals from humans. To me, we're all related, even to the grass" ("Spirituality, Sexuality, and the Body" 94). Though Anzaldúa does not necessarily discuss nonhumans as she develops her theory of la facultad, this concept has potential to be also understood as a shift in perception that could allow one to see beyond the surface of nonhuman existence to access the vibrancy housed within. The conceptualization of la facultad as a sense that enables the recognition of nonhuman animacy connects to Anzaldúa's notion of a rhythm or vibration of beings ("Within the Crossroads" 100). Anzaldúa asserts, "[T]he idea that everything is spiritual, that I'm a speck of this soul, this creative conscious, this creative life force; and so is a dog, a rock, a bird, this bedspread, and this wall," indicating the potential that attunement to spiritual connections can be accessed through la facultad ("Within the Crossroads" 100). The overlap between la facultad and enchantment further focuses the lens through which one may conceive shifts in human/nonhuman relationships. As I hope this paper suggests, the nascent dialogue between Anzaldúan theory and vital materialism makes important contributions to efforts that challenge ontological hierarchies and Cartesian dualisms. The cross-pollination between Anzaldúa's and Bennett's theories creates new avenues to advocate for social justice for all beings.

NOTES

1 As I explain later in this paper, I draw my definition of spirituality from Anzaldúa's articulation of the concept as a "relational activity leading to deep bonds between people, plants, animals, and the forces of nature" ("Foreword" 229).

2 Anzaldúa acknowledges many facets of her identity, while at the same time challenging the categorical approach to identity labels. In "La Prieta," Anzaldúa likens her identity to Shiva: she is "a many-armed and -legged body with one foot on brown soil, one on white, one in straight society, one in the gay world, the man's world, the women's, one limb in the literary world, another in the working class, the socialist, and the occult worlds" (45–46).

3 In "Risking the Personal," AnaLouise Keating discusses scholars' hesitancy in examining the spiritual aspect of Anzaldúa's work (8). Likewise, Juan D. Mah y Busch asserts that the segmented reprinting of Anzaldúa's texts works to over-emphasize certain aspects of her theories, while obscuring others (147).

4 "The flesh sings" (Anzaldúa, "Dream of the Double-Faced Woman" 71).

5 For further readings see: "Within the Crossroads: Lesbian/Feminist/Spiritual Development: An Interview with Christine Weiland (1983)" 100, 118–119; "Lesbian Wit: Conversation with Jeffner Allen (late 1980's)" 132; "Last Words? Spirit Journeys: An Interview with AnaLouise Keating (1998-1999)" 284; "*Tihueque*" 19; "El paisano is a bird of good omen" 51–69; "Spirituality, Sexuality, and the Body: An Interview with Linda Smuckler" 75, 94; "The New Mestiza Nation" 211; *Borderlands* 48, 58.

WORKS CITED

Anzaldúa, Gloria E. *Borderlands/La Frontera: The New Mestiza*. 4th ed. San Francisco: Aunt Lute Books, 2012. Print.

---. *The Gloria Anzaldúa Reader*. Ed. AnaLouise Keating. Durham and London: Duke University Press, 2009.

---. "Dream of the Double-Faced Woman." *The Gloria Anzaldúa Reader.* Keating 70–71.

---. "El paisano is a bird of good omen." *The Gloria Anzaldúa Reader.* 1982. Keating 51–69.

---. Foreword. *Cassell's Encyclopedia of Queer Myth, Symbol and Spirit. The Gloria Anzaldúa Reader.* 1996. Keating 229–231.

---. "La Prieta." *The Gloria Anzaldúa Reader.* 1981. Keating 38–50.

---. "The New Mestiza Nation." *The Gloria Anzaldúa Reader.* 1995–2002. Keating 203–216.

---. "Speaking Across the Divide." *The Gloria Anzaldúa Reader.* 2002. Keating 282–294.

---. "Spirituality, Sexuality, and the Body: An Interview with Linda Smuckler." *The Gloria Anzaldúa Reader.* 1983. Keating 74–96.

---. "Tihueque." *The Gloria Anzaldúa Reader.* 1976. Keating 19.

Anzaldúa, Gloria E. *Interviews/Entrevistas*. Ed. AnaLouise Keating. New York: Routledge, 2000.

---. "Lesbian Wit: Conversation with Jeffner Allen (late 1980's)." *Interviews/Entrevistas.* Keating 129–150.

---. "Last Words? Spirit Journeys: An Interview with AnaLouise Keating (1998–1999)." *Interviews/Entrevistas.* Keating 281–291.

---. "Within the Crossroads: Lesbian/Feminist/Spiritual Development: Interview with Christine Weiland (1983)." *Interviews/Entrevistas.* Keating 71–128.

Bennett, Jane. *The Enchantment of Modern Life: Attachments, Crossings, and Ethics*. Princeton and Oxford: Princeton University Press, 2001. Print.

---. *Vibrant Matter: A Political Ecology of Things*. Durham and London: Duke University Press, 2010. Print.

Descartes, René. *Meditations on First Philosophy in which are demonstrated the existence of God and the distinction between the human soul and body*. April 2007. Web. 9 September. 2013. <http://www.earlymoderntexts.com/pdf/descmedi.pdf >.

Grosz, Elizabeth. *Volatile Bodies: Toward a Corporeal Feminism*. Bloomington and Indianapolis: Indiana University Press, 1994. Print.

Keating, AnaLouise. "Risking the Personal." In *Entrevistas/Interviews/ Gloria Anzaldúa.*

Keating. 1–16.

Keating, AnaLouise and Gloria González-López, "Building Bridges, Transforming Loss, Shaping New Dialogues: Anzaldúan Studies for the Twenty-First Century." *Bridging: How Gloria Anzaldúa's Life and Work Transformed Our Own.* Eds. AnaLouise Keating and Gloria González-López. Austin: University of Texas Press, 2011. 1–16. Print.

Latour, Bruno. *We Have Never Been Modern.* Trans. Catherine Porter. Cambridge: Harvard University Press, 1993. Print.

Mah y Busch, Juan D. "Gloria Evangelina Anzaldúa (1942–)." In *Latino and Latina Writers.* Ed. Alan West-Durán, María Herrera-Sobek, and César A. Salgado. New York: Charles Scribner's Sons, 2004. 139–159. Print.

Torres, Monica. "'Doing Mestizaje': When Epistemology Becomes Ethics." *EntreMundos/AmongWorlds: New Perspectives on Gloria Anzaldúa.* Ed. AnaLouise Keating. New York: Palgrave, 2005. 195–203. Print.

ARCHIVES AND TRAJECTORIES OF ANZALDÚAN THOUGHT

BORDER DWELLERS, LLORONAS, AND NEPANTLERAS

BRIDGING THE ANZALDÚA ARCHIVE AND MERCEDES FLORESISLAS'S *TAMALES DE PUERCO*

TREVOR BOFFONE

In summer 2014, I was awarded a research fellowship at the LLILAS Benson Latin American Studies and Collections for my project, *Bridging Women in Mexican-American Theater from Villalongín to Tafolla (1848–2014)*.[1] After two weeks of analyzing the collections pertaining to Mexican-American theater and performing arts, such as the Carlos Villalongín Dramatic Company Records, the Tomás Ybarra-Frausto Papers, the Estela Portillo-Trambley Papers, and the Carlos Morton Papers, I had several days to spare and the Gloria Evangelina Anzaldúa Papers became my new playground.

While the collection's size is humbling (125 linear feet),[2] I mostly focused on Anzaldúa's correspondence with fellow feminists of color Norma Alarcón, Cherríe Moraga, Chela Sandoval, and Luisah Teish. I especially enjoyed Anzaldúa's back-and-forth with AnaLouise Keating, a part of the collection that features boxes of correspondence that are rich in content in their own right. Naturally, my mind began to wander. As anyone who has spent time in the Anzaldúa archive will tell you, it is both exhilarating and overwhelming. Ideas (some brilliant, most average at best) popped into my head with each new document. And then, at the very end of my fellowship, I discovered Anzaldúa's work on La Llorona. As soon as I saw her drawing of La Llorona entitled "The Body as La Llorona, Body as

Text," I was mesmerized and immediately knew that this was a project that I had to unpack and come to understand. As anyone who has spent time in the archive knows, the deeper one digs the more questions seem to arise.

In the pages that follow, I engage with the Gloria Evangelina Anzaldúa Papers to better understand contemporary Latin@ theater and performance. My aim is to open up a dialogue with other scholars about how we can collectively work together to fill the gaps in the archive. My argument is that Anzaldúa's Llorona as seen in "The Body as La Llorona, Body as Text" does not limit itself to Llorona stories in the traditional sense, but can converse with many Latina identities within a performance context. To bridge Anzaldúa's Llorona with contemporary Latin@ performance, I look to the work of emerging playwright Mercedes Floresislas's groundbreaking play *Tamales de Puerco* (2013),[3] which has the distinction of being the first Latin@ play to completely integrate English, Spanish, and American Sign Language (ASL) as they intersect with Deaf Latin@ identities.[4]

In the following work, I apply Anzaldúa's theory of La Llorona as a border-dwelling shape-shifter to Floresislas's play. I begin by analyzing Anzaldúa's Llorona as it appears in unpublished documents in the Anzaldúa archive that focus on La Llorona as a metaphorical border-dweller. I then turn to Floresislas's *Tamales* to underscore the ways in which the archive can converse with contemporary Latin@ theater and performance. *Tamales* tells the story of Norma, a mother to a Deaf child, who must learn to navigate both Hearing and Deaf worlds to create opportunities for her son. All the while, she must contend with an abusive husband, homelessness, undocumentedness, and increased injustices at the hands of local and state authorities. Norma becomes a shape-shifter, an Anzaldúan Llorona of sorts, who uses her positionality to overcome the many hardships she faces. Noticeably, *Tamales* is *not* a Llorona story; I have chosen to focus on Floresislas's play to demonstrate the reach and scope of Anzaldúa's work. I contend that Anzaldúa's Llorona is not relegated to Llorona stories in the traditional sense, but is a framework that can be applied to a variety of contexts. Ultimately, by examining *Tamales*'s Norma under an Anzaldúan lens, I propose that Anzaldúa's Llorona goes beyond conventional Llorona stories and opens up a new dialogue as to how the archive converses with contemporary Latin@ theater performance.

FINDING LLORONA IN THE ANZALDÚA ARCHIVE

While Anzaldúa's archive features several projects focusing on La Llorona, I find her unfinished dissertation project at the University of California at Santa Cruz titled "Lloronas—Women Who Wail: (Self)Representation and the Production of Writing, Knowledge and Identity"[5] to be the most compelling.

Anzaldúa's project is not only pertinent to classic tales of La Llorona:[6] indeed, in the project description, dated May 20, 2002, Anzaldúa elaborates on her theories surrounding the possibilities of using La Llorona as a critical framework to investigate how post-colonial cultural Others negotiate discursive spaces. This work questions voice and representation, looking to understand who has power and who does not. Anzaldúa uses La Llorona as a metaphor "to track how certain mythic components of identity have become part of the cultural language of the mestiza / Chicana and to link the various aspects of identity" ("Lloronas"). In the same vein, Anzaldúa addresses how these women "were constructed by colonialism and are constrained by neo-colonialism and how they constitute themselves as subjects and objects" ("Lloronas"). This project explores what grounds must be crossed and negotiated in order for a Mestiza to shift from being a consumer to a producer.

Part of "Lloronas—Women Who Wail" includes the unpublished essay titled "*Nomos*, the Feeding Place, the Dwelling Space" in which Anzaldúa conflates the body with La Llorona. In "*Nomos*," Anzaldúa claims "*La Llorona*, the ghostly body, carries the ***nagual*** possessing *la facultad*, the capacity for shape-changing and shape-shifting of identity." In this way, the body, as both home and the site of all intersections, serves as a shape-shifting and shape-changing entity, reminiscent of La Llorona. La Llorona functions both as the body and as a moveable site, a crossroads that enables recovery and the transition from a consumer to a producer. "*Nomos*" features a diagram of La Llorona titled "The Body as La Llorona, Body as Text," in which Anzaldúa writes the word "CROSSROADS" across Llorona's ghost-like head.[7] At first glance, one immediately notices that Anzaldúa has drawn two bodies on top of one another. [8] While some parts match up, others, such as the arms and feet, are in different areas. Over the legs the words "the juncture/plane of coexistence" are typed above "Nagual—shape-changer, shifter" (Anzaldúa, "*Nomos*"). This image addresses how the subject is constantly in a state of flux and is given the possibility to adapt to her surroundings. Put simply, La Llorona is a shape-shifter. She is invariably in a state of Nepantla. She is the definitive nepantlera.

Anzaldúa's work on La Llorona as a shape-shifting body presents some of the intricacies of the Gloria Evangelina Anzaldúa Papers. In many cases, Anzaldúa's final intentions are largely unknown because the works in the archive are incomplete drafts with comments and doodles here and there. This presents several problems (and gaps) in the archive. Some things can never be fully understood because they are missing or, in fact, never actually existed. In a way, these gaps parallel Anzaldúa's problems with the academy; she was not given support to focus on and finish these works. Her early and untimely death only reinforces this point. While her contemporaries, such as Norma Alarcón and

Cherríe Moraga, have been able to respond to their early work, fill gaps, and advance their scholarship and standing in the field, Anzaldúa's work must evolve posthumously and now relies on scholars to maintain her legacy and bring new knowledge to light.[9] By entering Anzaldúa's archive, we can begin to uncover her work and further dispel any notion that *Borderlands/La Frontera* is her only work that *truly* matters, *que vale la pena*. Adventurous and innovative scholarship has the potential to (re)write Anzaldúa's legacy and further cement her place in the academy as a body that matters, as an archive that matters, as a *living* archive.

AN UNLIKELY LLORONA IN *TAMALES DE PUERCO*

When I first encountered Mercedes Floresislas's *Tamales de Puerco*, I identified the protagonist Norma as a Nepantlera. As a mother to a Deaf child, Norma becomes a border-dweller whose experiences are marked by sociolinguistic liminality between English, Spanish, and ASL. She is not enough of anything. But in this third space, she can become whole, complete, and accepted.

In the play, Norma constantly shifts between Hearing and Deaf worlds to overcome her position as an undocumented, homeless, single mother to a Deaf child. Due to being undocumented, she does not have access to state institutions and, therefore, must tap into notions of Nepantla to navigate and overcome her surroundings. Given these premises, I argue that Norma embodies the qualities of an Anzaldúan Llorona. As a border-dwelling, shape-shifting Llorona, she straddles both cultures, is always between two worlds, and, thus, does not truly have a home. Her home is her body and her relationship with her son. Subsequently, due to being homeless and undocumented, she is always looking (wandering) for home. After all, La Llorona is the definitive homeless woman. Therefore, homelessness works both literally and metaphorically. Only by embracing her Llorona, her Nepantlera, does she bridge the disparate parts of her identity and forge community and home, and lose both senses of homelessness. In this way, Nepantla becomes a tool of empowerment. Living on this border makes her the powerful one who can exist and thrive in both worlds at the same time. We see this in Norma's story as she shifts between English, Spanish, and ASL. Nevertheless, her code-switching is not merely a sign of fluency, but more so demonstrates her strategy of survival. As a Nepantlera, Norma becomes a shape-shifter who navigates between disparate worlds with different masks intact. I find Anzaldúa's use of the word "masks" to be compelling in regards to *Tamales*. As a Nepantlera, Norma's masks are sociolinguistic: English masks, Spanish masks, ASL masks.

After seeing a group of Deaf people of color signing, Norma follows them into an Alcoholics Anonymous meeting exclusively for Deaf people. Here, she is able to learn ASL for free and, therefore, begin to communicate with her son

Mauricio. While her goal is to simply speak to her son and provide for him, having access to ASL and Deaf culture proves to be an unexpected and strategic defense mechanism. Aside from the obvious benefits of learning ASL for Mauricio, ASL plays a key role in the scene in which Norma's abusive husband Reynaldo returns. Given their history and Norma's separation from the corrosive relationship, she does not want him back in her life. This leads to an uncomfortable conversation because, ultimately, she decides to remain silent. The silence enhances their body language, manifesting how awkward this is for both. She is confused about his motives for being there while he is forcing the feeling of normalcy that disregards how verbally and physically abusive he was to both Norma and Mauricio. His push for a normal relationship fails, which leads to an uncomfortable encounter that bleeds into the audience's perception of the scene. Even though Norma and Reynaldo say nothing, we know, as Floresislas writes in the stage directions, that "THEIR WORDS WOULD BE REDUNDANT" (66). Although Norma remains confident and resists Reynaldo's attempts at gaining acceptance in this family, his presence alone destabilizes the environment that she has worked so hard to establish. Because he does not sign, he ignores the social codes of this community. The effect is jarring as Norma speaks to Mauricio at the end of the scene. Her mind in a different place, she verbally tells him, "Mauricio, get inside you're going to get wet!" (68). This is the *only* time in the play that Norma forgets to sign to her son.

Nevertheless, Norma fixes this problem by subconsciously embracing Nepantla. The next time Reynaldo appears unannounced at her home, Norma ignores his presence and converses in ASL with Mauricio and Karla, a social worker. As Norma explains who he is to Karla, Reynaldo is bothered by his lack of understanding. His confusion parallels the confusion that his son feels toward him: "What's...happening, what are you telling her?" (Floresislas 76). This environment mirrors the one of the outside world. Here, Reynaldo is the linguistic minority who misunderstands the conversations taking place around him. In this situation, Norma seamlessly shifts between different languages and registers and communicates with everyone. This dynamic reflects the power relationships ingrained in language. Norma is the one with power in this relationship, a process whereby she loses her Otherness. As a result, Reynaldo is left standing to the side, awkwardly observing the action taking place. Without any doubt, he is troubled and uneasy.

The preceding linguistic and visual aspects of the performance come together in the climax of the production. When Norma and Mauricio enter the home, Reynaldo is there. He has stolen all of her savings and demands tamales. Now empowered due to tapping into Nepantla, Norma asserts her independence: "I'D RATHER BE HOMELESS AGAIN OR DEAD THAN SPEND ONE

MORE DAY LOOKING AT YOU. […] NOW GET OUT! AND I NEVER WANT TO SEE YOU AGAIN!" (Floresislas 91). Their fight culminates in a visual and linguistic cacophony in which the signifiers of all three languages converge into a hybridized performance in which no single language stands alone. As Norma reaches for the phone to call the police, Reynaldo pulls her hair and they begin fighting. In this moment, Karla arrives and begins ringing the doorbell frantically; the red lights flash through the fighting, creating an auditory and optical sense of urgency. The audience can see Karla through the window desperately trying to open the door while ringing the doorbell. With the red light flashing and the doorbell ringing, Reynaldo tries to punch Norma but misses and knocks out Mauricio. Norma grabs a wooden rod and hits Reynaldo over the head, killing him instantly. As blood oozes from his head, the red light stops flashing. The urgency of the doorbell's ringing ceases as this red imagery shifts to the new locus of frantic desperation: the dead body at hand. Once Karla and Tana, a street vendor, enters, the three women break a moment of stunned silence with panic. At this juncture, all three languages come together to heighten the visual and linguistic cacophony. Karla talks to herself in ASL, Tana in Spanish, and Norma code-switches rapidly between all three, speaking a hybrid version of ASL and Spanglish that represents *all* facets of her identity as she becomes "in all cultures at the same time" (Anzaldúa, *Borderlands* 77).

In this instance, Norma becomes the border-dwelling Llorona. As Karla and Tana stand on opposite sides of Norma, speaking ASL and English respectively, Norma linguistically shape-shifts. She is the only one on stage capable of code-switching between the languages and, therefore, becomes the most powerful figure. Norma embraces Nepantla as a realm of possibility in which she experiences reality as "fluid, expanding, and contracting," and she becomes "exposed, open to other perspectives, more readily able to access knowledge derived from inner feelings, imaginal states, and outer events, and to 'see through' them with a mindful, holistic awareness" ("now let us shift…the path of conocimiento…inner work, public acts" 544). As a result of living in the borderlands between multiple cultures, Norma has access to all of the cultures that surround her and, subsequently, is able to shift in and out of these worlds to gain power and oppositional consciousness.[10]

CONCLUDING REMARKS

While this essay is not comprehensive, it reveals some of the many possibilities of the Anzaldúa archive by helping us to understand how we can begin to bridge Anzaldúa's less-discussed theories and contemporary Latin@ theater and performance, to which I would add literature and cultural studies. Under an Anzaldúan lens, La Llorona becomes a third space that allows the border-dweller in question to begin to make theory, develop strategies of oppositional consciousness, and, ultimately, survive. In the end, we see how Norma learns to navigate both aural and silent worlds, with a claim in both. She enters the silent world to forge a better path for her son and the aural world to forge a better path for herself. But to be whole, these two worlds *must* converge. She must find a way to connect, intertwine, and link these seemingly disparate parts of her identity. With her new-found knowledge intact, Norma not only survives in her conditions, but she *thrives*. Norma completes the journey from object to subject, from consumer to producer, from passive to an active agent, and, thus, becomes an Anzaldúan Llorona.

NOTES

1 I would like to thank the Center for Mexican-American Studies at the University of Texas at Austin for generously funding this research, for, without their support, this project would not have been possible.

2 I owe much thanks to Micaela Díaz-Sánchez for labeling the archive as "humbling" in an August 2015 Facebook post. Since my time in the archive, I had been searching for the right word to describe how the experience felt, and it was not until Díaz-Sánchez's post that I truly understood how I felt in the Anzaldúa archive.

3 Tamales de Puerco had its world premiere in 2013 at CASA 0101 Theater in Boyle Heights, Los Angeles, under the direction of Edward Padilla and the artistic mentorship of Josefina López. For more information, see my study in Sounding Out!: The Sound Studies Blog, "Deaf Latin@ Performance: Listening with the Third Ear."

4 I use the capitalized versions of Deaf and Deafness. A standard dictionary definition of "deaf" represents one who is partially or unable to hear (deaf and hearing impaired are essentially interchangeable). "Deaf" with a capital D, however, refers to the community that self-identifies as belonging to the Deaf culture. Deafness, therefore, is a sign of health and prognosis of well-being among sign language-dependent hearing-impaired people. Likewise, "hearing" versus "Hearing" represents a similar biological/cultural binary.

5 Anzaldúa's committee consisted of Helene Moglen (Chair), José David Saldivar, Donna Haraway, and Norma Alarcón.

6 For the most comprehensive study of La Llorona to date, see Domino Renee Perez's seminal work, There Was a Woman: La Llorona from Folklore to Popular Culture (2008).

7 In Teresa de Lauretis's feedback on this work, she cites this diagram as the "theoretical core of the project" and "truly a postmodern representation," and "what holds the various parts together, both conceptually and stylistically."

8 It should be noted that other versions of this drawing exist, some with more figures drawn on top. These other renderings involve complicated arrows, circling. As with the rest of the archive, it seems that the more information Anzaldúa gives us, the cloudier the archive becomes. Furthermore, these folders also contain other renderings of La Llorona.

9 This is not to say that Anzaldúa's work is not evolving. The recent publication of Light in the Dark/Luz en lo Oscuro demonstrates how new publications are still emerging from the archive and transforming Anzaldúa's place in the field.

10 With regard to Nepantlerismo, Anzaldúa proposes that "Living between cultures results in 'seeing' double, first from the perspective of one culture, then from the perspective of another" ("now let us shift" 549).

WORKS CITED

Anzaldúa, Gloria. *Borderlands/La Frontera: The New Mestiza*. San Francisco: Aunt Lute Books, 1987. Print.

---. Gloria Evangelina Anzaldúa Papers, Benson Latin American Collection, University of Texas Libraries, the University of Texas at Austin.

---. *Lloronas—Women Who Wail: (Self)Representation and the Production of Writing, Knowledge and Identity*. Box 93, Folder 14. Gloria Evangelina Anzaldúa Papers, Benson Latin American Collection, University of Texas Libraries, the University of Texas at Austin.

---."*Nomos*, the Feeding Place, the Dwelling Space." Box 93, Folder 2. Gloria Evangelina Anzaldúa Papers, Benson Latin American Collection, University of Texas Libraries, the University of Texas at Austin.

---. "now let us shift...the path of conocimiento...inner work, public acts." *This Bridge We Call Home: Radical Visions for Transformation*. Ed. Gloria Anzaldúa and AnaLouise Keating. New York: Routledge, 2002. 540–78. Print.

Boffone, Trevor. "Deaf Latin@ Performance: Listening with the Third Ear." *Sounding Out!: The Sound Studies Blog*. 3 Aug. 2015. Web.

Díaz-Sánchez, Micaela. "nothing humbles like the archive. 'making altars mediates the making of changes.' - Box 103, Folder 27. Anzaldúa Archives, Benson Library." Facebook. 21 Aug 2015. Web. 30 Sep 2015.

Floresislas, Mercedes. *Tamales de Puerco*. 2013. TS.

Perez, Domino Renee. *There Was a Woman: La Llorona from Folklore to Popular Culture*. Austin: University of Texas Press, 2008. Print.

COLLECTIVE *TESTIMONIOS*

GLORIA ANZALDÚA'S CO-EDITED, MULTI-GENRE, IDENTITY-BASED ANTHOLOGIES

ANNETTE PORTILLO

This essay examines the three major collections of work edited and co-edited by Gloria Anzaldúa: *This Bridge Called My Back: Writings by Radical Women of Color* (co-edited with Cherríe Moraga and referred to as *Bridge* throughout this essay), *Making Face, Making Soul/Haciendo Caras: Creative and Critical Perspectives by Feminists of Color*, and *this bridge we call home: radical visions for transformation* (co-edited with AnaLouise Keating). In contrast to canonical anthologies of American literature, these identity-based, multi-genre collections hold a marginal status within colleges and universities, because they are rarely required reading, especially not within, for example, many traditional English departments. One would more likely find these anthologies taught in Ethnic Studies or Women's Studies courses. And, many times, only excerpts of the anthologies are assigned, which disconnects them further from their original context. The marginalization of these works in academia is certainly a result of the editor's intentions to reach those outside the academic community by including "first-generation writers" whose works "range from extemporaneous stream of consciousness journal entries to well thought-out theoretical statements; from intimate letters to friends to full-scale public addresses" (*Bridge* xxiv). Neverthe-less, I argue that these collections are "collective *testimonios*" that serve as sites of resistance and transformation where writers provide readers with women of color epistemologies as they call their audience to action.[1] The earlier collections were originally rooted in urgent calls for the contributors to write themselves into the dialogue of the mainstream women's movement and against middle-class paradigms of feminism from the 1970s and early 1980s. The stories told within these collections articulate shared lived experiences of oppression suffered by working-class-identified women of color. The contributors resist silence and repression by writing *testimonios*, essays, poetry, and prose that in some cases serve as strategies for survival and healing. By naming themselves collectively, the contributors carve out a space for truth-telling as they raise the reader's political consciousness about issues pertaining to "third world" feminists of color.

THIS BRIDGE CALLED MY BACK: WRITINGS BY RADICAL WOMEN OF COLOR

It is important to first call attention to how *Bridge* was originally envisioned. After attending a women's retreat in San Francisco in 1979 and being made to feel like she was invisible and not worth listening to, Anzaldúa wanted to create a narrative space in which these racist and classist issues could be addressed. The call for writings to be included in the anthology read as follows:

> We want to express to all women—especially to white middle-class women—the experiences which divide us as feminists; we want to examine incidents of intolerance, prejudice and denial of differences within the feminist movement. We intend to explore the causes and sources of, and solutions to these divisions. We want to create a definition that expands what "feminist" means to us. (xxiii)

If we look at the first two editions of *Bridge* (1981, 1983), the cover is an outline of a naked faceless woman bent over on her hands and knees. The words "This Bridge Called My Back" are resting on a woman's back and shoulders. The woman seems to be in motion as she moves forward. This mobile female body is representative of the crossings that these writers and their readers must take in order to better understand each other's differences. As Toni Cade Bambara states in the foreword:

> This Bridge documents particular rites of passage. Coming of age and coming to terms with community—race, group, class, gender, self—its expectations, supports, and lessons. And coming to grips with its perversions—racism, prejudice, elitism, misogyny, homophobia, and murder. [...] This Bridge can get us there. Can coax us into the habit of listening to each other and learning each other's ways of seeing and being. (vii)

Although this "bridge" can manifest a source of empowerment that allows for dialogue and cross-cultural understanding, it also embodies pain and conflict as women of color are "walked over," bearing the weight of injustice. Cherríe Moraga notes in her preface that she "dreamed of a bridge," one which would quell the "myriad voices that live inside me" (xviii).

More importantly, the editors wanted to formulate an identity-based community that was not exclusively limited by academic theory. According to Moraga,

> The materialism in this book lives in the flesh of these women's lives: the exhaustion we feel in our bones at the end of the day, the fire we feel in our hearts when we are insulted, the knife we feel in our backs when we are betrayed, the nausea we feel in our bellies when we are afraid, even the hunger we feel between our hips when we long to be touched. (xviii)

The second section of the anthology is titled "Entering the Lives of Others: Theory in the Flesh," a theory described by the editors as that which means "one where the physical realities of our lives—our skin color, the land or concrete we grew up on, our sexual longings—all fuse to create a politic born out of necessity" (23). This section is key to the entire anthology as it articulates a framework for reading *Bridge*. The physical and material realities these women face, such as racism, classism, and sexism, are important to understanding the conceptual struggle of articulating moments of anger and pain through writing. The anthology allows for women to transform their life experiences and bodies into language that is then read and internalized by others in their community. In "Speaking in Tongues: A Letter To 3rd World Women Writers," Anzaldúa encourages her readers, *hermanas*, to "write in the kitchen [...] write on the bus or the welfare line, on the job or during meals [...] while you wash the floor or clothes listen to the words chanting in your body. When you're depressed, angry, hurt, when compassion and love possess you. When you cannot help but write" (170). This "call to write" by working class women was the basis for *Bridge*'s goal in creating a space for women outside of academia. Women are asked to "write their bodies" as they formulated subjectivities that resisted invisibility. Anzaldua states: "The act of writing is the act of making soul, alchemy. It is the quest for the self, for the center of the self, which we women of color have come to think as 'other'—the dark, the feminine" (169). It is through this process of writing that the contributors to *Bridge* become more aware of their multiple social locations as they are moved to better understand themselves.

The first section of *Bridge,* titled "Children Passing in the Streets: The Roots of Our Radicalism," is introduced as a *testimonio* characterized by heteroglossia, as there exists a multitude of voices from a variety of locations. The intro reads, "We are women from all kinds of childhood streets: the farms of Puerto Rico, the downtown streets of Chinatown, the barrio, city-Bronx streets, quiet suburban sidewalks, the plains, and the reservation" (5). The five poems and prose pieces that follow address the difficulty in coming to terms with one's own identity. In the poem titled "When I Was Growing Up," Nellie Wong writes:

> I know now that once I longed to be white.
> How? you ask.
> Let me tell you the ways.
> when I was growing up, people told me
> I was dark and I believed my own darkness
> in the mirror, in my soul, my own narrow vision
> when I was growing up, my sisters
> with fair skin got praised
> for their beauty, and in the dark
> I fell further, crushed between high walls
> . . . .
> when I was growing up, people would ask
> if I were Filipino, Polynesian, Portuguese.
> They named all colors except white, the shell
> of my soul, but not my dark, rough skin. (7–8)

Wong addresses the issue of internalized self-hatred as a result of imposed social constructions of race. Her poem reflects colonialist notions of whiteness and her "longing" to be white as she sees her sisters being praised for their "fair skin" and, certainly, acknowledges that colorism exists even within one's own community. Similar to other women of color, Wong's sense of identity becomes a site of crisis, a location of pain that is not simply eliminated by acculturating and adopting those values that are deemed valuable and mark her as a full citizen. Although she desires to be seen within a particular "Americanized" context and claim a particular capital power and move freely without fear, she realizes that she can never erase her skin color and deny her Chinese heritage. It is "dark, rough skin," that becomes her identifier; those who inquire if she is Filipino, Polynesian or Portuguese are unable to see beyond her body as a marker of identity. The editors strategically follow Wong's poem with that of Mary Hope Lee, who expresses her desire to be dark. Her poem "on not bein" relates the struggle of a young girl who is ostracized because of her "light" skin and her ability to "pass":

> she never wanted
> no never once
> did she wanna
> be white/to pass
> dreamed only of bein darker

she wanted to be darker
not yellow/not no high brown neither
but brown/warm brown
. . . .
momma took her outta
almost all black lincoln high
cuz she useta catch hell
every day in gym class. (9)

The ability to pass becomes a burden for this young girl who is treated as "some / kinda gawdawful allergy" (9). Her light skin and her body become sites of pain as whiteness within an all-black school is seen as a threat. Her color is read as privilege and her ability to pass, whether willingly or not, complicates her "black" identity, ironically marking her as other. This personal narrative becomes a lens in which to actually see how one's skin color signifies something different within different societal contexts and speaks to the complexities of naming oneself even within communities of color.

The essay that follows, by Chicana feminist Cherríe Moraga, is titled "La Güera," and it echoes similar feelings of displacement as a result of passing. She writes, "I was educated, and wore it with a keen sense of pride [...] but more than this, I was 'la güera': fair-skinned. Born with the features of my Chicana mother, but the skin of my Anglo father, I had it made" (28). The struggle with identity for these two women becomes apparent in their recognition that their bodies are marked. But Moraga problematizes her subjectivity and identity formation by consciously acknowledging that her ability to pass would never allow her to escape the life of her mother. Moraga's mother attempts to "bleach" her of any color she had in order to protect her from poverty and illiteracy. It is not until Moraga "lifted the lid" to her lesbianism that she completely comes to consciousness about her mother's oppression as a woman of color. She writes, "My lesbianism is the avenue through which I have learned the most about silence and oppression [...] the joys of looking like a white girl ain't so great since I realized I could be beaten on the street for being a dyke" (28–29). Moraga's subjectivity is inextricably linked to her sexuality and her coming-to-consciousness about her own social-political location. More importantly, it is through her personal experiences with multiple identities that Moraga has a specialized knowledge that allows her to discuss internalized oppression. And she acknowledges that her own classism and racism prompted her to work on *Bridge*. In a letter to Barbara Smith, Moraga recalls attending a Ntozake Shange reading that made her realize "that for years I had disowned the language I knew best—ignored the words and rhythms that were the closest to me" (31). Moraga recognizes her own participation in excluding the other and questions her own "right to even work on an anthology which is to be written 'exclusively by Third World women'" (33). Moraga confronts her anxiety and critically analyzes how she herself "identified with and aspired toward white values" (34). But she also acknowledges and asserts the difficulty in affirming her mixed-blood identity. Her essay calls for dialogue among radical feminists who might resist one another: "The real power, as you and I well know, is collective" (34). Thus, a U.S. Third World Feminist movement demands coalition and bridge-building. And this can only be achieved by deconstructing the categories of ethnicity, gender, and class. These goals are what *Bridge* sets out to achieve in its non-linear approach to collecting voices from those typically marginalized.

The essay following Moraga's in the second section is also important to understanding the objectives of *Bridge*. In her essay "Invisibility is an Unnatural Disaster: Reflections of an Asian American Woman," Mitsuye Yamada discusses the difficulty of teaching such anthologies as *Bridge* when she reflects upon her own classroom experience.

> Last year for the Asian segment of the Ethnic American Literature course I was teaching, I selected a new anthology entitled *Aiiieeeee!* compiled by a group of outspoken Asian American writers. During the discussion [...] one of my students blurted out that she was offended by its militant tone and that as a white person she was tired of always being blamed for the oppression of all the minorities. (35)

Surprisingly, the students admitted that they were not "offended" by the Black American, Chicano, or American Indian writings because they understood and empathized with their oppression. For Yamada, the reactions of her students paralleled the attitude towards Asian Americans she had received from other administrators in her college. She was involved in an academic due process procedure that she filed against the administrators at her college. Yamada's colleagues were surprised at her grievance because, as they stated, "this is so uncharacteristic of her; she seemed such a nice person, so polite, so obedient, so non-trouble-making"(36). Yamada's experiences address and problematize the stereotype of Asian Americans as passive and unassertive. Yamada states:

> In this age when women are clearly making themselves visible on all fronts, I, an Asian American woman, am still functioning as a "front for those feminists" and therefore invisible. The realization of this sinks in slowly. Asian Americans as a whole are finally coming to claim their own, demanding that they be included in the multicultural history of our country. (36)

Yamada likens her "invisibility" to the hero in Ralph Ellison's novel *The Invisible Man*, where she internalizes and "adapts" to not being seen by white America. Throughout her essay, she argues that her community needs to resist this type of acceptance, as "invisibility is not a natural state for anyone" (40). Yamada's *testimonio* is also characterized by a communal voice as she relates her childhood experiences during WWII. Yamada recounts the years she and her brother left the concentration camp in Idaho to work and study at the University of Cincinnati. Although her brother Mike, a U.S. citizen, was expelled after a short time, she, an "enemy alien," was allowed to remain. In 1945, Yamada left Cincinnati for New York University, "hoping to leave behind this and other unpleasant memories gathered there during the war years," but she found her political activism fell short of any meaningful change (38). Yamada argues that her experiences as an activist student, whose demonstrations and protest went unheard, created a sense of powerlessness in her own life. "We must remember that one of the most insidious ways of keeping women and minorities powerless is to let them only talk about harmless and inconsequential subjects, or let them speak freely and not listen to them with serious intent" (40). Thus, Yamada ends her *testimonio* by calling her readers to raise their voices, "even as they say to us 'This is so uncharacteristic of you'" (40).

These "collective *testimonios*" and "theories in the flesh" continue in *Bridge* with Max Wolf Valerio's essay in which he recounts his lived experience as a Native American.[2] Valerio asks,

> Just what is it to be an 'Indian'—Native American—a Skin...& more importantly how do I—half blood Indian and half Chicana relate to it all? [...] It seems too conceptual [...] Yet—I cannot forget and I don't want to. It's in my blood, my face my mother's voice [...] it's the shape of my legs and though I am light skinned it is my features—my eyes and face shape...it must even be the way I sweat! (42)

He echoes many of the contributors who question their own identities, who at times may feel alienated from their own communities as a result of colonialism and internal racism. Valerio continues, "Yes, I've been denied. What a shame not to speak Blackfoot. It was my mother's first language" (42). These feelings of loss and longing to reclaim language speak to the collectivist situation of U.S. Third World Women. For many, the pain of losing one's language and, subsequently, their "claim" to a cultural heritage problematizes their identity formation. Valerio discusses his first participation in a sweat at the age of sixteen. He recalls the emotions he expressed that resulted from the ceremony:

> The emotions seem to come out of some primeval cavity—some lonesome half-remembered place. It seems when I cried it was more than an individual pain. The weeping was all of our pain—a collective

> wound—it is larger than each individual. In the sweat it seems as though we all remember a past—a collective presence—our past as Native people before being colonized and culturally liquidated. (43)

This passage recalls a shared form of remembering. Unlike an "official" written historical narrative, Valerio recalls a "collective" memory of struggle and pain at sixteen. Similar to Yamada, his childhood experiences, his community, and his family inform his identity, however complex.

In her essay "Gee, You Don't Seem Like An Indian From the Reservation," Barbara Cameron also recalls her initial consciousness of an "Indian" identity. She explains how one of the first words she learned as a child in her Lakota language was "wasicu," which designated white people (46). By the first grade, after witnessing an Indian man gunned down in the back by police and an elderly Indian man beaten by white teenage boys, her "hatred for the wasicu was solidly implanted" (46). It was after visiting several "white towns" outside of her reservation that Cameron became more conscious of her Indian identity in relation to others. As a result of experiencing racial violence, she panics at even the thought of being alone in a room full of whites. This entrenched fear is something that cannot easily be explained or theorized. For Cameron, her fear translates into a form of survival or a defense mechanism used as protection against those who might harm her. Cameron also recognizes that certain misconceptions, such as those she has about Blacks, Chicanos, and Asians, serve only as a detriment. She acknowledges that many of her racist perceptions come from television, books, movies, and newspapers, and the only way to begin forming alliances between third world groups is to speak openly and honestly about these inaccurate images. Thus, *Bridge* becomes that medium where these women's voices, often marginalized, are allowed to relate their personal *testimonios*, allowing for readers to actively participate in "activism" and dialogue with each other.

Bridge is an anthology that represents lesser-known writers and marginal voices and serves as an oppositional stance toward mainstream academia. Although the contributors are directly addressing the white middle-class reader and feminist movement, its non-linear structure and *testimonio* writing counters the formal theoretical works that are usually assigned in history or English courses. Cynthia Franklin notes how the academy does not recognize the theoretical form of *Bridge* and, therefore, it is less likely to be assigned in graduate classes on feminist theory or even on lists for oral examinations. She notes that *Bridge* is rarely cited in standard academic feminist essays as theoretical insight, but rather only as a signifier of women of color's entry into feminism (42). Thus, the form itself and the "less theoretical" works have caused these anthologies to be seen as inferior in relationship to careerist academic feminism. But it is also important to note that the editor's initial vision of *Bridge* was, in fact, grounded in this counter-academic stance as it sought to be more inclusive of marginalized or less-known writers of color. The result was the publication of women whose works might never be accepted by mainstream presses. It is literally a "theory in the flesh," as Moraga states: "This book is written for all the women in it and all whose lives our lives will touch. We are a family who first only knew each other in our dreams, who have come together on these pages to make faith a reality" (xix).

MAKING FACE, MAKING SOUL/HACIENDO CARAS

Ten years after *Bridge* was published, in 1990, Anzaldua co-edited another anthology, *Making Face, Making Soul/Haciendo Caras*. In the introduction, she states that she was tired of waiting for someone else to publish a book that would continue where *Bridge* left off. This book reflects and responds to a different moment in feminism as it had become more established within and outside the university. In contrast to *Bridge*, *Making Face, Making Soul* shows the authors as active and confrontational, making "political subversive gestures" (xv). This is first represented in the title and introduction, where the bridge metaphor is replaced with the metaphor for carving out one's own face. As Franklin notes, the editors are "no longer willing to serve as a bridge to be walked upon," and the contributors look the world defiantly in the face, proclaiming themselves in charge of their own making (44). For Anzaldúa, "*haciendo caras*," or "making faces," is a phrase that is much more subversive, as it can also mean "the piercing look that questions or challenges, the look that says, 'Don't walk all over me,' [...] 'Get out of my face'" (xv). She further theorizes the face as a marker of one's self by stating that the "world knows us by our faces, the most naked, most vulnerable, exposed and significant topography of the body" (xv). Thus, through their writings, the anthology's contributors counter invisibility and silence as they rid themselves of the masks they have been forced to wear and use this space collectively to create their own subjectivity. "We begin to acquire the agency of making our own *caras*. 'Making faces' is my metaphor for constructing one's identity" (xvi). Many of the writings are self-reflective, as the writers address their social locations as second-class citizens and subsequently work toward a communal understanding of each other.

The works in Section One, "Still Trembles Our Rage in the Face of Racism: There Is War: Some Losses Can't Be Counted," address racism and its relation to dominance. I argue that the second poem in this section, "Poem For The Young White Man Who Asked Me How I, An Intelligent, Well-Read Person, Could Believe In The War Between Races" by Lorna Dee Cervantes, embodies the main concerns of contributors. She articulates the reality of racism and a sense of hopelessness for its end, because although she does "not believe in the war between races," "in this country / there is war" (5). She writes,

> I believe in revolution
> because everywhere the crosses are burning,
> sharp-shooting goose-steppers round every corner,
> there are snipers in the schools...
> (I know you don't believe this.
> You think this is nothing
> But faddish exaggeration. But they
> Are not shooting at you.)
>
> I'm marked by the color of my skin.
> The bullets are discrete and designed to kill slowly.
> They are aiming at my children.
> These are facts.
> Let me show you my wounds: my stumbling mind, my
> "excuse me" tongue, and this
> nagging preoccupation
> with the feeling of not being good enough. (4–5)

Cervantes relates a sense of urgency and a sense of unapologetic assertiveness that addresses the "horror" of racism and the effects on those who are its victims. As Anzaldúa notes in her introduction:

> Racism is a slippery subject, one which evades confrontation, yet one which overshadows every aspect of our lives. And because so few (white) people are directly and honestly talking about it, we in the book have once again had to take on the task. Making others "uncomfortable" in their Racism is one way of "encouraging" them to take a stance against it. (xix)

This first section continues with similar thematic concerns and contributions by Judith Ortiz Cofer, Mitsuye Yamada, Barbara Smith, María Lugones, and Chela Sandoval, to name a few. In "Something About the Subject Makes It Hard to Name," Gloria Yamato outlines definitions of racism, oppression, and internalized oppression. She defines oppression as the "systematic, institutionalized mistreatment of one group of people by another for whatever reason. The oppressors are purported to have an innate ability to access economic resources, information respect, etc." (20). And with internalized oppression, "members of the target group are emotionally, physically, and spiritually battered [...] believ[ing] that their oppression is deserved" (20). Yamato's descriptive essay on social hierarchies and various "isms" is not simply informative, but calls her audience to action: "So, what can we do?"(23). She answers her question by asking her audience to acknowledge that racism exists and then reclaim the ethnic heritage they may have lost. In addition, she asks that we challenge oppression by taking a stand against it, especially internalized racism. For both her white and women of color audiences, she asks that they educate themselves about how different groups have been oppressed and how they resisted that oppression and more importantly that they "[c]elebrate the inevitable end of racism" (24). Similar to essays in *Bridge,* Yamato's essay reveals the desire to create bridges and cross-cultural understanding.

The last series of essays in this section directly address the state of women's studies and institutional racism. Similar to *Bridge*, this collection's contributors question the academy's inability to fully accept the specialized knowledge of students and faculty who theorize their lived experiences in academic work as opposed to abstract elitist theories that are intangible to many readers in their own communities. For example, Barbara Smith argues that "racism is a feminist issue," and defines feminism as the "political theory and practice that struggles to free all women: women of color, working-class women, poor women, disabled women, lesbians, old women—as well as white, economically privileged, heterosexual women. Anything less than this vision of total freedom is not feminism, but merely female self-aggrandizement" (25). Smith is adamant about her critique of women's studies programs that simply diversify their curriculum to include material on Third World Women, yet do not fully comprehend the "subtleties" of institutional racism and how it "distorts and lessens your own lives as white women—that racism affects your chances for survival, too, and that it is very definitely your issue" (26). More importantly, she questions how women's studies programs and how academic feminists relate to the grassroots community of the women's movement:

> How do we bring our gifts and our educational privilege back to it [grassroots/community]? Do we realize also how very much there is to learn in doing this essential work? Ask yourself what the women's movement is working on in your town or city. Are you a part of it? Ask yourself which women are living in the worst conditions in your town and how your work positively affects and directly touches their lives? If it doesn't, why not? (27)

In the second section, "Denial And Betrayal," the contributors discuss their complex identities that do not fit into neat categories. In "Notes From a Fragmented Daughter," Elena Tajima Creef begins her essay by recalling incidents in her life directly related to her ethnicity. She remembers being asked by someone at an art gallery if she made any of the food (sushi, chow mein, egg rolls, etc.) because "I notice you look kinda Asian" (82). Or when she "buries" her Japanese mother and pretends to be Mexican, because it is safe and "I love it when people ask if I am Español"—until one night in Santa Cruz, when she attends a screening of "'Tampopo'—your basic Japanese noodle western" and she cannot help but to respond to the white, middle-aged man who tells her he loves Asian girls and is traveling to Taiwan to meet one he has been corresponding with. He continues by stating, "I really prefer Oriental women to American because (he whispers) there are so many 'feminists' in this town. You are Asian, aren't you?" (83). Tajima Creef responds to this remark by stating, "Idiot. I am the daughter of a World War II Japanese war bride who met and married my North Carolinan hillbilly father one fine day in 1949 [...] Nine months out of the year, I pose as a doctoral student—a historian of consciousness" (83). She contextualizes her self-identity and says her mother was a "war bride," one of those 45,000 Japanese women who married American servicemen after World War II and immigrated to the U.S. In interviews she has conducted with these women for her oral history collection, she states that the women resent the term "war bride" and would much prefer to be called *Shin Issei* or New Immigrants. The anxiety of a racially mixed identity and the desire for acculturation is a common theme in the essays that follow as the writers grapple with their "otherness." What does it mean to constantly be "othered" or feel unsafe in one's own flesh? This internalized colonialism is confronted in a much later poem by Joy Harjo, "I Give You Back." She proclaims,

> I release you, my beautiful and terrible
> fear. I release you. You were my beloved
> and hated twin, but now, I don't know you
> as myself. I release you with all the
> pain I would know at the death of
> my daughters.
>
> You are not my blood anymore.
>
> I give you back to the white soldiers
> who burned down my home, beheaded my children,
> raped and sodomized my brothers and sisters.
> I give you back to those who stole the
> food from our plates when we were starving. (151)

Harjo purges her fears, those feelings of self-hatred that have betrayed her and a community whose history is inextricably linked to a colonial past. She exclaims that she is not afraid to be white, black, hated, angry, or loved. This poem is appropriately placed in the section "(De)Colonized Selves: Finding Hope Through Horror: Turning the Pain Around: Strategies for Growth." Harjo's poem is a rebirth of her identity as she "releases" those negative aspects of her life that had instilled fear. Similarly, in "Journeys of the Mind," Anne Waters writes,

> You cannot
> extricate
> my Indiannness
> my Jewishness
> my Lesbianness.
> You cannot
> reach in and
> exorcise that
> pain, or joy. (159)

These women embrace their multiple identities and utilize poetry as a strategy to cope with their shared experiences.

Making Face, Making Soul takes on an oppositional stance toward the academy similar to that of *Bridge*. It is obvious from the non-traditional structure of these two anthologies that the editors and contributors were not concerned with reaching an audience that was primarily academic. Although the last section of *Making Face, Making Soul* is comprised of "theoretical" pieces, and Anzaldúa herself admits to being seduced by academic language, she states that this anthology avoids the oftentimes hard-to-access, jargonistic language that blocks communication (xxiii). Therefore, Anzaldúa claims that feminists of color are in the process of formulating their own "marginal" theories and new in-between positions:

> What is considered theory in the dominant academic community is not necessarily what counts as theory for women-of-color. Theory produces effects that change people and the way they perceive the world. Thus, we need *teorias* that will enable us to interpret what happens in the world, that will explain how and why we relate to certain people in specific ways, that will reflect what goes on between inner, outer and peripheral "I"s within a person and between the personal "I"'s and the collective "we" of our ethnic communities. *Necesitamos teorías* that will rewrite history using race, class, gender and ethnicity as categories of analysis, theories that cross borders, that blur boundaries—new kinds of theories with new theorizing methods. (xxv)

Anzaldúa is describing a type of (re)writing and (re)reading that includes one's lived experience, a specialized knowledge.

It should be noted that the final section, "'Doing' Theory in Other Modes of Consciousness," includes not only "traditional" academic essays by Barbara Christian, Tey Diana Rebolledo, and Norma Alarcón, but also poems and prose by Pat Mora and Alice Walker. Thus, the fixed boundaries of what constitutes "theory" are blurred further. One could argue that, in their entirety, the anthologies themselves are representative of a "mestizaje" theory. The essays by Christian and Rebolledo, although written in the late 80s, still resonate with relative concerns regarding academic hegemony and the displacement of creative writers by literary criticism. Both question their own relationship as literary critics to the literature they study. Christian objects to the "race for theory," whereas Rebolledo objects to theory as a means of validating and legitimizing "our literature." Christian asks, "For whom are we doing what we are doing when we do literary criticism?" (343). She pointedly answers by stating, "How I write is done to save my own life [...] for me literature is a way of knowing that I am not hallucinating, that whatever I feel/know *is*" (343). This call for creating new theories that are more inclusive continues with Anzaldua's next collection of works co-edited with AnaLouise Keating.

THIS BRIDGE WE CALL HOME: RADICAL VISIONS FOR TRANSFORMATION

In the collection *this bridge we call home* (2002), the contributors continue to tell their stories of lived experiences through "collective *testimonios*" as they discuss pressing issues facing women of color feminists twenty-one years after the publication of *Bridge*. In the introduction, Anzaldúa and Keating claim their focus is on agency as opposed to victimhood:

> Twenty-one years ago we struggled with the recognition of difference within the context of commonality. [...] [*this bridge we call home*] questions the terms *white* and *women of color* by showing that whiteness may not be applied to all whites, as some possess women-of-color consciousness, just as some women of color bear white consciousness. (2)

Thus, even the category "women of color," which is used to distinguish these multi-genre identity-based anthologies from others, becomes more flexible and inclusive as the editors expand the original objectives of *Bridge* by incorporating more "underrepresented voices such as those of transgendered people, and Arab and South Asian/Indian Americans" (3). Although Anzaldúa notes that some women of color may not want whites or males to be included in this collective consciousness, "we risk their displeasure" (3). She argues that, although many consider *Bridge* to be a "safe space" they call "home," no safe spaces really exist, and this collection wishes to create bridges that will loosen the borders rather than close them off (3). Therefore, even in the face of conflict and criticism, Anzaldúa and Keating choose to challenge further those fixed identities and categories that might be infinitely exclusive.

Chela Sandoval's foreword to this new collection recalls that *Bridge*, in its historical moment, was meant as a tool "to call up and recognize experiences—

and to make them matter differently. [...] 'Radical feminists of color' became women of words, speaking, writing, commanding, directing, giving meaning to silence" (22). Now, twenty years later, we must ask, "Where is this political movement that calls itself a 'women-of-color' movement? Who mobilizes within it? And on what terms?" (22–23). These are the questions that the contributors attempt to address and answer. And the silencing that was felt by some women of color in the original *Bridge* collection was taken into consideration for *this bridge we call home.* Anzaldúa defines this anthology as a way for contributors "to heal las rajaduras split open by mistrust, suspicions, and dualisms" (4). For these writers, "to bridge is an act of will, an act of love, an attempt toward compassion and reconciliation" (4). The first section is dedicated to acknowledging the impact that *Bridge* has had on this collective community and future of third world feminism. Many writers recall the first time they encountered *Bridge,* whether it be in a used bookstore or their women's studies course. Although many of these *testimonios* celebrate the text that helped them to work though their own conflicting identities, Deborah A. Miranda recalls how she felt excluded as a "mixed-blood Indian woman" (192). Even though *Bridge* included a few Native voices, she exclaims, "I wanted more. I wanted to belong to this book, own this book, I wanted my struggles as an *Indian woman* to be present and *part of* this beautiful, incredible book!" [italics in original] (192). Miranda felt the stories she was reading were not hers, and, in order to claim its power, she had to become a generic woman of color and lose her Indianness (192). "First Peoples are not gone! My question here, then, is not only who has been silenced? but whose ears have been denied sound and song? What has been hidden even from you, my sisters of color? What do you not know about the land you stand on? Why don't you know it? How can you learn it?" (193).

Another contributor, Nada Elia, addresses a similar issue as Miranda, and states that, "with regard to what may well be the most invisible minority group in the United States, namely Arab-American feminists," *Bridge* did not help her (223). She notes that, although Arab-American writers are published in volumes on Islam or the Middle East, these voices rarely appear in anthologies featuring U.S. women feminists. She emphasizes the need for more inclusion on all levels, especially within academia. "As women of color insistently denounced white feminism, [...]Arab-Americans must today denounce the myopia of women of color, minus one shade. We must denounce it, and not keep our bitterness to ourselves, contained in anthologies of Arab-American writing" (230). Thus, the women's voices present in this latest collection are simply telling their stories, their histories, and creating new subjectivities. Their collective lived experiences, or "theories in the flesh," culminate in a specialized knowledge. I would argue that *this bridge we call home,* similar to its predecessors, builds a community not only of contributors, but of readers as well. After all, survival and healing depends not only on the telling of these stories, but also on the listeners and readers engaging and reacting to them.

I argue that all three collections are "collective *testimonios*" where the act of storytelling results in "community building" between contributors and readers alike. The contributors produce what Anzaldúa calls "marginal *teoría*" that provides an active space for working through the process of decolonization. Although readers may not identify with all the essays, poems, or short stories, their interaction/reactions to the narratives will raise their consciousness in multiple ways. And the contributors form an oppositional identity that is defined as a "third world feminism" which resists assimilation to a hegemonic feminist model. More importantly, I see these texts as sites of activism that call their readers to action and coalition-building.

NOTES

1 I am utilizing the term *testimonio* as defined by John Beverly. He states the genre is a narrative "told in the first person by a narrator who [...] witnesses the events he or she recounts, and tells of a significant life experience" (92–93). In addition, the narrator not only represents the individual subject, but also a group or class situation that is marked by marginalization, oppression, and struggle" (103). See: John Beverley, "The Margin at the Center On *Testimonio* (Testimonial Narrative)." I extend this definition further to include the definition of *testimonio* as defined by the Latina Feminist Group, who argue for the "importance of *testimonio* as a crucial means of bearing witness and inscribing into history those lived realities that would otherwise succumb to the alchemy of erasure" (2). They call themselves "professional testimoniadoras or (producers of *testimonios*), whether as oral historians, literary scholars, ethnographers, creative writers, or psychologists" (2). See Latina Feminist Group, eds., *Telling to Live: Latina Feminist Testimonios.*

2 I utilize the pronoun "he" for Valerio who identified as a Chicana-Native American lesbian feminist when the first edition of Bridge was published. He has since written about his experience as a transsexual man of color in his book *The Testosterone Files: My Hormonal and Social Transformation from Female to Male* (2006) and published an essay "Now That You're a White Man': Changing Sex in a Postmodern World—Being, Becoming, and Borders" in *this bridge we call home: radical visions for transformation* (2002).

WORKS CITED

Anzaldúa, Gloria, ed. *Making Face, Making Soul/Haciendo Caras: Creative and Critical Perspectives by Feminists of Color.* San Francisco: Aunt Lute Books, 1990. Print

Anzaldúa, Gloria E. and AnaLouise Keating, eds. *this bridge we call home: radical visions for transformation.* New York: Routledge, 2002. Print.

Beverly, John. "The Margin at the Center On *Testimonio* (Testimonial Narrative)." *De/Colonizing the Subject: The Politics of Gender in Women's Autobiography.* Eds. Sidonie Smith and Julia Watson. Minneapolis: University of Minnesota Press, 1992. 91-114. Print.

Franklin, Cynthia. *Writing Women's Communities: The Politics and Poetics of Contemporary Multi-Genre Anthologies.* Madison: University of Wisconsin Press, 1997. Print

Latina Feminist Group, eds. *Telling to Live: Latina Feminist Testimonios.* Durham: Duke University Press, 2001. Print.

Moraga, Cherríe, and Gloria E. Anzaldúa, eds. *This Bridge Called My Back: Writings by Radical Women of Color,* 2nd ed. New York: Kitchen Table: Women of Color Press, 1983. Print.

WORKING WITH ANZALDÚA'S WRITING NOTAS

AN ARCHIVAL EXPERIMENT IN THREE PARTS

ANALOUISE KEATING, KELLI ZAYTOUN, BETSY DAHMS

Gloria Anzaldúa's archive is enormous, consisting of 125 linear feet of material that literally spans Anzaldúa's life—from birth certificates to obituaries, and beyond. From this huge collection, we focus on a single item: "Writing Notes H37, H47–H98," located in Box 103, Folder 4. Writing notes—collections of quotations, speculations, autobiographical self-reflections, and so on—were an important part of Anzaldúa's creative process, serving at least two purposes: (1) They functioned as a type of storage where Anzaldúa collected material that she hoped to later include in her essays, autohistorias, and fiction; and (2) they enabled her to brainstorm freely and play around with ideas which she would later incorporate into her theories and drafts or use to generate entire projects. Because Anzaldúa's writing process was epistemological, intuitive, and communal, her writing notes represent rich sites of knowledge creation.[1] And, she left hundreds—if not thousands—of pages of writing notes (or what she labeled on her hard drive and described in conversations as her "notas").

Written between December 1998 and early April 1999—during the time when Anzaldúa was developing her theory of conocimiento, drafting "now let us shift... the path of conocimiento... inner work, public acts," beginning to edit *this bridge we call home: radical visions for transformation,* and working on several other projects—"Writing Notes H37, H47–H98" offers an intimate glimpse into Anzaldúa's thought process. By focusing on such a small slice of her unpublished work—only seventeen single-spaced typed pages!—we adopt a self-imposed constraint designed to generate additional insights while, perhaps, enacting Anzaldúan archival methods. As Suzanne Bost suggests in her important article on the Gloria Evangelina Anzaldúa Papers, Anzaldúa's archive—with its enormous proliferation of materials—reminds us that an archive is not a "passive storehouse of history" just waiting to be read by researchers; an archive is, rather, an agent in the research process. Anzaldúa's archive contains "multiple material actants at work"—materials that go beyond paper documents, and include apparently random objects, like "doorknob placards, ticket stubs, [and] appointment cards," that play active roles in knowledge production (617, 616). Drawing on her experience of the archive as an individual researcher, Bost asserts that the challenge of navigating "the huge and messy archive" expanded and enriched her work (618). We add to Bost's idea of the "messy materiality" of archival work by engaging with the archive as a research collective, demonstrating the rich variety in knowledge production that can unfold even when multiple researchers are working with the same material. At the same time, in working together, we discovered links and overlaps in what we wrote as individuals, and the process produced further insights, revisions, and recreations—truly collaborative thinking and writing facilitated by Google Docs, Facebook messages, phone calls, and Gloria Anzaldúa's words.

In the following discussion, "Writing Notes H37, H47–H98" functions as inspiration, evidence, jumping-off points, corrections, and more for our short analyses. We each engage with a distinct aspect of this material and enact a different, though related, approach. Our approaches were shaped by our previous scholarship on Anzaldúa and by our personal intellectual interests. Putting "now let us shift" into dialogue with Anzaldúa's intense self-reflections, AnaLouise Keating investigates Anzaldúa's innovative decolonial onto-epistemology and its implications for contemporary scholar activists. Focusing on Anzaldúa's references to shamanism and James Hillman's work, Betsy Dahms uses archetypal psychology to explore Anzaldúan writing as transpersonal, animist prayer. And, drawing on Anzaldúa's shapeshifting theory of imagination, Kelli Zaytoun analyzes, through a new materialist lens, "Writing Notes H37, H47–98," and offers new evidence for Anzaldúa's theory of self and its invaluable place in critical conversations on subjectivity, agency, and social justice work.

TRANSFORMING DESPAIR, DECOLONIZING EPISTEMOLOGIES: ANZALDÚA'S RELATIONAL ONTOLOGY

AnaLouise Keating

In the opening paragraph of "now let us shift...the path of conocimiento... inner work, public acts," Anzaldúa recounts her daily walk across a public park, Lighthouse Field, which is located about two blocks from her home in Santa Cruz, California. Writing in second person, she affirms the spirit-infused quality of her surroundings: "You experience nature as ensouled, as sacred" (540). Significantly, she does not try to prove nature's ensoulment by offering logical arguments, detailed analyses, references to Western philosophical/theological traditions, or discussions of indigenous knowledge systems. Instead, she simply affirms a cosmic sacredness and uses this affirmation to initiate the relational ontology, epistemology, and ethics (or what, borrowing from Karen Barad, we could call her "onto-ethico-epistemology") she describes and enacts in "now let us shift." She offers a theory-practice designed to decolonize herself and her readers.

Drawing from indigenous (Nahuatl, Olmec) philosophies and esoteric teachings that precede conventional Western divisions between the secular and the religious, Anzaldúa sidesteps monotheistic religious and Cartesian injunctions. In so doing, she enacts the decolonizing advice she gave herself in "Writing Notes H37, H47-H98": "Step out of your cultural trance. It limits one kind of relationship you can have with spirit." She posits a non-religious, non-secular, entirely ensouled world in which all nature is sacred; all nonhuman beings—even rocks and dirt—are vibrantly alive. Throughout "now let us shift," Anzaldúa enacts a metaphysics of interconnectedness[2] that replaces modernist divisions between subject/object, spirit/matter, body/soul with a post-secular, post-religious animism.

As I use the term, "animism" represents an immanent materialism in which everything that exists is interconnected, conscious, and imbued with/composed of spirit, awareness, mind. With its origins in ethnocentric nineteenth-century anthropology, "animism" has negative connotations that have been only partially redeemed by what Graham Harvey calls the "new animism."[3] However, I'm convinced that animism's dynamic, inspirited world most accurately describes Anzaldúa's philosophy. Moreover, because the term "animism" was invented as part of a colonizing ontological process, using it to describe Anzaldúa's *de*colonizing process demonstrates the post-oppositional nature of her work and reminds us that decolonial thinking can borrow from and revise intellectual colonization rather than rejecting it entirely. In what follows, I use Anzaldúa's reflections in "Writing Notes H37, H47–H98" to briefly explore her innovative approach (especially in her development of a metaphysics of interconnectedness) and speculate on its implications for contemporary scholar-activists and other social actors.

An examination of her published and unpublished work from the late 1970s until her death indicates that Anzaldúa was developing this animistic philosophy for much of her life. She forged her metaphysics of interconnectedness through personal-cultural trauma and the desire to address and transform social injustice, enacting a hybrid, post-oppositional strategy. She did not entirely reject Cartesian and other status-quo stories, but worked through them in order to address social injustice at a root level—to decolonize and, thus, transform the worldview (ontology, epistemology) that, she believed, was foundational to social injustice.[4]

"Writing Notes H37, H47–H98" illustrates the intense self-reflection necessary for Anzaldúa's post-oppositional approach. In the face of her ongoing health crisis (diabetes, gastro-intestinal reflex, Charcot foot, neuropathy, blurred vision, thyroid malfunction, and insomnia) and intermittent depression, or what she describes in this document as her "particular black hole," Anzaldúa maintains (and, arguably, strengthens) her metaphysics of interconnectedness.[5] She turns *toward* it through her research, as she develops ways to live out her beliefs. In short, her philosophy is tested and endures.

I view this aspect of Anzaldúa's work as a type of empirical experimentation. Take for example the following assertion: "I'm addicted to self-pity and to suffering. I have to challenge the consensual beliefs that make us suffer and that we use to punish ourselves—through the form of self-rejection, guilt, shame, and anxiety."[6] Observe the direction in this trajectory as Anzaldúa ties inward with outward. She sees a problem in herself but doesn't dwell on this personal limitation. Rather, she shifts her focus to investigate the underlying paradigm and "cultural trance" which fosters this self-pity and impacts us all in various ways. As in "now let us shift," with its simultaneous "inner work" and "public acts" (seen both in the title and in Anzaldúa's movement through the seven stages of conocimiento), Anzaldúa uses her internal "spiritual crisis" as the grist for her philosophical mill. As she states in the section titled "LOSS":

> I became interested in meditation through depression and despair—I wanted something other. I was dissatisfied with what and who I was and so looked for this other. I searched for a state of peace, of love, of bliss, a state that would be better than what I had. I looked for meaning in what I found—in the states, in the experiences. I created descriptions, explanations and instructions. From these I created a philosophy, a spirituality.

Anzaldúa neither denies nor becomes paralyzed by self-despair, but instead uses it as an engine to invent an alternative worldview.

As part of this philosophical creation, Anzaldúa read widely in a variety of wisdom traditions. She believed that "[c]reating a bridge to ancient traditions of knowledge can help us live our lives more closely." To build this bridge, she combined scholarship with self-reflection and developed a belief system for herself and others. As she asserts in a February 16, 1999 entry:

> By pondering and reinterpreting cultural myths, I can explore human processes, stages of life, and learn to see myself and others and our life issues in different ways. I try to correlate psychotherapy, shamanism, science and philosophy, [and] spirituality to come up with patterns that inform the needs of human beings and reveal the Creative Life Force and Intelligence that permeates all living things by putting a 21st Century face on ancient myths. How people relate to this Creative Intelligence. Myths that speak to our conditions. I use affirmations, repetition of thoughts in the form of words to establish the belief system I want.

This statement—and "Writing Notes H37, H47–H98," more broadly—demonstrates four key characteristics of Anzaldúa's metaphysics of interconnectedness: its monism, its energetic materialism, its polytheism, and its dynamism. I briefly discuss these traits in the remainder of my section.

First, Anzaldúa's metaphysics is a panpsychic monism: Everything that exists (visible, invisible, semi-visible) is composed of one thing, which takes an infinite variety of forms. In "Writing Notes H37, H47–H98," Anzaldúa references this compositional substance in multiple ways: "the Creative Life Force and Intelligence," "The Universal Mind, the Creative Mind," "consciousness," "Spirit," "the universal Intelligence," "cosmic consciousness," "cosmic creativity," "Knower," "Gods." Despite each term's distinctiveness, they all underscore a type of fluid awareness. Significantly, Anzaldúa does not equate this awareness exclusively with human beings; it is "[n]ot human consciousness but cosmic consciousness or cosmic creativity." Cosmic consciousness exceeds us but is also found within us: "The Universal Mind, the Creative Mind is constantly acting as the collective and individual thoughts of all people." Anzaldúa distinguishes her philosophy from anthropomorphic theories that view humans as a type of culminating sentience: "Consciousness is woven into the fabric of the universe and not something that emerges as an accident after years of evolution. Not simply an epiphenomena as naturalists say."

Second, Anzaldúa's metaphysics of interconnectedness is an energetic materialism. She maintains that "[t]he material universe is not made up of things—it is only energy and lines of force continuing to produce temporary forms that are in a state of continuous flow." As this passage suggests, Anzaldúa does not deny materiality but instead redefines it in energetic terms. Third, this metaphysics is an immanent polytheism: "The distinction between 'out there' and 'in here' (within) is artificial. The same reality (of Gods) can be discovered within." And fourth, Anzaldúa's metaphysics is a dynamic, nondual process: "The watchers and the watch disappear and the watching the awareness is all. Awareness, and the object of awareness come together and consciousness is formed. Consciousness is an interaction . . . . Who we really are has no edge." Note that consciousness here is a verb, not a noun. It's action, doing, being aware. The opening paragraph of "now let us shift" illustrates this dialogic enactment, a consciousness-as-doing in which knowledge is produced through creative interaction between Anzaldúa, the surroundings, and language (the words which emerge as she tries to recount the experience). She illustrates philosopher Alva Noë's assertion that "[c]onsciousness of the world around us is something that we do: we enact it, with the world's help, in our dynamic living activities. It is not something that happens in us."

Anzaldúa's post-oppositional decolonizing process has important implications for social justice work, facilitating the formation of affinity-based coalitions and nepantlera politics. Indeed, it's possible that Anzaldúa's radically inclusive politics and nepantlera theory (developed in "now let us shift) were, in part, forged through these intellectual-spiritual excavations and others which we'll find in the notas.

"ENCHANTING THE WORLD" WITH WORDS: ANZALDÚAN WRITING AS TRANSPERSONAL ANIMIST PRAYER

Betsy Dahms

I approach "Writing Notes H37, H47–H98" as a liminal text. Downloaded from Anzaldúa's desktop folder on her writing laptop computer to be preserved in her archive at the University of Texas, Austin, the content of this folder is neither personal journal nor polished text ready for publication, but something in between. "Writing Notes H37, H47–H98" is organized by date and by bolded subheadings referencing authors, topics, and locations. When authors are listed, many of whom work with shamanism and psychology, the notes that follow are not direct citations properly punctuated, but rather Anzaldúa's notes on their texts, signaling a collaborative process of knowledge formation. Prompted by Anzaldúa's longstanding interest in archetypal psychology, especially the work of James Hillman,[7] I explore the author's relationship with language and subjectivity in her published work and archival folder "Writing Notes H37, H47–H98" to posit her writing as an attempt to ensoul the world via transpersonal animist prayer.

Shamanic references and explicit mentions of the soul are frequent throughout Anzaldúa's work, as is the idea of the liminal space of borderlands. Archetypal psychology, as described by Hillman, aims at "the development of a sense of soul, the middle ground of psychic realities, and the method of therapy is the cultivation of the imagination" (*Archetypal Psychology* 4). Positioning the soul in the liminal space between body and spirit, Hillman argues for the importance of the imagination and the primacy of images. The imagination and images are essential to "making soul" in Hillman's articulation of recovering soul, a principal objective in archetypal psychology. Hillman argues that the loss of soul, both individual and communal, has lead Western society to concentrate and amplify the individual subject, which manifests in egocentrism.[8] Anzaldúa discusses the connection of images to her writing in *Borderlands/La Frontera* when exploring what she calls "The Shamanic State" of writing; she declares, "But now I realize it is my job, my calling, to traffic in images" (69–70). Furthermore, some of Anzaldúa's theories are illustrated as images in her archive as well as published in *The Gloria Anzaldúa Reader*. And we need only remember the title of her second anthology, *Making Face, Making Soul/Haciendo Caras: Creative and Critical Perspectives by Feminist of Color*, to see Anzaldúa's preoccupation with the soul.

Academic discussions of soul are tricky, but this short investigation does not intend to debate the existence or merits of soul. Instead, by tracing Anzaldúa's use of the soul and connecting the importance of images and soul to both Anzaldúa and Hillman, I explore Hillman's influence on Anzaldúan language and selfhood. According to Hillman, archetypal psychology's function is to find the logos for the psyche or "to provide soul with an adequate account of itself" (*Archetypal Psychology* 16). In "Writing Notes H37, H47–H98," Anzaldúa makes copious notes on shamanism, concluding that a shaman's task was to ensoul the world, "to enchant the world." Writing in the tradition of the shaman, Anzaldúa confronts the daunting tasks of recovering her individual soul and, in the process, recovering the world's soul.

Anzaldúa explored the process of recovering individual and collective soul in her 1999 essay, "Putting Coyolxauhqui Together," by rewriting the Aztec myth of Coyolxauhqui. The quest to define selfhood, however, was a lifelong process for Anzaldúa as her theorization of selfhood was dynamic and always in flux. According to Hillman, "there must be a shift in cosmos so that one actually feels an expanded sense of identity" (*Healing Fiction* 124). Following the trajectory of Anzaldúa's theorizing over the course of her life, it is evident that she expanded her concept of self from identity politics to cosmic or planetary citizenship. In "now let us shift," Anzaldúa states, "You share a category of identity wider than any social position or racial label" (558). Anzaldúa's use of second person narration allows the reader to see how the author accounts for her multiple subjectivities and her connection with the reader. Perhaps building on Jung's theory that "every personality is essentially multiple," Anzaldúa explores plurality within the individual (Hillman, *Archetypal Psychology* 51). Expanding her sense of identity necessarily includes, but goes beyond, the human, as she records research notes from Margaret Bullitt-Jonas, a practitioner of environmental spirituality in the Episcopal Church and from environmentalist James A. Swan in "Writing Notes H37, H47–H98." Anzaldúa's connection to the environment is evident in her omnipresent references to the sea and water in general. In her expansive and expanding view of self, Anzaldúa remarks: "Who we really are has no edge." This awareness is not selfish transcendence, but rather seeks community, both human and other than human. From this point, she moves to connect the individual and the individual soul to the world soul, the *anima mundi*. This posthuman connection expands to encompass all animisms in an ensouled world.

Anzaldúa's animism and expanding consciousness inform her writing process, and her personal journey to "know thyself" is directed outward to her readers, encouraging them to travel a similar path of discovery. She instructs herself in "Writing Notes H37, H47–H98," "WRITING TECHNIQUES … beginning at the inside and proceeding out." Viewing the world as ensouled, I argue, motivates Anzaldúa's writing. Through her writing, Anzaldúa reminds herself and her readers of our interconnection. Yet this is not a one-sided lesson from teacher to student or author to reader. This process is complicated by a shared consciousness, which Anzaldúa imagines as el cenote, making the process of consciousness individual AND collective. This two-way movement of conocimiento is stressed in "now let us shift" when Anzaldúa insists on "inner work" and "public acts." As such, readers must co-create the reality Anzaldúa presents in her writing.

Referencing the linguistic work of Ferdinand de Saussure in that "all of our language is based on differentiation," Anzaldúa is aware of linguistic poststructuralism, but seems to employ language to connect, rather than differentiate. As Anzaldúa focuses on both her own material reality and material reality in general in her writing, I argue, she also engages language (verbally, in the form of words; physically, in the form of printed words; and mentally, in her thoughts) as material and materializing. She works through this idea in "Writing Notes H37, H47–H98": "With my words/thoughts I create everything that happens in my life—or at least I co-create everything that happens." Following this monist, new materialist view of language, Anzaldúa posits, "We channel meanings into our bodies, negative meanings can kill." This statement raises the question: If negative meanings can kill, can positive meanings heal?

Rather than herbs or pharmaceuticals, Anzaldúa's medicine of choice is words. Keating's statement that "Anzaldúa approached her writing like a ritual or a prayer" ("Reading Gloria Anzaldúa" 7) aligns with Anzaldúa's research in psychology and points to Anzaldúan writing as transpersonal prayer. Citing the work of Larry Dossey, which proposes that "through prayer people have changed biological functions, metabolic activities," Anzaldúa explores the material effects of language on our bodily processes ("Writing Notes H37, H47–H98"). With its emphasis on healing, Anzaldúa's writing reads as a prayer with the intention of healing both the author's wounds and the world's. This simultaneous healing is possible because the individual soul and the world soul, in Hillman's terms, are intricately connected: "[I]n Neoplatonic thought, soul could be spoken of as both my soul and world soul, and what was true of one was true of both" (*Archetypal Psychology* 11). I do not intend to limit Anzaldúa's writing by pointing to the connections with transpersonal and archetypal psychology, but rather I point to these influences in an attempt to understand the multilayered and far-reaching work her words do in readers and, thus, the work her words do in the world. While cognizant of intentional fallacy, I am interested in the possible goals Anzaldúa had for her words and how these goals affected the way she wrote. Reading Anzaldúa's writing as a reminder to ensoul or resoul the world, the reader may shift consciousness along with the author and, furthermore, might conceive of the power of language differently. Hillman's archetypal psychology highlights the power of the image in meaning-making, reminding us that "experience is never raw or brute; it is always constructed by images which are revealed in [...] narrative" (*Archetypal Psychology* 45). The narrative that Anzaldúa creates seems to intrigue many different types of readers, perhaps because it speaks to familiar images and encourages psychic healing.

Because we seldom return to the images of the soul, Hillman suggests that the soul wants healing fictions. His approach to psychology as fiction, or narrative, highlights the fictional nature of subjectivity and, instead of trivializing psychology as merely fiction, illuminates the fictional nature of reality. It is fitting, then, that Anzaldúa would use fiction to share soul and co-construct reality. In a 1998–1999 interview with Keating, Anzaldúa addresses the link between thoughts, words, and the power of prayer:

> [W]e must have very concrete, precisely worded intentions of what we want the world to be like, what we want to be like. We have to first put the changes that we want made into words or images. We have to visualize them, write them, communicate them to other people and stick with committing those intentions, those goals, those visions. Before any change can take place you have to say and intend them. It's like a prayer, you have to commit yourself to your visions. (*Interviews/Entrevistas* 290)

In reading "Writing Notes H37, H47–H98" as a liminal text that elucidates Anzaldúa's thought process, it is important to draw attention to a statement located under the subheading of "Self & consciousness," wedged between her notes on Larry Dossey, cited above on the medical effects of (remote) prayer, and Jean Houston, who worked on the Human Potential Project and LSD research. Anzaldúa writes: "There are three levels of healing: 1) mechanistic, drug healing, 2) working with images, meaning, 3) remote praying and other funny business (paralogical, paradoxical)." Here we catch a glimpse of Anzaldúa's thought process, as she was both intrigued by, but perhaps still skeptical of, the "funny business" of remote prayer and the implications of expanded consciousness. My analysis of Anzaldúan writing as transpersonal animist prayer speaks to Anzaldúa's metaphysics of radical interconnection, her interest in Hillman's archetypal psychology, and perhaps what Anzaldúa viewed as our communal task. Writing in the tradition of the shaman, Anzaldúa works to ensoul the world through her words and her actions. Anzaldúa was still working with/through this idea in "Writing Notes H37, H47–H98," but her essay "now let us shift" begins with an offering and ends with "ritual…prayer…blessing…for transformation" (574), suggesting a possible adoption of the "funny business" of remote prayer.

EMBODIED AND EMBEDDED:[9] ANZALDÚA'S INTRICATE THEORY OF THE SELF

Kelli D. Zaytoun

In the preface to *Borderlands/La Frontera*, Gloria Anzaldúa unapologetically acknowledges that the "inner life of the Self" was one of her "preoccupations." According to Anzaldúa, selfhood is vital to social justice work; she says, "You make the inner changes first, and then you make the outer changes. I've always believed that" (*Interviews* 101). In a time when "the self" is held suspect—and rightly so—by anti-essentialists, postmodern and postcolonial thinkers, and other critics of Cartesian selfhood, Anzaldúa does not dismiss the self, but transforms it, honoring our complex inner experience as individuals, while, at the same time, dismantling modern conceptions of individual personhood and subjectivity. Analyzing "Writing Notes H37, H47–H98" with new materialist lenses and the shamanism that inspired Anzaldúa offers new evidence for Anzaldúa's intricate theory of self, its invaluable place in critical conversations on subjectivity, the concept of the individual, and the "work for transformation" to which Anzaldúa was so fervently dedicated ("now let us shift" 574).

To Anzaldúa, the self is always rooted in and constituted through relationships not only with humans but also with nonhuman matter, and holds capacities beyond those conceived of by Western belief systems. Of our rootedness, she says in "Writing Notes H37, H47–H98," "We cannot function separately from the system in which we are embedded—we can't do to nature that [which] we don't do to ourselves or do to other nations because it will boomerang back to us." This statement might be read as consistent with new materialist approaches,[10] for instance, with a posthumanism that rejects both the uncritical wielding of human supremacy over nonhuman life forms and matter, and the privileging of the rational human thought and transcendence associated with liberal humanism. Yet Anzaldúa also honors individual persons, which is still narrowly considered the realm of humanism, in a complex rendering of the power of the imagination and other psychological and communicative capacities of embodied, embedded selfhood. Anzaldúa helps us to envision new understandings of selfhood that retain an interest in the psychological even as they expand its traditional, liberal limits.[11] We can turn to Anzaldúa for an example of how to recast the individual in new terms outside of humanistic unity, as Barad suggests we do when she says, "'Individuals' do not *not* exist, but are not individually determinate. Rather, 'individuals' only exist within phenomena (particular [...] materializing relations) in their ongoing iteratively intra-active reconfiguring" [emphasis mine](77). Through such intra-actions, individuals, as Barad sees them, are "particular material articulations of the world" in particular moments in time and location (77). To dismiss the individual, to dismiss the self, or how one experiences being a single person with an inner life of thoughts, imagination, dreams, memories, and emotions, is to miss out on a large part of Anzaldúa's vision of "work for transformation" ("now let us shift" 574).

Anzaldúa's work on the self provides, in part, a way of thinking about the self as complex, multiplicitous, unfixed, and decolonial, but not necessarily ontologically plural. To her, the self, though made up of multiple components, maintained a sense of consistency that was bound to and participated in a larger constituent. Indeed, Anzaldúa was a monist, as Keating describes. Of all the claims Anzaldúa makes of the self in "Writing Notes H37, H47–H98," this point is the most clear. She believed not just in a self among selves or in the "knower [that] is always with you" ("now let us shift" 20), but she also believed that this self participated in what she called in these notas "the great pattern of existence." She says, "Something about us is omnipresent, infinite in space and time, eternal and immortal. Something that behaves like a soul that doesn't die with the body"; she refers to "a plan greater than ourselves" and "the totality of existence." Her theory of the tie that binds self with surroundings is consistent with Rosi Braidotti's take on a "contemporary monism" involving "zoe" or "a dynamic and generative force" (86) that is "vitalist, [and] self-organizing" (82). Anzaldúa says, "I feel like I am being hammered and chiseled into shape by the experiences that my soul guides me to. It has a plan for me." On the process of being shaped, she says, "Consciousness is an interaction," a continuous interaction that extends beyond human interaction and participates with a creative source.

Anzaldúa departs from Braidotti in her emphasis on the materially transformative power of language; Braidotti claims that the posthuman is not postmodern because it is not "deconstructivist" or "linguistically framed" (51).

I argue that Anzaldúan subjectivity is materialist, vitalist, and embodied, but also deconstructivist and powerfully shaped, in concrete ways, by language and discourse. Influenced by nagualismo, an Olmec-inspired shamanistic belief system and practice that held that thought and language were functions of the body and had the power to transform material realities, Anzaldúa maintained that a person's imagination was a significant concrete vehicle for enacting palpable change.[12] Contrary to the Cartesian cut that splits mind and matter, thoughts and bodies are always linked for the Anzaldúan subject. She says in her notas, "[...] the energies that bring forth fantasy come from the organs of the body." Invoking and articulating the imagination, therefore, is a primary function of Anzaldúan subjectivity. Writing, of course, what she called "a visceral activity," becomes a primary practice for her in this regard, a practice in which her readers participate. Fantasies, dreams, thoughts, words in the head as well as on the page, take material forms to her: "Suddenly a thought, an insight blazes a trail through our body mind like a jet leaving a vapor line in the sky, like the sudden clap of a wave to our body"; and, "All maintenance begins with my thoughts for it is thoughts that shape the form my realities take. With my words/thoughts I create everything that happens in my life—or at least I co-create everything." In terms of its embeddedness, the self therefore participates with the co-constitutive force of language and thought in its making.

Shamanism's influence on Anzaldúa also informed her monism and animism. In these notas she says, "Animism: everything is alive, goes back to the shamans. The interconnection of all life. One talks to the rocks, to the spirits. See spirits as mind creations or as separate life forms. It depends on your worldview." Shamanism is raised here as a critical, often-overlooked, source of inspiration for much of Anzaldúa's theorizing and worldviews. Nagualismo, in particular, inspired Anzaldúa's theorizing on "la naguala," the function of selfhood that "arouses the awareness that beneath individual separateness lies a deeper inter-relatedness"; la naguala, the shapeshifter, is a physical, cognitive, emotional, and spiritual practice that transforms boundaries between the self and other human and nonhuman matter, a shift to a "larger vision, a less-defended identity," that of nepantleras ("now let us shift" 571).[13] Her concept of la naguala helps to explain her position on the self as multiplicitous and decolonial. By way of the imagination, the naguala invokes a shift in the self, a temporary merger of the self with the emotions of other people, with the characters about which the writer writes, and with a variety of states of consciousness, like dreams, for example (569). Anzaldúa's choice to write in second person—which she does in "now let us shift" and "Putting Coyolxauhqui Together," the two essays in which she elaborates most on the naguala—suggests a complex multiplicitous and unfixed selfhood in which the reader and the resistant oppressed participate.

Lastly, Anzaldúan selfhood can be read as a decolonial project, an attempt to decolonize the Western subject-self and provide new visions for coalition work and resistance to oppression. As Norma Alarcón has stated, Anzaldúa's "telos was a quest for personal and political decolonization" (189). In her description of conocimiento, Anzaldúa provides a rich and complex theory of an embodied and embedded self in relationship that honors the potentially transformative work that is initiated by the inner life and imaginations of persons; at the same time, she subverts the modern understanding of individual personhood. As Anzaldúa doesn't "try to prove nature's ensoulment by offering logical arguments [or] references to Western philosophical/theological traditions," as Keating stated, Anzaldúa doesn't try to prove "the self" through such traditions either. For Anzaldúa, the self is vitalist, embodied, embedded, multiplicitous, and decolonizing. Given the complexity and enormity of the self, one can see how these notas provided for Anzaldúa not only "sites of knowledge creation," as we assert in our introduction, but sites of self-creation as well.

(IN)CONCLUSION

As our experiment in three voices demonstrates, focusing so specifically on a single unpublished document from Anzaldúa's extensive archives can yield a wide variety of insights and perspectives. We each brought our specific scholarly and personal interests to this project and used these interests as we interacted with Anzaldúa's words, inviting her words to expand on our views. In so doing, we enact a relational, dialogic method that demonstrates the rich potential in Anzaldúa's vast unpublished work.

We would like to thank Robyn Henderson-Espinoza for their contribution to the creation and development of this essay.

NOTES

1 For a more extensive discussion of Anzaldúa's writing process, see Keating's "Re-Envisioning Coyolxauhqui."

2 For an early discussion of Anzaldúa's metaphysics of interconnectedness see Keating, "Risking the Personal"; for a later, more developed discussion, see Keating, "Re-Envisioning Coyolxauhqui."

3 The term "animism" was coined by Edward Tyler and used to represent a type of backward "primitivism." For a discussion of animism's history, see Graham Harvey's *Animism.*

4 See, for example, Anzaldúa's assertion in *Borderlands/La Frontera:* "In trying to become 'objective,' Western culture made 'objects' of things and people when it distanced itself from them, thereby losing 'touch' with them. This dichotomy is the root of all violence. Not only was the brain split into two functions but so was reality. Thus people who inhabit both realities are forced to live in the interface between the two, forced to become adept at switching modes" (37).

5 See Appendix 2, "Anzaldúa's Health," in Anzaldúa's *Light in the Dark/Luz en lo oscuro*, for a more detailed discussion of Anzaldúa's health during these years.

6 All unreferenced quotations throughout our chapter are from Anzaldúa's "Writing Notes H37, H47–H98."

7 Anzaldúa recorded reading James Hillman as early as July 15, 1979, and her work shows a sustained interested in his writing (Personal communication with AnaLouise Keating).

8 Anzaldúa described the loss of soul as "susto." See, for instance, "Light in the Dark" 27.

9 Rosi Braidotti frequently uses the language of "embodied and embedded" in her work on posthumanist subjectivity. However, I borrow the language from Anzaldúa, whose mention of embeddedness and attention to the body throughout these writing notes inspired my use of the terms.

10 The term "new materialism" emerged in the late 1990s to refer to approaches that critique and expand traditional notions of matter/materiality and distinctions between the human body, human experience (including thought), and its material context. See Diana Coole and Samantha Frost's *New Materialisms: Ontology, Agency, and Politics* and Rick Dolphijn and Iris van der Tuin's *New Materialism: Interviews and Cartographies*, anthologies that showcase the work of theorists who engage with what is referred to as the new materialist turn.

11 I want to credit Mariana Ortega, whose writing on the self has a strong influence on my thinking about Anzaldúa's work and on my own theorizing on self. Her ideas about self and ontological pluralism, in particular, informed the assertions I put forth in this paper. See her book *In-Between: Latina Feminist Phenomenology, Multiplicity, and the Self.*

12 AnaLouise Keating explores the material effects of language, including evidence for Anzaldúa's linking of language and imagination to physical outcomes in "Speculative Realism, Visionary Pragmatism, and Poet-Shamanic Aesthetics in Gloria Anzaldúa—and Beyond" and in "Living (with) Language."

13 I offer a more detailed discussion of Anzaldúa's la naguala in Zaytoun, "'Now Let Us Shift' the Subject: Tracing the Path and Posthumanist Implications of La Naguala/The Shapeshifter in the Works of Gloria Anzaldúa."

WORKS CITED

Alarcón, Norma. "Anzaldúan Textualities: A Hermeneutic of the Self and the Coyolxauhqui Imperative." *El Mundo Zurdo 3*. Eds. Larissa Mercado-López, Sonia Saldívar-Hull, and Antonia Castañeda. San Francisco: Aunt Lute, 2013. 189–208. Print.

Anzaldúa, Gloria E. *Borderlands/La Frontera: The New Mestiza*. San Francisco: Spinsters/Aunt Lute, 1987. Print.

---. *Interviews/Entrevistas*. Ed. AnaLouise Keating. New York: Routledge, 2000. Print.

---. "now let us shift...the path of conocimiento...inner work, public acts." *this bridge we call home: radical visions for transformation*. Eds. Gloria E. Anzaldúa and AnaLouise Keating. New York: Routledge, 2002. 540–78.

---. "Writing Notes H37, H47–98." Box 103, Folder 4, Gloria Evangelina Anzaldúa Papers. Nettie Lee Benson Latin American Collection, University of Texas, Austin.

Anzaldúa, Gloria E. and AnaLouise Keating, eds. *this bridge we call home: radical visions for transformation*. New York: Routledge, 2002. Print.

Barad, Karen. *Meeting the Universe Halfway: Quantum Physics and the Entanglement of Matter and Meaning*. Durham, NC: Duke U P, 2007. Print.

---. "Intra-actions." Interview by Adam Kleinman. *Mousse* 34.13 (2012): 76–81. Web. 5 May 2015.

Bost, Suzanne. "Messy Archives and Materials That Matter: Making Knowledge with the Gloria Anzaldúa Papers." *PMLA* 130.3 (2015): 615–30. Print.

Braidotti, Rosi. *The Posthuman*. Cambridge: Polity, 2013. Print.

Coole, Diana, and Samantha Frost, eds. *New Materialisms: Ontology, Agency, and Politics*. Durham: Duke UP, 2010. Print.

Dolphijn, Rick, and Iris van der Tuin. *New Materialism: Interviews and Cartographies*. Ann Arbor: Open Humanities Press, 2012. Print.

Harvey, Graham. *Animism: Respecting the Living World*. New York: Columbia UP, 2005. Google Play Book.

Hillman, James. *Archetypal Psychology: A Brief Account*. Dallas: Spring Publications, Inc. 1985. Print.

---. *Healing Fiction*. Woodstock, CN: Spring Publications, Inc., 1983. Print.

Keating, AnaLouise. "Living (with) Language." *Hypatia* 30.3 (2015): 628–635. Web. 21 Sept. 2015.

---. "Reading Gloria Anzaldúa, Reading Ourselves...Complex Intimacies, Intricate Connections." *The Gloria Anzaldúa Reader*. Gloria E. Anzaldúa. Ed. AnaLouise Keating Durham, NC: Duke University Press, 2009. 1–15. Print.

---. "Re-envisioning Coyolxauhqui, Decolonizing Reality: Anzaldúa's Twenty-First-Century Imperative." *Light in the Dark/Luz en lo oscuro: Rewriting Identity, Spirituality, Reality*. Gloria E. Anzaldúa. Durham, NC: Duke University Press, 2015. ix–xxxviii. Print.

---. "Risking the Personal: An Introduction." *Interviews/Entrevistas*. Gloria E. Anzaldúa. Ed. AnaLouise Keating. New York: Routledge, 2000. 1–15. Print.

---."Speculative Realism, Visionary Pragmatism, and Poet-Shaman Aesthetics in Gloria Anzaldúa—and Beyond." *WSQ: Women's Studies Quarterly* 40.3–4 (2012): 51–69.

Noë, Alva. *Out of Our Heads: Why You Are Not Your Brain, and Other Lessons from the Biology of Consciousness*. New York: Hill and Wang, 2009. Kindle Edition.

Ortega, Mariana, *In-Between: Latina Feminist Phenomenology, Multiplicity, and the Self.* New York: SUNY Press, 2016. Print.

Zaytoun, Kelli. "'Now Let Us Shift' the Subject: Tracing the Path and Posthumanist Implications of La Naguala/The Shapeshifter in the Works of Gloria Anzaldúa." *MELUS* 40.4 (2015). Web.

MARASSA AND MESTIZA CONSCIOUSNESS

COMPARING DANTICAT AND ANZALDÚA

MICHAEL REYES SALAS

Contemporary writings of diasporic and indigenous women of color across the Americas that thematize healing often possess threads of connection with respect to syncretic spiritual practices. These interrelations lead me to question how ritual symbolism, a transcultural legacy of the borderlands, plays into the creation of selfhood. This avenue of inquiry informs my study of worldviews that express relations to non-human life in Gloria Anzaldúa's non-fiction writings and the historical fiction narratives of Edwidge Danticat. As I draw this comparison, I aim to explore the boundaries of borderlands. Some guiding questions are: Can notions of borderlands theory become overly generative? Are there transcultural exceptions to Anzaldúan borderlands?

Since the borderlands of Haiti/Dominican Republic (DR) possess histories of struggle distinct from the México/US context, I proceed with this comparison cautiously. Although the colonial history and the development of capitalist nation-states vary within these countries, the more heavily militarized countries in each coupling, the DR and the US, respectively, possess xenophobic attitudes that underlie their common settler-colonialist policies. The violent founding of these racist nation-states has issued reverberations of violence throughout the hemisphere, to which women of color have been particularly susceptible.

Anzaldúa and Danticat are bound by their reclamation of ancestral spiritual traditions in efforts to convey ways of knowing conducive to healing the wounds generated by this violence.

While Danticat approaches African-inspired traditions, mainly Haitian Vodou, as a fiction writer, Anzaldúa approaches *curanderismo* as a practitioner. As a result of colonialism—the DR as France's *Saint Domingue* and México as Spain's *Nueva España*—both writers also engage with folk-Catholic traditions. Reading Danticat and Anzaldúa in tandem, we encounter religiosity through *lwas*, saints, and spirits. Both writers demonstrate cultural survival against xenophobic nation-state campaigns of terror. Consequently, the narratives of Danticat and Anzaldúa point toward epistemological shifts of consciousness.

While Anzaldúa articulates a sense of mestiza consciousness in *Borderlands/La Frontera* (1987), recent scholarship has drawn attention to how the concept of *marassa* consciousness is a useful method of interpreting Danticat's works (Bragg 169). In spite of these overlapping themes, several critics view Anzaldúa and Danticat as doing completely different, even antithetical, work in their writing (Shemak 158–159). I argue that mestiza and *marassa* consciousness each serve to textually represent a subjectivity of transition constantly enduring border-crossing experiences both literally and figuratively. My cross-cultural examination of *marassa* and mestiza consciousness creates bridges among writers of colors whose worldviews resemble one another.

La facultad and *el conocimiento* are premised on the notion that we are bound to *la madre naturaleza*. As a condition of being, mestiza consciousness is "a state of perpetual transition," which posits plurality as a virtue (Anzaldúa 100). Influenced by José Vasconcelos's notion of *la raza cósmica* as a biological phenomena, a syntheticrace, produced in the violent crossings of European, Indian, and African blood, Anzaldúa's own notion of mestizaje encompasses cultural, spiritual, and epistemological mixing as a source of empowerment. The symbols of mestizaje come to embody dedichotomization, the undoing of binaries. This holistic feature of mestiza consciousness activates strength where purists see disorder. Anzaldúan mestiza consciousness possesses avenues for healing via its strategic capacity to challenge structural violence.

In the introduction to the 25th anniversary edition of *Borderlands/La Frontera*, Norma Cantú and Aída Hurtado acknowledge the specific conditions that Anzaldúa lived in. They explain that she theorized "as the daughter of farmworkers living in extreme poverty in South Texas" (7). Cantú and Hurtado also acknowledge that "[borderlands] theory also applies to any kind of social, economic, sexual, and political dislocation" (7). From this position, the regional particularities of Anzaldúa's borderlands do not make her case exclusive or exceptional. From the non-fiction circumstances of Anzaldúa's upbringing to

Danticat's historical fiction, the broadness of borderlands activates resonances across the Americas:

In the Borderlands
    you are the battleground
    where enemies are kin to each other;
    you are at home, a stranger,
    the border disputes have been settled
    the volley of shots have shattered the truce
    you are wounded, lost in action
    dead, fighting back;
. . . .
To survive the Borderlands
    you must live *sin fronteras*
    be a crossroads. (Anzaldúa 216–217)

This excerpt captures a sense of borderlands ambiguities, such as being a stranger at home, "dead" and "fighting back," while also conveying the sense of active crossings on a battleground. The embodied experience of being at a crossroads is an attribute of subjectivities formed in the borderlands. This poetic description serves as an intersectional profile of the borderlands in Danticat's narrative fiction. The Caribbean borderlands of Hispaniola, as depicted by Danticat's historical fiction *The Farming of Bones* (1998), are characterized by displacement and exile. Danticat's itinerant textual subjectivities often have their vantage point in the Haitian/Dominican borderlands, where "enemies are kin to each other" (Anzaldúa 216).

The protagonist of *Farming of Bones* is Amabelle, a young Haitian woman working as a servant at a Dominican hacienda situated in the small town of Alegría. Amabelle becomes an orphan after she witnesses her parents drown in the Massacre River (which marks the separation of Haiti and the DR). Shortly after, she begins working at the hacienda owned by Señor Pico Duarte, a colonel in the Dominican dictator Rafael Leonidas Trujillo's military, who lives there with his father-in-law, Papi (aka Don Ignacio), and his wife, Señora Valencia. While working for this land-owning Dominican family of Spanish descent, a social elite during this time, Amabelle becomes the companion of Señora Valencia and midwife of her twins, Rosalinda y Rafael. Amabelle also develops a romantic relationship with a fieldworker, Sebastien Onius, who is disappeared during the beginnings of the 1937 Parsley Massacre.[1] Due to the wave of anti-black violence, Amabelle crosses the border into Haiti to seek refuge.

In the *Farming of Bones*, Danticat depicts *marassa* consciousness in subtle ways. For example, she opens the text with an epigraph that references a *lwa* (ancestral and nature spirits in Haitian Voudou tradition). Amabelle dedicates the story in the following way: "In confidence to you, Metrès Dlo, Mother of the Rivers." By honoring the *lwa* Metrès Dlo, an iteration of Ezili Danto,[2] Amabelle acknowledges her own spiritual reality based in the African-inspired traditions of Haitian Voudou. Danticat's representations of Voudou draw on the multifaceted traditions it is composed of, which "existed as profound religious systems before contact with Europeans and remained cosmologically intact afterwards," even if often rewritten for a nationalist purpose (Bellegarde-Smith and Michel 463). Instead of creating a teleological overemphasis of Voudou's role in the Haitian national narrative, Danticat evades functionalist representations of Voudou as cultural resistance to instead create a textual world conducive to the survival of Voudou worldviews, which are informed by interaction with non-human life such as a river spirit.

VèVè A. Clark's influential study "Developing Diaspora Literacy and Marasa Consciousness" elaborates how *marassa* consciousness informs contemporary Caribbean textual production. Clark situates *marassa* consciousness in the historical context of the early twentieth-century "epistemological break away from the predominance of Euro-American influences on black texts" happening in the Caribbean literary scene (9). This shift prompted Caribbean writers to create new literary forms, resulting in authors drawing from vernacular traditions of Vodoun ceremonies (and other indigenous rituals) and developing what Clark calls a *marassa* principle to engage in African diaspora criticism. The writing that exhibits *marassa* consciousness "points to the transformation of cultural oppositions in plantation societies [...] [although] relief from contradictions was certainly not guaranteed" (13). This emphasis on inner conflict in *marassa* consciousness is what becomes the nexus that links Danticat and Anzaldúa.

The *marassa jumeaux* figure in *Farming of Bones* appears when Rosalinda and Rafael are born as divine twins. The omen of a twin birth is compounded by Amabelle's observation that Rafael's umbilical cord was wrapped around the neck of Rosalinda at birth, "as if the other one tried to strangle her" (19). Ironically, although Doctor Javier discloses his anxiety about Rosalinda's health to Amabelle, it is actually Señor Pico and Señora Valencia's firstborn son, Rafi, who "stopped breathing" soon after being born. Doctor Javier later admits, "I thought Rosalinda was the one in danger, but he was the one whose strength failed" (90). It bears mentioning that the infant's death takes place in the context of Señor Pico's recent hit-and-run incident, in which reckless driving on the road while returning home after receiving news that his wife was giving birth resulted in the death of Joël, the only son of Kongo, a local Haitian farmworker. Consequently, Rosalinda becomes an only child. Within this plantation society context, Danticat engages *marassa* to point to transformation in social relations as the patriarchal family genealogy is disrupted by Rafi's death and Rosalinda's survival.

Marassa consciousness—and its association with divine twins—is also evident in Danticat's novel *Breath, Eyes, Memory* (1994). Set in present-day Brooklyn, Sophie, a twelve-year old Haitian immigrant, arrives from Haiti to reunite with her mother, Martine Cacao, whom she had not seen since infancy. Sophie soon discovers that Martine suffers chronic nightmares. Afterwards, Martine confesses the source of her nightmares: the trauma of Sophie having been conceived through rape. In *Breath, Eyes, Memory*, stories are embedded on the bodies of women characters. During her adolescence, Martine begins to police Sophie's virginity by "testing" her hymen, a form of abuse she learned from Sophie's grandmother. As Martine "tests" Sophie, she recounts a tale of the *marassas* in an effort to warn Sophie that pursuing relations with a man would result in giving up a lifetime with her mother (84–85). In this way, Martine transmits intergenerational trauma to Sophie. In the case of *Breath, Eyes, Memory*, the divine twins are mother and daughter. After seeking therapy at a sex-phobia group, Sophie intensifies her efforts at healing by returning to Haiti.

Although *Farming of Bones* and *Breath, Eyes, Memory* are both fictional texts, the historical element of *Farming of Bones* calls attention to exile during *El Corte*, while *Breath, Eyes, Memory* explores contemporary intergenerational trauma. Anzaldúa's non-fiction prose in *Borderlands/La Frontera* similarly possesses both historical reference points with regard to colonial history and ongoing struggles faced in contemporary society. Instead of creating a narrative with fictional characters, Anzaldúa's writing references herself along with relatives, ancestors, and spirits. While Danticat's text is primarily in English, her prose is interspersed with French and Haitian Creole. Overall, a borderlands consciousness articulated via prose becomes the commensurable through line that links the fiction and nonfiction of Danticat and Anzaldúa.

The transcultural applicability of Anzaldúa's borderlands theory is evident in its detailed textual account of the impacts that accompany straddling several different cultures. As a queer Chicana activist and writer who grew up near the Texas-México border, Anzaldúa's literary style blurs the content/form binary. The poetics of *Borderlands* are emblematic of the transversal self-identity Anzaldúa generates: at times it is autobiographical, historical, and the prose often turns into poetry written in verse. More linguistically varied than Danticat's prose style, Anzaldúa's writing deliberately operates on several linguistic registers, from English, Español, Spanglish to *Nahuatl*, as she conscientiously writes for a multilingual readership. This style, which reconfigures fragments of contemporary and precolonial cultures, represents one way in which Anzaldúa overcomes the dispossession and violence experienced at the border.

In contemporary textual creations of diasporic and indigenous women subjectivities across the Americas, the struggle of intergenerational cultural transmission of empowerment is a perpetual challenge. The embodied conflicts found in the above quote from Anzaldúa's "To live in the Borderlands means you" include: being a stranger at home, being dead and fighting back, and living *sin fronteras* in spaces defined by their borders. These experiences necessitate the exploration of healing by breaking "the silence around female sexual victimization" (Bragg 179). Anzaldúa and Danticat construct subjectivities from the figures of mestiza and *marassa* to inform the worldviews evident in their literature, which critically confront the focal point where patriarchal systems of oppression, racialization, and colonization meet. Instead of being taken down by this violence, survivance pervades the texts produced by these authors. References to stories from diasporic and indigenous vernacular traditions represent their efforts to continue bearing *el conocimiento* of ancestral ways of knowing.

The plurality of mestizaje and mestiza consciousness has opened up room for their critiques. One example is in the 2011 book *Asylum Speakers: Caribbean Refugees and Testimonial Discourse* by April Shemak, who analyzes Anzaldúa's theories in relation to Danticat's representations of the borderlands. Shemak interprets Anzaldúa's "celebration" of the borderlands as a site of empowerment as too facile and misleading a depiction, while crediting Danticat with challenging such premature celebrations (159). Shemak accuses Anzaldúa of romanticizing and idealizing mestizaje by "construct[ing] a stagnant, mystified indigeneity [...] [that] can be (and has been) manipulated by nation-states to reproduce deleterious ethnic/racial formations to bolster nationalism" (158). With reference to her studies on the Dominican Republic, Shemak claims that Anzaldúa loses sight of how indigeneity is co-opted by Latin American governments that foster mestizaje nationalism.

For a critique specifically about Anzaldúa's usage of indigeneity, María Josefina Saldaña-Portillo argues that, since Anzaldúa is a first-world minority and not a third-world subaltern, "when she resuscitates this particular representation of indigenous subjectivity to be incorporated into contemporary mestiza consciousness, she too does so to the exclusion and, indeed, erasure of contemporary indigenous subjectivity" (282). She frames Anzaldúa's work through the theory of internal colonialism and is especially skeptical about claims made by Anzaldúa regarding "Chicanos [being] originally and secondarily indigenous to the Southwest" (27). Grappling with these critiques has taught me about where I position myself in this discourse on indigeneity.

As I reviewed the arguments of Shemak and Saldaña-Portillo, I found a fundamental dissonance between their understanding of Anzaldúa's mestizaje and my own. These critics equate Anzaldúa's mestizaje with the mestizaje exemplified in the prevailing statecraft that has resulted in Latin American exceptionalism (a claim that countries where miscegenation has prevailed and institutionalized racial segregation has not been established are racial democracies). In these efforts to detail the pitfalls of Anzaldúa's vision, Anzaldúa is framed as a champion of colonial miscegenation and of the erasure of contemporary indigenous subjectivities.[3] What I infer from this skewed perception of Anzaldúa's vision is a narrow-minded conception of what constitutes indigeneity. Implying that the mestizo's claim to indigeneity silences the non-mestizo indigenous subjectivity privileges a narrow biological concept of indigenous identity. Such totalizing notions lead us to fetishize genomic science and reinforce our reliance on a blood quantum metric to answer the questions: Who among us is a settler? Who among us is indigenous? These notions of indigeneity draw attention away from other significant elements of indigenous identity, such as the formation and consistent nurturing of communities and families connected through ancestral ways of knowing how to relate with non-human life through language, storytelling, and spirituality.[4]

As a point for concluding reflection, I continue to investigate how the epistemological implications of mestiza and *marassa* consciousness resonate with us today. The limited scope of this essay leaves much to be addressed regarding the discourses of indigeneity, which I aim to explore in future studies. I will continue to compare the writings of Danticat and Anzaldúa with emphasis on other similar themes including the dangers and risks of creative artistry in the borderlands, and how feminine deities activate figurative and literal queer crossings. By articulating worldviews premised on syncretic religious practices, Gloria Anzaldúa and Edwidge Danticat explicitly and implicitly critique prejudicial attitudes within their respective borderlands cultures while cultivating cultural survival. My literary comparison of *marassa* and mestiza consciousness from a hemispheric vantage point is an effort toward fostering decolonial solidarity in the Americas between African diasporic, Chican@, and Indigenous communities.

NOTES

1 The Parsley Massacre, also known as *El Corte*, was a government-sponsored genocide executed by Trujillo, referred to in the story as the Generalissimo, who was infamous for his anti-Haitian attitudes.

2 Ezili (Erzulie) is a *lwa* of "love and sensuality," often "depicted visually in Catholic terms as the Virgin Mary in her manifestation as Our Lady of the Sorrows" (Conner and Sparks 39).

3 For further studies that challenge this claim, please look to "The Borderlands of *Borderlands*: Tres Vistas" by Lydia A. French.

4 For further reference see the "Peoplehood model" of Indigenous communities explained by Taiaiake Alfred and Jeff Corntassel in *Being Indigenous: Resurgences against Contemporary Colonialism*, which emphasizes sacred history, ceremonial cycles, language, and ancestral homelands as interconnected factors foundational to the Indigenous identity (609).

WORKS CITED

Alfred, Taiaiake, and Jeff Corntassel. *Being Indigenous: Resurgences against Contemporary Colonialism*. Oxford: Blackwell, 2005. 597–614.

Anzaldúa, Gloria. *Borderlands/La Frontera: The New Mestiza.* 4th ed. San Francisco: Aunt Lute Books, 2012. Print.

Bellegarde-Smith, Patrick and Claudine Michel. "Danbala/Ayida as Cosmic Prism: The Lwa as Trope for Understanding Metaphysics in Haitian Vodou and Beyond." *Journal of Africana Religions* 1.4 (2013): 458–487. Print.

Bragg, Beauty. "Edwidge Danticat's *Breath, Eyes, Memory*: Historicizing the Colonial Woman." *Literary Expressions of African Spirituality*. Eds. Carol P. Marsh-Lockett and Elizabeth J. West. Lanham: Lexington Books, 2013. 163–182. Print.

Cantú, Norma and Aída Hurtado. Introduction. Borderlands/La Frontera: The New Mestiza. 4th ed. San Francisco: Aunt Lute Books, 2012. Print.

Clark, VèVè. "Developing Diaspora Literacy and Marasa Consciousness." *Theatre Survey* 50.1 (2009): 9–18. Print.

Conner, Randy P., and David Hatfield Sparks. *Queering Creole Spiritual Traditions: Lesbian, Gay, Bisexual and Transgender Participation in African-Inspired Traditions in the Americas*. New York: Harrington Park Press, 2004. Print.

Cotera, María Eugenia and María Josefina Saldaña-Portillo. "Indigenous But Not Indian? Chicana/os and the Politics of Indigeneity." *The World of Indigenous North America.* Ed. Robert Warrior. New York: Routledge Press, 2014. 549–568. Print.

Danticat, Edwidge. *Breath, Eyes, Memory*. New York: Vintage, 1994. Print.

---. *The Farming of Bones*. New York: SOHO, 1998. Print.

French, Lydia A. "The Borderlands of *Borderlands*: Tres Vistas." *Indigenous Cultures Institute.* n.p. n.d. Web. 15 October 2015.

Saldaña-Portillo, María Josefina. *The Revolutionary Imagination in the Americas and the Age of Development.* Durham, NC: Duke University Press, 2003. Print.

Shemak, April. *Asylum Speakers: Caribbean Refugees and Testimonial Discourse*. NY: Fordham University Press, 2011. Print.

ANZALDÚA'S UNCONDITIONAL HOSPITALITY[1]

CRISTINA GARRIGÓS

"Perhaps the impossible is the only possible chance of something new"
(Jacques Derrida, The Politics of Friendship 36)

We take the word hospitality for granted. Hospitality is a virtue that we are supposed to have. We receive friends and family in our houses, and we share with them food and lodging, which makes us feel generous and part of a community. But is this the real meaning of generosity, or a very comfortable, albeit limited one? Real hospitality implies acceptance, recognition, and reconciliation with "the other," beyond tolerance, since tolerance does not necessarily imply acceptance. Tolerance is a stance of mutual non-interference (Young 246). Real hospitality is about deconstructing the very otherness that allows for separation and for borders. It implies accepting the unknown, the unfamiliar, the stranger, and sharing space and resources with others. It means accepting that there is some common ground between apparently different people, where issues of ethnicity, gender, and national identity are dissolved and we recognize each other in our common humanity. Real hospitality means to discard hostility, fear, and suspicion and to replace it with identification. Hospitality, according to Seyla Benhabib, refers to "all human rights claims which are cross-border in scope" (*Another Cosmopolitanism* 149). Hospitality is a matter of both states and civil societies (150). It implies an act of receptivity towards the other, which is ultimately the "fundamental act of the ethical" (157).

These ideas can be found in the thought of Gloria Anzaldúa. Throughout her life Anzaldúa tried to move beyond binary divisions, positioning herself simultaneously inside and outside several identity categories. In her early work she recognized the conflict and tension between dichotomies as a personal and a collective hindrance. Since all her writing is to be understood as part of a life process, as she acknowledged herself (*Interview/Entrevistas* 268), we can observe that there is an evolution from the first texts in *This Bridge Called my Back*, through *Borderlands/La Frontera*, to *This Bridge We Call Home*, in the way she approached her search for understanding (*conocimiento*) and "spiritual activism" (Keating "I'm a Citizen"). It is my contention that much of Anzaldúa's thought can be better understood when related to the concept of hospitality, a critical idea that was discussed by Kant, Levinas, and Derrida, and that has recently been instrumental to understanding immigration laws and cosmopolitanism. In other words, it is my belief that Anzaldúa's thoughts could and should be considered together with those of the above-mentioned philosophers, since her theories provide a fruitful insight into the theory of hospitality.

In the West, hospitality has always been concerned with rights, duties, and obligations, following a lineage from the Greco-Roman world through the Judeo-Christian tradition and the political philosophies of Kant and Hegel (Derrida, *Of Hospitality* 77). Derrida takes on Kant's ideas on hospitality, which he sees as the foundation and the principle of ethics (*Adieu* 50). According to him, hospitality is culture itself (*On Cosmopolitanism and Forgiveness* 16); hospitality magnetizes questions related to the historical, ethical, political, juridical, and economical ("Hostipitality" 3). It is thus related to all areas of human endeavour. It is about how we understand and articulate our relationship with the others in our houses (actual houses, but, metaphorically, also family, nation, city, language, etc.), and about our positions as guests in other people's houses.

The idea of the home is central to Anzaldúa, to the extent that it is in the title of several of her texts, both as author and editor. Throughout her work she tries to find a space, a place, where the conflicts she sees around her and within her can generate something positive. She works with the idea of the bridge and the threshold as spaces of separation, but also of connection. The term hospitality invokes the figure of the host and the guest, but, as we will see, the relation between these two roles is quite complex. Anzaldúa is aware of the inner struggle (*la lucha*) that is necessary to act collectively: "We carry this bridge inside us, the struggle, the movement toward liberation" ("Acts of Healing," xxviii). The struggle inside us is provoked by the confrontation between our roles as hosts and guests. In order to create something new, we need to overcome the confrontation and contradiction inherent in the term so that we can cross the threshold. This is a recurrent thought in Anzaldúa, which I believe is inextricably linked to the concept of hospitality.

The conflict, or the tension between host and guest, is to be found in the etymology of the term hospitality itself. The word "hospitality" carries its opposite within itself: *hospitalitas* derives from the Latin word *hospes* which, as Benveniste remarks, is divided into two elements *hostis,* which originally means "stranger" (*hostilis*), and which is also the origin of words such as hostility and hostile, and *pet (*or *potis, potentia*), to have power, mastery. According to Benveniste, *hospes* means *guest-master.*[2] However, the word "guest" in romance languages also derives from *hospes: huésped (*Spanish), *hôte* (French). Thus, hospitality refers both to the guest and the host, uniting two contradictory or at least diametrically opposed notions: one inviting and welcoming; the other, asking for accommodation. The combination host/guest implies a temporal value (before-after) and a spatial one (here/on this side-beyond) (Raffestin 166). As Ranjana Khana points out,

> The host is someone who opens up frames or borders. Rather like a parergon, the host/guest is a supplement to that which is protected within the frame. And the host "community," like the ergon, is challenged by the arrival or presence of a supplement at its borders . . . . The Latin ostio is a door with a frame, a starting gate, the entrance into the underworld . . . . The doubled-edged nature of the term "host," like the double-edged nature of the term "frame" (protector/excluder, host/guest, communication/failure of communication, naturalized/formulated, internal structure/outer rim), indicates how hospitality and hostility vie with each other, because the "Law" of unlimited hospitality conflicts with its actualized laws. (19-20)

From the Ancient times on, hospitality has been considered a virtue in the Western world. In Greece, it was synonymous with civilization, since it was the duty of the citizens to provide food and shelter to strangers. Taking into account that there were no hotels, it was normal to offer your house to travellers. As Benito and Manzanas explain, "In ancient Greece the stranger was initially looked upon as an enemy in possession of a powerful fetish, or just as a sorcerer or a being endowed with supernatural powers" (Bolchazy 1), but this initial perception changed as strangers were gradually viewed as ordinary human beings. Once this view of the other changed, the host could offer him/her protection as a sign of generosity, altruism, and civilization, which implied giving something to a complete stranger".[3] However, this hospitality is regulated: that is, it is ruled by laws and is therefore conditional (Westmoreland 1). The stranger (*xenos*) had some rights, but these are established by the city. Thus, the state divides people between citizens and non-citizens, hosts and guests (Westmoreland 2).

Hospitality has always been regulated by the state and has always been juridical. Immanuel Kant addressed the relation of hospitality to politics, law, and economics in the third article of *Perpetual Peace* (1795). The German philosopher states that the "*Cosmopolitan Right* shall be *limited* to *Conditions* of *Universal Hospitality*" (my italics) and that "No one originally has any greater right than anyone else to occupy any particular position of the earth" (105). For him, hospitality is not about philanthropy, but about right: "The right not to be treated with hostility when he arrives on someone else's territory" (105). This right has some implications, of course, for it presupposes that the stranger is a peaceful one. Peace is then a prerequisite for peace. But I would like to focus here on two terms that Kant uses in the title and that are very contemporary: "cosmopolitan" and "universal." As he indicates, there are limitations and conditions to universal hospitality, a notion that is developed further by Jacques Derrida in his writings on hospitality.

Derrida establishes a distinction between conditional and unconditional hospitality. Most well-intentioned conceptions of hospitality entail a distance between the host (master of the house) and the guest (stranger), and a relationship where the owner is in control, while the guest is subject to his/her rules. For Derrida, this is the "normal" hospitality, and the one that best exemplifies the tension inherent in the name. The other one, the unconditional, is aporetic, impossible, because in order to be hospitable, one has to abandon all claim of mastery, thereby, circumventing any possibility of hosting anyone: "The law of hospitality, the express law that governs the general concept of hospitality, appears as a paradoxical law, pervertible or perverting. It seems to dictate that absolute hospitality should break with the law of hospitality as right or duty [...]" (*Of Hospitality* 25). Ideal hospitality is unconditional, relying more on visitation than invitation. As such, it is related to somebody who is neither expected nor invited. This is, of course, ideal and impossible, according to Derrida, since it would mean to give what you have to the person who is in your house, to make him/her feel (s)he is at home (literally). The impossibility of absolute hospitality is based on the constitution of power relationships, since it can only exist outside the law. For Derrida, "it is as though the laws (plural) of hospitality [...] consisted in challenging and transgressing *the* law of hospitality, the one that would command that the "new arrival" be offered an unconditional welcome" (*Of Hospitality* 77).

Transgressing the law of hospitality is for Derrida an aporia, but this is not negative. This paradoxical state is necessary in the sense that in order to be hospitality, there must be a door, a threshold; but if there is a door, complete hospitality is unviable. Thus, "hospitality can only take place beyond hospitality, in deciding to let it come, overcoming the hospitality that paralyzes itself on the threshold which it is" ("Hostipitality" 14). In other words,

> Hospitality limits itself from the threshold on its own threshold, it always remains at its own threshold, it governs the threshold—and in its measure it prohibits in some ways crossing the threshold that it seems to allow crossing. It becomes the threshold [. . . .] This apparent aporetic paralysis on the threshold 'is' what needs to be overcome, it is the impossibility there that has to be overcome [. . . .]
>
> Hospitality can only take place beyond hospitality, only by deciding to make it come from beyond, by surmounting hospitality, which paralyses itself on the threshold where it is. (Derrida, *Adieu* 39-40)

Derrida's threshold becomes in Anzaldúa's thought, Nepantla, the space of change and possibility. What Derrida sees as impossible and aporetic (the paralysis of the threshold), albeit necessary in order to transgress the conventional and contradictory nature of hospitality and reach the ideal one, is for Anzaldúa a prerequisite for crossing over and reaching true *conocimiento.* As Paola Zaccaria says, the notion of hospitality in Anzaldúa (even if she does not mention the term) is very similar to the idea of reconciliation, forgiveness, and understanding that Derrida sees as impossible, and that he explores through translation (177). The role of the translator of cultures as mediator is that of the border-crosser, a Nepantla figure, who helps and establishes a bridge between cultures. As Anzaldúa proclaims, "Bridging is the work of opening the gate to the stranger, within and without" ("now let us shift" 3). As opposed to border hospitality, conventional hospitality implies the existence of limits that the guest cannot trespass (conventions ruled by the house—state, nation, city, language—property rights, requisites that the guest must follow so that (s)he can be allowed to cross the threshold or the door), Anzaldúa seems to be pleading for a borderless hospitality, transitional and transnational (Zaccharia 177). We must recognize, however, that borderless hospitality is a contradiction in terms, an aporia, since the border/threshold is an element needed to create the conditions for hospitality. If there were no borders, no sense of possession, nobody would be the host or the guest. Everybody would belong. Aware of this paradoxical state, Anzaldúa believes that real acceptance (ideal borderless hospitality) requires a shift in our mentalities, which implies trespassing established categories. As AnaLouise Keating says, "Anzaldúa positions herself on the thresholds—simultaneously inside and outside a number of groups—and uses her threshold perspective to challenge the status quo" ("From Borderlands" 6). Borderless hospitality implies the dissolution of the threshold and the invalidation of the role of the guest and the master, which become one and the same. This is what is effected in Nepantla:

> Anzaldúa was a nepantlera—a term she coined to describe a unique type of visionary cultural worker. Nepantleras are threshold people: they move within and among multiple often conflicting, worlds and refuse to align themselves exclusively with any single individual, group, or belief system. The refusal is not easy; nepantleras must be willing to open themselves to personal risks and potential woundings, which include, but are not limited to, self-division, isolation, misunderstanding, rejection, and accusations of disloyalty. Yet the risk-taking has its own rewards, for nepantleras use their movements among divergent worlds to develop innovative, potentially transformative perspectives. They respect the differences within and among the diverse groups and, *simultaneously,* posit commonalities. ("From Borderlands" 6)

But before exploring the meaning of Nepantla, which she did later in her work, Anzaldúa worked on the idea of hospitality in her early texts, although not using explicitly that term. In "Speaking in Tongues" she asks the following question: "Who gave us permission to perform the act of writing?" (164). Permission is needed when somebody is the master of the house, in this case of writing. The master grants the guest permission to cross the threshold and enter a space that is not his/hers. This permission is conventional, ruled by right and laws, which were established by the master. If the guest complies with the rules, (s)he can stay in the house as long as this stay is temporary. Anzaldúa believes that white people have mastered the house of writing for too long. She urges women of color to subvert the guest position that they have been given and trespass the threshold to occupy the master's house. This implies entering a space where they are not welcome, that is, breaking the rules or the norms established by the master, by refusing to remain in the comfortable stereotypical image whites have created in their minds. Instead, Anzaldúa asks them to revolt against that:

> The Third World woman revolts: We revoke, we erase your white male imprint. When you come knocking on our doors with your rubber stamps to brand our faces with DUMB, HYSTERICAL, PASSIVE PUTA, PERVERT, when you come with your branding irons to burn MY PROPERTY on our buttocks, we will vomit the guilt, self-denial and race-hatred you have force-fed us into us right back into your mouth. We are done being cushions for your projected fears. We are tired of being your sacrificial lambs and scapegoats. ("Speaking in Tongues" 165)

This text shows a rejection of the violence imposed upon Third World women by the hosts (men and white women) who are the ones setting the rules and maintaining control. At this point for Anzaldúa there is no possibility for reconciliation: "We are not reconciled to the oppressors who whet their howl on our grief. We are not reconciled" ("Speaking in Tongues" 171). As we saw before, peace is a prerequisite for peace. In this case, since the master is not peaceful, peace cannot be expected from a guest who resists the role of being guest in a house that (s)he believes belongs to everybody. Following Kant, she believes that, "No one originally has any greater right than anyone else to occupy any particular position of the earth" (Kant 105).

However, Anzaldúa seems to be aware that violence is not a solution. In "La Prieta," for instance, she looks for a way towards recognition and acceptance. She sees herself as "a wind-swayed bridge, a crossroad inhabited by whirlwinds. Gloria the facilitator, Gloria the mediator, straddling the walls between abysses" (205). Although she relates to the Mundo Zurdo—Third World women, lesbians, feminists, and feminist oriented men of all colors (209)—she admits that she does not exclude whites from the list of people she loves (206), and that there is an enormous contradiction in being a bridge. But it is precisely this contradiction that allows her to evolve and make possible the impossible: a door open for reconciliation.

The concepts of the frontier and the mestiza in *Borderlands/La Frontera: The New Mestiza* (1987) have been subject of much analysis already, as this text is considered Anzaldúa's most important work. However, I agree with AnaLouise Keating in that despite its indisputable relevance to understand identity-based issues, among other things, this work should be contextualized as part of a life-long project. In *Borderlands,* Anzaldúa struggles to give visibility to Chicanos/as, to call attention to their role as guests in a land that belongs to them. Appropriately enough, the first chapter is about "The Homeland". The *hostipitality,* to use Derrida's term mixing hostility and hospitality ("Hostipitality"), towards Chicanos/as is evidenced in the treatment they receive by their hosts. They are treated like strangers by the master of the house (United States) who is also the master of language (English). Women and queers are also guests in a culture where power is in the hands of a few (power in the sense of *posis* [power/spouse]). The law of hospitality in the borderlands is imposed by the master who will grant the guest permission to cross the threshold and stay as soon as (s)he conforms to the rules. The queer Chicana, the new mestiza, is not welcome in the community because she does not follow the rules of the master. This position can only lead to paralysis, and to be left in the threshold, "the ultimate rebellion she can make against her native culture is through her sexual behaviour" (19). Entering the house means adapting and renouncing an important part of her identity. Aware of the pain and suffering caused by this situation, Anzaldúa believes that real hospitality means complete acceptance and recognition of the other, that is, not mere tolerance or philanthropy, which are but forms of colonization.

In "now, let us shift…the path of conocimiento…inner work, public acts," she argues for going beyond the comfort zone, a work that implies looking into yourself and recognizing the conflict and contradictions in you in order to be able to have real communication with others. She vindicates the figure of the nepantlera as helper in this process, mediator, translator of cultures. Nepantla, the second stage towards *conocimiento,* is the place "where the outer boundaries of the mind's inner life meet the outer world of reality, is a zone of possibility" ("now, let us shift" 544). Nepantla implies an opening, a mindful holistic awareness, but also "un aislamiento spiritual" (Rosario Castellanos, *Los narradores* 93).[4] As such, it is a site of conflict, but also home: "You realize that 'home' is that bridge, the in-between place of nepantla and constant transition, the most unsafe of all spaces. You remove the old bridge from your back.... nepantla is the only place where change happens" ("now, let us shift" 574).

For Anzaldúa, it is through spiritual activism and through the role of the nepantlera that ideal hospitability can be reached: "Las nepantleras know their work lies in positioning themselves—exposed and raw—in the crack between these worlds, and in revealing current categories as unworkable" ("now, let us shift" 567). Ideal hospitality requires dismantling your most deeply ingrained beliefs. Most of the people are comfortable living with what they take as certainties. However, for Anzaldúa, this was not possible. She lived in Nepantla, "the place where different perspectives come into conflict and where you question the basic ideas, tenets, and identities inherited from your family, your education, and your different cultures" ("now, let us shift" 548). Living between cultures means that you see something from two (or more) different angles, making your body (your mind) a battleship. But this conflict, this split consciousness, is necessary if we are to reach beyond traditional positions that only lead to separation, misunderstanding, and discrimination.

Nepantla is not an undemanding space if it is to be understood as a site of change and transformation. Likewise, if we think of the perfect hospitality that Derrida proposed, it is neither easy for the host, who has to change his/her attitude and frame of mind, nor for the guest who must abandon the position of inferiority and resist any categorization of identity. For Anzaldúa, you have "to rethink yourself in more global-spiritual terms instead of conventional categories of color, class, career" ("now, let us shift" 561). The awareness of interrelatedness (what Anzaldúa calls "la naguala"), the belief that we are united, not separated, is a necessary step if we want to reach a real change. Humanity provides the common link. We are the other. As Monika Kaup points out, "by shifting the site of the struggle between identity and difference from communities to the conflict within the individual, Anzaldúa's model makes significant progress in dissolving boundaries that are ... the foundations of racism" (111). This movement implies, as we have seen, an inner struggle and also, according to Anzaldúa, what AnaLouise Keating calls "re(con)ceiving" the other (*Women* 75-81, quoted in

Anzaldúa "now, let us shift" 570). The idea of re(con)ceiving the other is central to the notion of unconditional hospitality that I am discussing here. You receive the other; you are the host. You reconceive your position, and his/her otherness, and you become aware that you are also a guest. But this relation is not dual. As Mustaka Dikeç points out,

> Hospitality is not about the rules of stay being conditioned by a duality of host and guest with unequal power relations leading to domination; it is about a recognition that we are hosts and guests at the same time in multiple and shifting ways, Hospitality, in this sense, is a refusal to conceive the host and the guest as pre-constituted identities. It is about the recognition that they are mutually constitutive of each other, and thus, relational and shifting as all identities are. (239)

Both guest and host happen simultaneously. Both are "mutually constitutive of each other" (Dikeç 239). This state is, according to Derrida, aporetic and impossible, but for Anzaldúa, although with extreme difficulty and hard work, it can be reached. It requires an important inner struggle in order to reset the information you have stored in you, to be able to connect, act, and effect change. As she says at the end of her piece:

> We are ready for *change.*
> Let us link hands and hearts
> Together find a path through the dark woods
> Step through the *doorways* between worlds
> Leaving huellas for other to follow,
> Build *bridges,* cross them with grace, and claim these *puentes* our
> "*home*"
> sí se puede, que así sea, so be it, estamos listas, vámonos.
> Now let us *shift.*
> contigo. ("now let us shift" 576)[5]

In her words we can see the importance of doorways (thresholds) and bridges (*puentes*) as elements of change, and the idea of the home as the place of encounter, of hospitality. Gloria Anzaldúa closes her essay with a memory of others whose backs served as bridges: Pat Parker, Audre Lorde, Toni Cade Bambara, Barbara Cameron, y tantas otras ("now, let us shift" 576). As the critic Suryia Nayak points out when speaking of hospitality related to the work of Audre Lorde, "Audre Lorde saw borders as limits that made her feel secure, stable: 'I rely on psychic borders for a delusion of stability' (Nayak 102). Eliminating these borders implies instability, suffering, and change. It is not easy. "The attempts of my race, gender, class, sexuality and age to play host and guest to each other, are caught up in Derrida's problematic, 'Is not hospitality an interruption of the self?' (Derrida 1999:51) (Nayak 92). As we saw before, for Derrida, absolute hospitality requires "that I open up my home and I give not only to the foreigner, but to the absolute, unknown, anonymous other ... without asking of them reciprocity (entering into a pact) or even their names" (*Of Hospitality* 25). In welcoming the guest this way, the self is interrupted: the host becomes the guest, the guest the host (25). Nayak sees the concept of hospitality in Lorde's notion of the Sister outsider, being both sister (proximity) and outsider (hostility). Re-reading Lorde's work as being simultaneously inside and outside "turns the whole house inside out" (Nayak 130).

Like Lorde's, Anzaldúa's model of identity is based on the recognition of the other in us. "Seeing through the eyes of the other" is the first step in the process that will enable us to make alliances (Koshy 158), and that will consolidate the interrelatedness between (human and non-human) beings that is so important for Anzaldúa. The nos/otras that Anzaldúa proposes is the equivalent of the tension in "hospitality." As AnaLouise Keating notices, "With nos/otras, Anzaldúa offers an alternative to binary self/other constellations, a philosophy and praxis enabling us simultaneously to acknowledge and to bridge the distance between self and other" ("From Borderlands" 10). The belief in the interconnectivity of all beings, - somos todos un país ("now let us shift") points towards inclusion, a holistic worldview (Keating, "I'm a Citizen" 54). I am a citizen of the universe, Anzaldúa says.

Even though Gloria Anzaldúa never used the term hospitality explicitly, her conception of Nepantla and spiritual activism is very close to what Derrida sees as the unconditional absolute mode of hospitality. According to the Algerian philosopher, this state is very difficult to reach, if not impossible. But I believe that Anzaldúa's ideas provide an insight as to where to start and how to work in that direction. In my opinion, her whole oeuvre is an attempt to try to find the way to trespass this threshold, by challenging and transgressing the law of hospitality as we know it. Her desire to reach what is beyond the known limits in the way we relate to each other, beyond hospitality as a convention, may well be the best way to finally reach universal hospitality.

NOTES

1 This article is part of the following research projects: "Historia crítica de la literatura étnica norteamericana: una visión intercultural," (funded by the Ministry of Economy and Competence FFI2012-31250. 2013-15. Project Leader: Jesús Benito, and "Las fronteras de la hospitalidad en los estudios culturales de Estados Unidos y Europa,") - (SA342U1.4. 2014-2016 funded by the Government of Castilla y León. Project Leader: Ana Mª Manzanas).

2 Moreover, as Benveniste notices, potis (master) is the root of both master and husband (posis > spouse). The master of the house was also the master of the family and of the wife (72). The patriarchal connotation which derives from this, and its repercussion in Western thought is obvious.

3 From the introduction of Jesus Benito and Ana Manzanas, Hospitality in American Literature and Culture: Spaces, Bodies, Borders. New York and London: Routledge, forthcoming.

4 Quoted by Gloria Anzaldúa in "now let us shift…the path of conocimiento…inner works, public acts" in this bridge we call home.

5 My italics.

WORKS CITED

Anzaldúa, Gloria E. "Acts of Healing." *This Bridge Called my Back: Writings by Radical Women of Color.* 1981. Eds. Cherríe Moraga and Gloria Anzaldúa. 4th ed. Albany, NY: SUNY P, 2015.xxvii-xxviii. Print.

---. "Speaking in Tongues: A Letter to Third World Women Writers." *This Bridge Called my Back: Writings by Radical Women of Color.* 1981. Eds. Cherríe Moraga and Gloria Anzaldúa. 4th ed. Albany, NY: SUNY P, 2015.163-172. Print.

---. "La Prieta." *This Bridge Called my Back: Writings by Radical Women of Color.* 1981. Eds. Cherríe Moraga and Gloria Anzaldúa. 4th ed. Albany, NY: SUNY P, 2015. 198-209. Print.

---. *This Bridge Called my Back: Writings by Radical Women of Color.* 1981. Eds. Cherríe Moraga and Gloria Anzaldúa. 4th ed. Albany, NY: SUNY P, 2015. Print.

---. *Borderlands/La Frontera: The New Mestiza.* Aunt Lute Books, 1987. Print.

---. "En rapport: cobrando cuentas a las nuestras." *Making Face/Making Soul, Haciendo Caras: Creative and Critical Perspectives by Feminists of Color.* Ed. Gloria Anzaldúa. Aunt Lute Books, 1990. 142-150. Print.

---. *Interviews/Entrevistas.* Ed. AnaLouise Keating. New York: Routledge, 2000. Print.

---. "now let us shift…the path of conocimiento…inner work, public acts." *This Bridge we Call Home: Radical Visions of Transformation.* Eds. Gloria E. Anzaldúa and AnaLouise Keating. New York and London: Routledge. 2002: 540-579. Print.

Benhabib, Seyla. "Hospitality, Sovereignty, and Democratic Interactions." *Another Cosmopolitanism.* Robert Prost, ed. Oxford: Oxford UP, 2006. 147-186.

Benveniste, Émile. Indo-European Language and Society, trans. Elizabeth Palmer. London: Faber, 1973.

Bolchazy, Ladislaus J. *Hospitality in Antiquity: Livy's Concept of its Humanizing Force.* Chicago: Ares, 1993. Print.

Derrida, Jacques. *Adieu a Emmanuel Levinas.* Trans. Michael Naas and Pascale-Anne Brault. Stanford: Stanford UP. 1999. Print.

---. "Hostipitality," *Angelaki: Journal of the Theoretical Humanities.* 5.3 (2000): 3-18. Trans. Barry Stocker with Forbes Morlock.

---. *On Cosmopolitanism and Forgiveness.* Trans. Mark Doodley and Richard Kearney. New York: Routledge, 2005. Print.

---. *The Politics of Friendship.* Trans. George Collins. New York: Verso, 2005. Print.

Derrida, J., & Dufourmantelle, A., *Of Hospitality.* Trans. Rachel Bowlby. Stanford: Stanford UP, 2000. Print.

Dikeç, Mustaka. "Pera Peras Poros: Longings for Spaces of Hospitality." *Theory Culture Society* 2002 19 (1-2): 227-247.

Kant, Immanuel. "Perpetual Peace: A Philosophical Sketch." *Kant's Political Writings.* Ed. H. Reiss. Trans H.B. Nisbet. Cambridge: Cambridge UP, 1970. Print.

Kaup, Monika. "Crossing Borders: An Aesthetic Practice in Writings by Gloria Anzaldúa." *Cultural Difference and the Literary Text: Pluralism and the Limits of Authenticity in North American Literatures.* Iowa City: U of Iowa P, 1997. Print.

Khana, Ranjana. "Frames, Contexts, Community, Justice." *Diacritics* 33.2 (2003): 11-41.

Koshy, Kavitha. "Nepantlera Activism in the Transnational Movement: in Dialogue with Gloria Anzaldúa's Theorizing of Nepantla." *Human Architecture. Journal of the Sociology of Self-Knowledge* 4.3 (2006) 147-161. Print.

Keating, AnaLouise, "From Borderlands and New Mestizas to Nepantlas and Nepantleras." *Human Architecture. Journal of the Sociology of Self-Knowledge* 4.3 (2006) 5-16.

---. "I'm a Citizen of the Universe: Gloria Anzaldúa's Spiritual Activism as Catalyst for Social Change." *Feminist Studies* 34 (2008) 53-69. Print.

---. Ed. *The Gloria Anzaldúa Reader.* Durham: Duke UP, 2009. Print.

Nayak, Suryia. *Race, Gender and the Activism of Black Feminist Theory: Working with Audre Lorde.* Routledge, 2014 Print.

Raffestin, Claude. "Reinventer l'hospitalité." *Communications* 65.1 (1997): 165-177.

Westmoreland, Mark W. "Interruptions: Derrida and Hospitality." *Kritique* 2.1 (2008): 1-10. Print.

Young, I.M. "Residential Segregation and Differentiated Citizenship." *Citizenship Studies* 3(1999): 237-52.

Zaccaria, Paola. "The Art and Poetic of Translation as Hospitality." *The Conditions of Possibility: Ethics, Politics and the Aesthetics on the Threshold of the Possible.* Ed. Thomas Claviez. New York: Fordham UP, 2013. 168-184. Print.

CREATIVE MESTIZAJE

DEAR SANTA

VERONICA SANDOVAL, LADY MARIPOSA

Dear Santa,

First of all, I want to thank you for the wonderful present you got me last year. I really liked my Vogue Girl, she came with her own cell phone and a long golden dress so I could change her out of the halter top and jeans she came in. It did not matter that her halter top showed off her chichis a lot, she looked like my Tia Veronica, who is always showing her chichis, and I like her. Her shirts and her skirts are always sparkly, I think because they are so tiny she must be able to buy lots of them. Mom says "Vero, te encuero," a lot and laughs. I don't know what that means, but I'm not supposed to tell Tia Vero that. Dad doesn't laugh with mom either; he is always looking at Tia Vero's outfits as well. I asked him about this once and he said he was really into fashion, mom says he's just really into D cups. When Erika came over for my slumber party I asked dad to borrow his D cups because I wanted to make some hot chocolate in the microwave. Dad didn't understand and gave us juice boxes instead.

I know that the Vogue Girl wasn't the Barbie I wanted, but mom already explained to me that since 9-11, international travel has become difficult and you haven't been able to get a visa. Mom says that that's why you're outsourcing

Santa duties to local pansones, and that probably some dropout named Fred is taking the money you gave him and spending it on huilas. I don't blame him, I really like kites, I'd spend my money on huilas too! But maybe you need to hire more pansones? Hey, my dad's name is Fred too! Maybe I'll tell him to apply for Santa duties next year. He is disabled for a living, I'm not sure what that means, but Mom says it involves scratching huevos. I didn't even know we had a chicken, but maybe we should get a new one, because the one we have must have pulgas.

The reason I'm writing this letter is because I wanted to let you know that I don't want a Barbie this year. This year for my present will you bring my mom something instead? I already made her a macaroni picture of a snowman, but I don't think she really likes those even if she does put them on the refrigerator. Mom's been crying a lot lately, and I can't seem to find the bola de animales who she says, live in our house and have ruined her life. Santa, Mom hasn't worn a pretty dress in a long time and that's why I was hoping that you could bring her one. I've seen some real nice ones at Wal-Mart, I have enclosed a picture of the dress I like in this letter. It is red and long because mom says girls shouldn't be running around like Tia Vero showing todo El Rancho to all of McAllen. However, if I had a rancho, I'd show it off, and I'd put a horse in it too, but I don't tell my mom this anymore because it makes her really angry.

Anyways, I was hoping you could bring her that pretty red dress because it will go great with the pair of shoes I got at the pulga for a quarter. They used to smell like patas, but now they smell like Fabuloso, and I don't think my mom will mind at all.

My friend Kim said that if I asked you to bring something for my mom instead of me, that you would probably still bring me a gift, because asking for stuff for other people practically guarantees you a Christmas miracle. If this is true I still want a Barbie, on account that I left my Vogue Girl in the truck last year and her patas melted off. Either way, I hope you have gotten your visa issues fixed because I've been wanting to meet you, and Fat Fred never does a good job.

As always I will leave the empanadas next to the tree.

Love
Sandrita

PS. Don't worry, that ugly brown thing is a border wall and mom says people are acting in dreams for it to be gone. Si diosito quiere as dad says, by Christmas, it won't bother you or Rudolf at all.

DÓNDE ESTÁ MI GENTE?

VERÓNICA SOLÍS

So I thought
By this time
By this age

**

I should say I was taught—
To be RID
Of the feelings I have
And I say have because
I STILL FEEL THEM
THIS IS STILL WHO I AM.
¿Quién soy?
La Vero
La Nueva
La Profeta

La Mera Neta
Romeo, también Julieta
Yo soy Alma y Corazón completa
La derecha a tu izquierda
So—
Con migo no chinguen.
Porque yo
De mi mami salí.
Soy mujer de mujeres
Y tú no me dices
Yo te digo a ti—
Qué dicen?
Ay sí muy chingona!
FUCK YEAH!!
And I'm leading this charge
Because I got people
In this country and
And in other countries too
Closeted.
STILL!
Queens, gays, bi-, transgender
And lesbianas REFUSING to bloom
Because!
...this is the part that pisses me off
They're getting killed and even
Killin' themselves
Since you say it ain't right with you
And then you justify it with "It ain't right with God."
You people need to understand
WE don't ASK for this!
But you blame and condemn us
For not fitting one or the other-
Here's your binary:
Fuck. You.

***

You know
I don't want to be angry.
The "angry lesbian."
What a fucking cliché.
Hmm. I don't have a dick, wah!
FUCK THAT SHIT!!!
Y'all got your peter and I got my chalice and it's all good.
You know some of you mutherfuckers
Are making it very difficult
For us to just live
Well guess what?!
Right now it's all equal opportunity.
Todos parejos cabrones.
'Cause I'm leading this charge.
Do unto others…
Is what I'm here to remind you
Cause I got it right
Y ¿quién eres tú?
Enséñame
También aprende
Que soy Verónica
Y acuérdate
That's MR. Solís to you.
So what the fuck?!
Dónde están?!
Salgan?!
Qué pinche onda?!
DÓNDE ESTÁ MI GENTE?! Ya sé que está mi Raza
Pero DÓNDE ESTÁ MI GENTE?
DÓNDE ESTÁ MI GENTE?

CONTRIBUTOR BIOGRAPHIES

Marisa Belausteguigoitia Rius has a PhD in Ethnic Studies with emphasis in women, race, and sexuality from the University of California at Berkeley. She is a Full Professor at the School of Humanities of the Universidad Nacional Autónoma de México (UNAM) in the programs of gender, culture and education. Marisa is an advisor to the México City Commission on Human Rights. She was chair of the center for gender studies at UNAM for ten years. Her work analyzes the relation of new pedagogies, art, and justice from a gender perspective. She centers her analysis in juridical, artistic, and pedagogical processes in women's prisons.

Trevor Boffone is the founding managing editor of the 50 Playwrights Project and a member of the National Steering Committee for the Latina/o Theatre Commons. Trevor has a PhD in Latin@ Theatre and Literature from the University of Houston. His first book project, *Eastside Latinidad: Josefina López, Community, and Social Change in Los Angeles*, examines the textual and performative strategies of contemporary Latin@ theatermakers based in Boyle Heights, Los Angeles.

Margaret Cantú-Sánchez is an instructor of English at St. Mary's University. She received her PhD in English, with a specialization in Latino/a Literature from The University of Texas San Antonio. Her research focuses on the identity conflict which Anglocentric institutions of learning impose upon Latino students. As an instructor at a Hispanic Serving Institution, she strives to include multicultural texts in all courses, especially those within the core curriculum.

Nicholas Centino holds a doctorate in Chicana and Chicano Studies from UC Santa Barbara. His work explores the deployment of memory through music, dance, and other forms of popular cultural practices. His current work explores work, labor and culture in Southern California as a postdoctoral research scholar with the UCLA Labor Center and the UCI Community and Labor Project.

Betsy Dahms is an assistant professor of Spanish at the University of West Georgia. Her work focuses on Anzaldúa and Anzaldúan theory in relation to identity, queerness and language. Her publications appear in *El Mundo Zurdo 3*, *Letras Femeninas*, and *Diálogo*. She is currently co-editing a volume of essays entitled *Queer Perspectives in Anzaldúa: Post/Borderlands.*

Cristina Garrigós is Associate Professor of English and American Literature at the National University of Distance Learning-UNED (Spain). She is the author of *John Barth: an Author in Search of Four Characters* and essays on Postmodernism, bilingualism, biculturality, and hybridity. Currently she is working on the notion of hospitality in Gloria Anzaldúa's work, and on a book provisionally titled *Postmodernism Revisited: A Report on the Literature of Replenishment.*

Sonia Hart Suárez is a PhD student in Comparative Ethnic Studies at the University of California at Berkeley. Her research brings together non-western healing practices, the history of science, and race and gender in medical and behavioral science. She takes a critical approach to mental healthcare for people of color by investigating the polemical mind-body divide. Her work submits race, gender, and health to the lens of alternative healing methods used by (Afro) Latin@s /Chican@s in day-to-day life.

Linda Heidenreich teaches at Washington State University. She is author of *"This Land Was Mexican Once": Histories of Resistance from Northern California*, and is currently working on a manuscript on Queer Latin@s in times of Nepantla. When she writes poetry she sometimes uses the pen name oneangrygirlfag. When she is not teaching or working on the manuscript, she enjoys poetry, hiking, and fighting imperialism.

Estee Hernández is a doctoral student in the Higher Education program at Florida State University. She currently serves as a graduate assistant within the Center for Leadership and Social Change. A native Tejana, she earned both her BA in French and her MSEd. in Higher Education & Student Affairs from Baylor University. Currently, her research focuses on the Latina doctoral student experience and social media counter-communities.

Yndalecio Isaac Hinojosa is an Assistant Professor of English at Texas A&M University - Corpus Christi. Prior to his employment, he served Northwest Vista College in San Antonio as an Associate Professor in the English and Reading Department. His areas of research involve Chicana/o Studies, Literacy Studies, and Writing Studies.

Sara Ishii is a third year doctoral candidate in Women's Studies at Texas Woman's University. She holds an MA in Feminist, Gender, and Women's Studies from York University in Toronto, Ontario and an MFA in Art and Technology from the University of Texas at Dallas. Her research interests include Anzaldúan visual and written work, feminist and womanist theories, new directions in continental philosophy, transdisciplinary approaches, arts-based research, feminist perspectives is game studies, and multimodal pedagogy.

Elizabeth Blomstedt Keating is a Teaching Fellow and PhD student in Rhetoric, Composition and Pedagogy at the University of Houston. She has a BA in Rhetoric and Writing from the University of Texas at Austin and an MA in English and American Literature from the University of Houston. Her research interests include first-year writing pedagogy, writing assessment, critical pedagogy, and the digital humanities.

AnaLouise Keating is professor of Women's Studies and director of the Women's Studies doctoral program at Texas Woman's University. Her work focuses on US women of color theories, womanist spiritual activism, and Anzaldúa. Her most recent book is *Transformation Now! Toward a Post-Oppositional Politics of Change*; she's edited several of Anzaldúa's books and co-edited with Anzaldúa *this bridge we call home*. She also edits the University of Illinois Press series *New Visions in Womanism, Feminism, & Indigeneity*.

Sylvia Mendoza Aviña is Visiting Scholar with the Center for Mexican American Studies at the University of Houston. Her research interests include Anzaldúan thought, Chicana/Latina feminisms and research methodologies, and Mexican American studies in K–12 schools.

Larissa M. Mercado-López is an Assistant Professor of Women's Studies at California State University, Fresno, where she teaches courses on women of color feminisms. Her research areas include Chicana Studies, Latina literature, maternal studies, and feminist fitness. Dr. Mercado-López is co-editor of *(Re)Mapping the Latina/o Literary Landscape: New Works and New Directions* and *El Mundo Zurdo: Volumes 3-5*, and is the author of a forthcoming children's book from Arte Público Press.

Roberto C. Orozco is Program Coordinator for Social Justice Programs at the University of Nevada, Las Vegas, overseeing the Center for Social Justice. He earned his MS in Higher Education from Florida State University. A native Iowan, he earned both a BS in Marketing & International Business and a BS in Psychology from Iowa State University. Currently, his research focuses on Latino male masculinity and his efforts have been geared towards social justice initiatives.

Domino Renee Perez is an Associate Professor in the Department of English and the Center for Mexican American Studies at the University of Texas at Austin. She regularly teaches courses in film, young adult fiction, popular culture, American Literature, and Mexican American literature and culture. Her first book, *There Was A Woman: La Llorona From Folklore to Popular Culture,* examines La Llorona, the weeping woman, one of the most famous figures in US/Mexican folklore.

Annette Portillo, Assistant Professor of English and Native American Studies at the University of Texas, San Antonio, received her PhD from Cornell University. Her interdisciplinary research focuses on life stories, *testimonios*, memoirs, and autobiographies by women of color. She has taught Chican@, Native American ,and Ethnic Studies courses at Cornell, Mount Holyoke, Oberlin, Nevada State, and UTSA. She is especially dedicated to student-centered learning and integrates *testimonio* into her classes where she values and validates everyone's lived experiences.

Michael Reyes Salas transferred from Citrus College in 2011, after which he completed his BA in English (minor in French) at UCLA in 2014. Reyes' community with indigenous students and his awareness of Jarocho Afro-Mexican ancestors inform his studies of modern Afro-francophone and contemporary First Nations literature. He is a Mellon Mays Alumni and Ford Predoctoral Fellow.

Sonia Saldívar-Hull, professor of English and Women's Studies at the University of Texas, San Antonio, is Director of the Women's Studies Program and the Women's Studies Institute. She received the 2016 UTSA President's Distinguished Diversity Award. Her publications include *Feminism on the Border: Chicana Politics and Literature*. She is the coeditor of *El Mundo Zurdo: Volumes 2-5* and coeditor of the Duke University Press book series *Latin America Otherwise*.

Veronica Sandoval is Lady Mariposa, a poet sCHOLAr from the Rio Grande Valley. She has a Spoken Word Album entitled: *Hecha en El Valle: Spoken Word & Borderland Beats*, and her work has appeared in publications from Texas A&M University Press, Aunt Lute Books, VAO Publishing, El Serape Press, Lamar University Press, and Savant Books & Publications. She is currently working on her PhD in American Studies at Washington State University.

Verónica Solís has been teaching for over ten years and is currently attending The University of Texas Rio Grande Valley, formerly known as The University of Texas Pan-American, where Gloria Anzaldúa received her undergraduate degree and left a profound legacy. Verónica began performing with WAKE-UP!—Women Artistically Collecting Experiencias-Unidas Prosperando! in April 2014 at the El Retorno Conference. She has since performed with the collective and individually while completing courses for her MFA in Creative Writing.

David Hatfield Sparks is a Chicago writer, musician, and gay father who has written and performed from Manhattan to San Francisco, where he has been active in queer artists/writing communities. A close friend and housemate of Anzaldúa, he, with his husband Randy P. Conner, helped organize and participated in the El Mundo Surdo Reading Series. His works appear in academic, feminist, spiritual, and LGBTQ publications, including, "The Birth of Xochiquetzal" to Anzaldúa, in the anthology *She Is Everywhere*.

Carla Wilson holds an MA in Women's Studies from Georgia State University. Carla teaches Gender and Social Change and Womanist Spiritual Activism at Texas Woman's University. Carla's research interests include compassionate listening as form of spiritual activism; Gloria Anzaldúan thought; feminist, womanist, and Indigenous epistemologies and pedagogies; and contemplative practices in higher education.

Kelli Zaytoun is associate professor of English, interim director of the Women's Center, and former director of Women's Studies at Wright State University. Her research and teaching focus on identity and narrative, multi-ethnic American literature, feminist theory, and memoirs. Her publications on Anzaldúa appear in *EntreMundos/Among Worlds New Perspectives on Gloria E. Anzaldúa*, the *NWSA Journal*, *Bridging: How Gloria Anzaldúa's Life and Work Transformed Our Own*, and *El Mundo Zurdo 3.*

Grażyna Zygadło is an assistant professor in the Department of American Studies and Mass Media and an associate in the Women's Studies Center at the University of Lodz (Poland). Her areas of expertise are in American studies, specifically minorities in the United States, and gender studies. She was a guest lecturer at universities in Spain, Finland, Sweden, as well as a recipient of grants from major US universities: University of Idaho, MIT, and Florida International University in Miami. Since 2009 she has been a member of the Society for the Study of Gloria Anzaldúa.

Aunt Lute Books is a multicultural women's press that has been committed to publishing high quality, culturally diverse literature since 1982. In 1990, the Aunt Lute Foundation was formed as a non-profit corporation to publish and distribute books that reflect the complex truths of women's lives and to present voices that are underrepresented in mainstream publishing. We seek work that explores the of the very different histories from which we come, and the possibilities for personal and social change.

You may buy books from our website or by phoning in a credit card order.

www.auntlute.com

Aunt Lute Books
P.O. Box 410687
San Francisco, CA 94141
415.826.1300
books@auntlute.com

This book would not have been possible without the kind contributions of the Aunt Lute Founding Friends:

Anonymous Donor

Anonymous Donor

Rusty Barcelo

Marian Bremer

Marta Drury

Diane Goldstein

Diana Harris

Phoebe Robins Hunter

Diane Mosbacher, M.D., Ph.D.

Sara Paretsky

William Preston, Jr.

Elise Rymer Turner